A Life Well Lived

A Life Well Lived

Berlin, Shanghai, and America

ERNEST GLASER

ISBN-13: 9781548618339
ISBN-10: 1548618330

Table of Contents

"...Jewish identity is a phenomenon of birth because ultimately we carry within us not only the hopes, tears, commitments and dreams of our ancestors... we are part of a story that began long before our birth and will continue after we are no longer here. More than identity is something we choose, it is something that chooses us. To be a Jew is to hear a voice from the past, summoning us to an often tempestuous and never less demanding future, and knowing that this is inescapable of which I am a part."

Jonathan Sacks, Past Chief Rabbi of Great Britain

Introduction

Some time ago I walked along a path and came upon a young boy picking up horse chestnuts. It reminded me of my youth, and I wondered whether this boy would carve little baskets and boats out of these chestnuts, as I did, or use them to "bean" a kid across the street, as I did.

As my mind wandered back, I remembered another day in the fall when my parents took me for a walk in a nearby forest. It was a beautiful, exhilarating fall day with red leaves piled high on the ground, and in my exuberance I climbed a little hill. As I started to run down hill toward my parents, I could see the fear in my father's eyes, that I would lose control and hurt myself. When he leaned forward to catch me, the impact knocked him down, luckily into a pile of leaves.

These were small, unimportant events, yet I remember them vividly. When we are young, we pay scant attention to our own history because we are attuned to the present and the future. But as we age we start to look back and become more introspective, wondering what factors shaped our personality and determined the course of our lives. Unfortunately, by that time events begin to blur in one's memory, and many of the key players in our lives have left us. So it is difficult, often impossible, to verify one's own recollections against those of others.

My generation lived through unusual, sometimes horrible, times. With these recollections I hope not only to portray my own experiences, but also attempt to convey an understanding of that era as well a flavor of the times; to recapture the background of events that influenced my young life and shaped my personality.

Today we see events within minutes of their actual happening miles or even continents away. In this context last week's news is history. So for today's generation, events that took place in the 1930's might as well have taken place during the period of the American Civil War. And the fast pace of today's events raises the interesting question whether my generation's experiences could repeat themselves in an age of instant global communications.

History never repeats itself exactly, but as Jews we are justified to always have our antennae up and our eyes and ears open. We see a new world order emerging after eighty years of communism, with nationalism coming to the fore in many parts of the world including the United States. The Balkans fell apart in ethnic and religious strife, the Arab Spring changed the political landscape of the entire Middle East, Israel is still fighting for its very survival, and our own country, the United States, is fighting external and internal terrorism. We are stuck in Afghanistan and we are trying to keep Iran from building an atomic bomb. Who knows in what direction such momentous changes will lead, whether the fragile flame of liberty will still burn a few years from now or whether it will be crushed?

Like a tree, we need our roots. My purpose then is to convey the importance of roots, perhaps to see relevance of some of my experiences in the lives of future generations and to be alert to the constancy of change and with it the need for flexibility and constant vigilance.

Throughout this autobiography, I will use German words and phrases, written in the German alphabet in italics, followed by a translation, in order to add flavor and authenticity. I worked on this autobiography, off and on, over a number years, never satisfied with the way it sounded, never quite ready to let go of it. But, as I said earlier, memories begin to fail and I want to finish it before mine are totally gone. Here then is my story.

One more word about this memoir. Today, invasion into people's privacy is a fact of life. Unintended, inadvertent, disclosure of one's birth date, mother's maiden, even last names have become tools used by crooks to invade bank accounts etc. Therefore, I omitted these from this narrative and, wherever appropriate, not used last names.

This then is the life's story of a penniless German-Jewish kid who spent the Second World War in China, was interned by Japanese authorities, came to the United States, graduated from two top American universities, raised a family and became a business executive.

One

EARLY YEARS

My family background

There is a Chinese curse that says: "May you live in interesting times." We do today but my parents certainly did, experiencing two world wars, the Great Depression, and the Hitler Years with exile from their homeland as penniless refugees. They also saw more innovations during their lifetime than the sum total of all previous developments. Their lives spanned a time during which kerosene lamps ultimately gave way to fluorescent lamps, and horse-drawn streetcars evolved into rapid transit systems. Knowledge in medicine exploded from the introduction of aspirin to the development of antibiotics, and age-old scourges like smallpox and whooping cough were totally eradicated. Horse and buggy gave way to automobiles, and continents were spanned by supersonic jets.

My father, Moritz, was born 1887 in Plathe, a small town in Pomerania about twenty miles east of Stettin. Today, the entire area is part of Poland, and the regional capital, Stettin, is now Szczecin, on the border of Germany. My paternal grandfather died at age thirty-seven, leaving my grandmother to care for the five little ones: two girls and three boys. A boy had died in infancy and the story was told (with some embarrassed snickering) that he was buried in a cigar box – an exaggeration I am sure but testifying to the fact they were very poor.

Public welfare systems did not exist, the Jewish community was too small and poor, so relatives had to pitch in since grandmother had no tangible means of support. Two boys were put into a Jewish orphanage in Stettin. My father, being the youngest, went to live with his grandfather in Stargard, about twenty miles South of Plathe, and the two girls stayed with their mother. My great-grandfather was a very strict and religious person. I do not know how long my father lived there, except that it was long enough for him to receive a solid religious education. In spite, or because of this, he developed a strong aversion to organized religion. Often, he would say: *"Man muss dem lieben Gott nicht die Füsse küssen"* (one need not kiss God's feet), equating excessive religious zeal with idol worship. His motto was: "All one needs to do to be a good Jew is to obey the Ten Commandments". Yet whenever I was with him in the synagogue, he participated fully. He readily answered calls to participate in Torah readings or to be part of a *minyan* (the required ten men for prayer services), and he generally seemed to enjoy the services.

My father attended a *Volksschule* (a grammar school) up to age twelve, which constituted his entire formal education. He was never taught a foreign language, yet he was an educated man. As a young man he was a voracious reader, and he was versed in many subjects throughout his life. At twelve years of age, he was sent to Stettin to be an apprentice in a dry goods store, "Swarsensky." Among the duties, which started at sunup, he had to look after the family's baby. As fate would have it, this baby grew up to become a leading rabbi in Berlin, made famous by a 1938 High Holy Day sermon in which he admonished the congregation to leave Germany because there was no future for Jews in Germany. During his rabbinical studies, however, young Swarsensky lived with my family in Berlin; he officiated at my Bar Mitzvah, and performed our wedding ceremony some twenty-five years later in Madison, Wisconsin.

Left: My father during military
service; approx. 1910

Below: My father taken right after
the war; 1919

Without higher education, my dad was drafted into military service at age twenty-one. According to his military record, he was assigned to a machine gun company and was discharged as a "reservist" two years later. He was proud of his military service and would often reminisce about it with innumerable anecdotes. A humorous one he often retold for my friends bears repeating because it demonstrates how little some aspects of military training have changed in the past seventy-five or so years. His company was often out on maneuvers, marching along country roads, the tallest in front the shortest making up the rear. Everyone carried a rifle and a rucksack that contained clothing, etc., with side pockets full of ammunition. As the day went on, the midday sun beating down on them, each soldier looked for ways to lighten his load, which felt heavier and heavier. One remedy was to open the side pockets and gradually "lose" some ammunition along the way. Unfortunately, my father was relatively short so he was positioned toward the rear of a long column. This meant that the road was full of ammunition, and my father was forced to walk as if on ice in order to avoid slipping. Whenever he told this story, he would demonstrate his gait to the amusement of my friends. Soldiers still go on long marches, still carry heavy packs, still care little about government property, and still brag about their experiences.

My father's business career began when he completed his apprenticeship and went to Berlin. He started at Hermann Tietz, the premier department store. It must have been quite a coup for a young man from the country to start in one of the largest department stores in Berlin in which the owner, Hermann Tietz, was a leader in Berlin's Jewish community. Probably, my dad had some contacts to help him land the job. The store is still in operation under the name Herti, of course under different ownership. I believe my dad was hired as a trainee and later promoted to buyer.

Hermann Tietz was the training ground for a large number of aspiring young businessmen, a number of them Jewish, and Tietz graduates could be found all over town as business owners or managers. They were like an alumni association. In later years my father looked to buy things "at wholesale" from Tietz alumni who, like himself, had gone on elsewhere to "make good". I remember shopping with my father for a suit for me as quite an experience. He would always ask for a certain manager or store owner, and after a hearty greeting the two would reminisce about "the old days" while I waited impatiently, only wanting to get the purchase over with.

Some time before or during the First World War, my father went into business for himself. I am not sure what prompted him to do so, except that corporate career opportunities were limited, especially for Jews.

Even though he had military training, he managed to stay out of the war. Today he would probably be called a draft dodger, or worse, a war profiteer. But I must say in his defense that he supported his mother and his two sisters, none of whom had any income. Later during the war, his sister was left a war widow with three very young children. His brothers were away fighting for the Kaiser so the task of supporting their mother and sisters fell mainly upon my father.

I do not know what business my father was engaged in at the time, but he must have done reasonably well. Living conditions were very crowded in wartime Berlin. The entire family, eight people in all, lived in one apartment in a middle class neighborhood in West Berlin.

He even managed to put some money away in newly issued government bonds; gold bonds at that. But within a few years he was nearly penniless because Germany, to pay for war reparations, defaulted on its bonds and high inflation wiped out the balance. It left an indelible mark on my father; he never again felt financially secure.

Dad enjoyed telling an anecdote about his war experiences. It was relatively easy for him to obtain draft exemption in the beginning because he supported his mother, sisters, and the three little boys, after Hannah lost her husband in the war. But as the war progressed and more men were needed on the front, things became tougher. He was able to bribe a series of minor military officials, but his last supervisor advised him to develop a limp and to carry a cane at all times so people would not find it strange to see a young, otherwise able-bodied man out of uniform. He often repeated a comment made by one of his neighbors: "I knew when the war was over; it was when Glaser stopped limping".

I have no idea as to what prompted my father to get into the agricultural supply business, but somehow he connected with several manufacturers of rope, twine, and jute belting. He established himself as a manufacturer's representative and sold merchandise to agricultural suppliers. There were few competitors and a high demand for agricultural products after the war, so it followed that things were going well.

My mother's family came from Saxony. She was born in Plauen, a town famous for its lace, which was exported all over the world. Grandmother often claimed that her family lived in the area a very long time; also that among our ancestors was a town mayor in the 14th or 15th century. More likely he was a *Schtadtlan* who spoke for the Jewish community (a court-Jew, or one with influence at the *Rathaus*, the city hall). My grandfather, Max (*Opa*), owned a dry goods store but didn't do well, and after the first World War he moved the family to Berlin, where he worked as a salesman representing a Plauen lace manufacturer. My maternal grandmother Elise's maiden name was Löwenthal. (I called her *Omi* as differentiated from *Oma*, my father's mother). Her birth certificate indicates that she was born in 1867 in Aschersleben, a small town in Saxony. Her brother Alex lived in Meissen, famous for its porcelain, near Dresden. He was the owner of a small department store and was financially well off.

My mother Erna was born in 1894, the eldest of four children. She attended the mandatory *Volksschule* (grammar school) until age ten, then transferred to a *Lyzeum*, a high school for girls. It was called a *Höhere Töchter Schule*. I'm not sure if it translates to a "school for daughters with a higher status background" or a "high school for daughters, i.e., girls". At any rate, higher education, especially for girls, was then a luxury.

I also remember her saying that she was one of very few Jewish girls at the Lyzeum and had to attend daily Protestant religious services. On the other hand, I never heard my mother talk about any Jewish education, although she could read Hebrew prayers. I am sure that, at the very least, my grandfather instructed her since he was an observant Jew. According to her records, she graduated in 1909 and started to work as a typist for a lace manufacturer. Among my memorabilia, I still have a letter of recommendation from her employer received upon leaving with her parents for Berlin.

Although Plauen was an industrial town, not a little country village, the move to Berlin must have been an exciting adventure for my mother. Years later, I remember her talking about her first experience taking a horse drawn streetcar. Because the vehicle never stopped, people had to get on and off while it was in motion which, being a young girl, was no problem for my mother but presented difficulties for my grandparents. She also talked about eating "strange" foods for the first time. Having never seen bananas until she came to Berlin, she said she had no idea, they required peeling. Needless to say, her first try, just biting into one, left her less than impressed. To me this story always seemed farfetched, but one has to remember that tropical fruits were an unfamiliar luxury at that time.

She also spoke of the family's first introduction to the telephone. Apparently, my grandfather wanted nothing to do with this new-fangled invention and when, after much coaxing, he did pick it up, he held the receiver far away from his ear, screaming into it from a distance. Of course I was amused by these stories because I grew up with electric streetcars, peeled bananas and dial telephones, but I don't laugh about them anymore, having experienced my own hesitancies in adopting modern innovations. To this day, I have difficulties programming electronics, and I was far behind the curve with computers and cell phones, just to name a couple.

My mother and Uncle Eric

My grandparents
mother and uncle Harry

Uncle Eric in France 1915

In Berlin, my mother worked as a foreign correspondent, which meant she handled export correspondence for a firm in French and English. My father was introduced to her in the early 1920's by my grandfather, a travelling salesman. *Opa* had met my father "on the road," and having an eligible daughter, he invited him home for dinner. At that time, my grandparents lived in an apartment on Pariser Strasse 50 in the middle class district of Wilmersdorf.

Before *Mutti* and *Vati* ("Mother and Father" as I called my parents) met, my father had a checkered social background. He seemed to have dated a lot, mostly non-Jewish women. My cousin Ruth sent me a clipping of a woman who supposedly had been very close to my father and who later emigrated to Israel. I only knew that he had been engaged to a non-Jew. She was part of the nobility; I was told she was a countess. I have no idea why the engagement fell through. It is not too farfetched to think that my father should have sought such a relationship with someone of German nobility. Even if impoverished, as many of the nobility were after the war, such a marriage would have elevated his own social status considerably.

I don't know anything about my parents' courtship, but I know that my grandfather was worried about my mother getting too old to find a husband. Yet she was a beautiful young lady, judging from pictures. According to my uncles, my mother had a number of suitors, but she was very selective—"none of the men were good enough for her." Furthermore, one of them was not Jewish, which was totally unacceptable to my grandfather. So when he met my father, he jumped at the opportunity of a *schiddach* (a match). Actually, knowing my mother was always a very fearful person, marriage probably scared her terribly. I presume this had to do with her strict upbringing, which prevented her from easily finding close relationships throughout her life. I don't know how long the courtship went on, but I recall hearing my mother caused my father's breakup with the countess.

My parents were married in May 1923, five days after my father's thirty- sixth birthday. My mother was twenty-seven. The ceremony was performed by Rabbi Winter at the Stier Strasse synagogue in Berlin, which was followed by a civil ceremony with my grandfather and my uncle Ludwig Weiss as witnesses. My parents could hardly have picked a worse time for getting married. My father had lost a great deal of money and my grandfather had lost his business before coming to Berlin. It was the height of inflation and Germany was in turmoil. A dowry was out of the question. The family joke was that my mother's dowry lasted from the wedding to the railway station. I still have a restaurant bill that my parents saved from their honeymoon: each item cost thousands of marks.

My Parent with Ernst Adolf Berthold

Mutti and *Vati* set up housekeeping in a small apartment in Pestalozzi Strasse, in Berlin's Charlottenburg district. It took courage to start a new life in times like those. Perhaps that accounted for their ability to cope with adversity in later life. They weathered the worst of the inflation and a few months later Germany stabilized its currency. My father's business must have prospered because, in addition to setting up a new household, he continued to support his mother and sisters. As mentioned, one sister was a war widow with three kids who received a small pension from the government, but which was insufficient, so my father pitched in.

My father introduced a fellow salesman to his unmarried sister; a man *Vati* had met travelling. As interest turned to courtship, my father offered to team up with the suitor in lieu of the traditional dowry; so Ludwig Weiss became my father's partner. Thereafter the business name was changed from Glaser to Glaser & Weiss. The partnership lasted a year or two. Both being rather strong-willed, they seemed to have trouble working things out. They split up but not on unfriendly terms. After Uncle Ludwig left the business, the firm's name remained Glaser & Weiss, and Uncle Ludwig set himself up in a parallel business, mostly covering a different territory. Although there was some competition between the two, it did not seem to carry into their personal lives. I cannot remember my parents ever saying anything negative about Ludwig, except perhaps that he was stingy.

As I mentioned earlier, my father sold products for agricultural applications. Draft horses were still in widespread use for pulling ploughs, and hay was still baled with twine, so the agricultural market for such products was large. His main supplier was located in Immenstadt, Bavaria. Although Bavaria, especially small town Bavaria, was known to be very anti-Semitic, the owners of this firm stuck by my father long into the Nazi period.

Family Relationships

My parents were happy with my arrival in their apartment in Pestalozzi Strasse. Mothers didn't go to hospitals to have babies in those days; hospitals were for sick people. My birth certificate identifies me as Ernst Adolf Berthold Glaser. My middle names related me to my deceased grandfather and great-grandfather. I remember my father talking about my birth in later years. He phoned the doctor to tell him that my mother was ready. The doctor told him to start boiling water and get some newspapers ready. My father thought this was strange, wrapping a newborn in newspaper, but he did as the doctor told him. What he found out, of course, was that newspapers were used in place of bed sheets because printer's ink supposedly sterilized the paper. I wished I could say that my interest in reading stemmed from my earliest contact with the printed word, but I was a poor reader. That I was born on a Sunday was of great significance to my mother. Apparently there existed a superstition that *Sonntagskinder* (children born on Sundays) were very fortunate and lucky throughout their lives. This superstition turned out to be true.

I was a bottle baby– breastfeeding had gone out of style. I must have inherited my dental problems from my mother's side of the family. My parents often told me that they were ready to get false teeth for me because it did not seem that I would ever have any real ones. I have always been dark-complexioned, and my mother said she was asked by strangers whether my father was from India. Knowing German racial prejudice, I am sure my mother did not take kindly to such remarks.

We did not live in the first apartment for very long but, strangely enough, I do remember that my ivory colored crib was in a room with blue wallpaper. My father must have been doing well financially as we moved to a nice, big apartment sometime between 1928 and 1929.

Although I had no siblings, or perhaps because of it, I formed a close attachment early on to Helga Rehmer. Our mothers met in the Lietzensee Park, which was a block away from the first apartment. Both were new mothers with similar problems. My mother and Frau Rehmer became good friends and still corresponded after the Second World War. I was told that I introduced myself to Helga as a toddler by running off with her little baby buggy. Nevertheless, Helga and I became good friends until about 1936 when her father, who was not Jewish (her mother was), decided to move to Holland to get away from the Nazis. I distinctly remember what she looked like at the time. She was a curly-haired blond with blue eyes, a little on the chubby side. Being the same age, we were also about the same height, but otherwise she was way ahead of me. I recall window-shopping with her while she pointed out the things we needed to set up housekeeping after we were married.

I lost touch with Helga, but through my mother's contact with her mother, I learned that, after Hitler overran Holland, Herr Rehmer decided to move back to Berlin. Somehow he was able to shield his wife and daughter all through the war. She survived, but as fate would have it, he died in an air raid on Berlin during the last few months of the war. Helga married another *Mischling* (a child of a mixed marriage) and last I heard she lived somewhere in the Rhine area.

On rainy or winter days we enjoyed playing *Kaufmann's Laden* (grocery store) at my home. Essentially it was a doll house game for boys. There was a wooden miniature grocer's shop with a little counter, a toy cash register, and lots of little drawers to store various items like rice, beans, lentils and nuts. We had make-believe money, and Helga and my other friends would come to do their shopping. It kept everybody busy for hours and we had fun.

The new apartment was located on the corner of Kant and Schlüter Strasse within walking distance of Kurfürsten Damm, the famous shopping boulevard. Ours was a corner apartment with six or seven rooms overlooking the busy street corner. My world was within easy reach. Both the kindergarten and the grammar school I attended and all my friends could be reached in minutes. I can still remember the apartment in some detail. As in all such apartment buildings, there was a *Portier* (a concierge) downstairs who made sure that no unauthorized individual entered the building. There were shops to the right and left of the street entrance. One of the stores was Etam, a chain selling ladies hosiery.

As was the fashion, my parents furnished much of the apartment with heavy oak furniture. The drawing room had a very large rounded picture window in front of which my father placed a large desk. There were also a heavy leather-upholstered sofa and two overstuffed, but exceedingly comfortable, armchairs. Along one wall we had a heavy bookcase and in the corner the standard grandfather clock. The bookcase contained the complete works of Germany's great classic writers: Göthe, Schiller, Heine, Kleist, and Schopenhauer are a few I remember. The room had the smell of success, a mixture of leather and tobacco. The dining room was furnished in quasi-French provincial mahogany furniture, lined with some aromatic wood that you smelled the minute a drawer was opened.

One entered the apartment through a large hallway. Living and dining rooms were divided by huge sliding doors with etched glass inserts of symmetric floral patterns. The only reason I remember so much about the doors is that one of the glass inserts developed a crack. We were insured, and the insurance representative came to inspect the damage. He took one look at me and said, "Let me tell you about a recent experience, young man, so you won't repeat it. This glass is very expensive and we had to replace one not too far from here. We brought the new glass panel and rested it against the wall for the carpenter to install the next day. A young fellow, about your age, came home, leaned his bicycle against the glass and broke it." And raising his finger he said that he hoped this would not happen here. This episode must have impressed me terribly because it stuck in my mind so vividly.

It was an elegant, older, four-storied building without an elevator, so the first floor was the best location, even though it was noisy being closest to street traffic. There was no central heating. All rooms were equipped with large tile stoves that occupied one corner of the room. These stoves were very elaborate with fancy tile decorations. The one in the living room had a built-in bench on one side.

My father's original base of operations was the whole Northeastern quadrant of Germany, with the exception of East

Prussia. He liked the area; it was home turf to him. He knew people's idiosyncrasies and spoke the dialect of the area, *Plattdeutsch,* which is akin to Dutch. Agriculture was predominant, the region being the breadbasket of Germany, so the need for the products my father sold was substantial. It was a logical area for him to serve, and he had lots of friends there.

Every year he purchased a *Reisepass,* a travel pass, that allowed unlimited travel throughout the region. I remember my father pouring over the timetables every Sunday, putting together a *Fahrplan* (travel plan) for the coming week. He would leave his itinerary with my mother, always staying at the same small hotels. The owners knew him well; he never needed advance reservations.

We had a live-in maid who probably started with us when we moved to Schlüter Strasse. Her name was Ella Lindner, and Ella and I became good buddies. My parents claimed she was a poor housekeeper, but she was good with me and I remember I had a lot of fun with her, and she spoiled me even more than my mother. She was a young woman with a very big heart. I would guess she was twenty or twenty-one years old when she came to us. Ella was from the country; her father lived in the district of Zehlendorf. Today it is a part of Berlin, but it was rural then. He had a little fruit orchard and was a carpenter by profession. Ella occasionally took me by train to Zehlendorf, and I spent part of one summer vacation there.

I looked forward to visiting Herr Lindner, and it was there that I developed my love for German shepherd dogs. He had a beautiful young shepherd named *Raudi* (Rowdy), who wouldn't hurt a fly but looked ferocious. Early one morning, he found a thief stealing apples in the orchard, scared the wits out of the fellow, and without ever touching him, chased him down the street into the arms of a policeman. The local policeman, who knew Raudi, later told us that the thief begged to be protected from this vicious dog. Herr Lindner, who was a widower, grew his own vegetables and had a big bowl of greens every day for lunch; obviously I remembered this because I never saw anybody eat such a "meager" lunch, or was he way ahead of his time?

By contrast, my mother's cooking was extremely rich, at least in my early years when supplies were still plentiful. Later, during the Hitler years, her menus changed drastically. Nobody ever heard of cholesterol or saturated fats in those days. Being overweight was a sign of prosperity and health. Breakfast consisted of bacon and eggs with rolls baked that day, or rolls with sausage and cheese for variety. Obviously, we did not keep Kosher. The main meal of the day was eaten at noon and usually consisted of soup, meat and potatoes with a side dish of vegetables, and a rich dessert. The evening meal was quite heavy as well. Open-faced buttered sandwiches with sausage and lots of cheese were pretty much standard. In between meals I occasionally picked up a piece of cake at the bakery to tide myself through the afternoon. I am sure that it was only because I was so active during the day that I was relatively skinny. But even in later years under the Hitler regime, when foodstuffs became scarce, our cooking was rich, at least by today's standards. Dad traveled a great deal until about 1935. He would leave on Monday morning and return Friday afternoon. My mother was a great worrier, and by Friday noon she became antsy. She would go out on the balcony to see whether she could spot my father coming down the street from the railway station. A great sigh of relief announced that she spotted him from afar. He always came home with a one-pound box of Fassbender chocolates, my mother's favorite brand, and we would feast on them for a couple of days. They seldom lasted longer.

There was another, less pleasant, routine related to my father's weekly return. My mother must have had a lot of trouble coping with her loneliness and my occasional bad behavior. After a short welcoming period she would relate each and every one of my transgressions in great detail. He would get ever more agitated while I stood in front of him, head drooping, knowing the punishment I could expect. At the end of her list of major and minor infractions, she would say, "Well, are you going to do something about this, or are you letting him get away with it?" Whereupon, in good German fashion, my father would start beating me, and I would scream to high heaven until my mother would interfere with, "Stop already before you kill him."

Yet, while I feared my father, I always looked forward to his coming home. The rest of the weekend was usually enjoyable, except for occasional fights between my parents. These were always related to my father's jealousy. My mother was quite attractive and my father was deeply in love with her. But he assumed all men found her desirable, and because of his long absences she would have many opportunities to be unfaithful. He had this obsession to the day he died.

I lost my maternal grandfather, Max, when I was only three years old. I have vague recollections of him; one is sitting on his lap, but his death did not seem to have a great impact on me. He died very suddenly from pneumonia, and it was a terrible blow to everyone around me, especially my grandmother. She was a determined and strong-willed woman, and after losing her husband she lived with her bachelor son Eric, for whom she kept house.

My mother's brother was a complex person, probably due to his wartime experience. Although he had friends and his work mandated rapport with people, he seemed remote and very critical of others. He had fixed views and spoke in a clipped military style. He had a very good position as sales manager for an apron manufacturer. The company furnished him a car and chauffeur, a real status symbol. I had a good relationship with him in spite of his reticence, as did my cousin. Since he was on the road a good deal of the time, *Omi* was alone during the week, as was my mother, so there was a lot of visiting back and forth. Fortunately, my grandmother did not live far from us on Wilmersdorfer Strasse.

There was a large city park within walking distance from our home. It was called the *Tiergarten* (a former royal hunting woods). It contained the famous Berlin Zoo and I spent many enjoyable hours there. The park contained a number of large inter-connected lagoons and lakes with rowboats for rent during the summer. Swans and ducks were in abundance, and in spring coveys of ducklings followed their mothers into and out of the water, much to everyone's delight. These were also my Uncle Eric's favorite excursions. *Omi*, too, loved to go for long *Spaziergänge* (leisurely walks) with the two of us to the *Tiergarten* and the zoo.

Things were different with Uncle Harry, my mother's second brother. Harry was about six feet tall, about six inches taller than his brother, and he was much more outgoing than Eric. He married someone whose mother was not Jewish which created a break with his father. Fortunately, the rift was not permanent and with my mother's help, father and son were reconciled about one year after the marriage. I do not know if my aunt "officially" converted, but I presume she did. I remember, though, my parent's conversation on the way home from a Shabbat dinner at Uncle Harry's home. Aunt Hilde had baked challah, blessed the candles, and seemed to know more of the ritual than Uncle Harry did. My parents commented on her being more Jewish than most Jews they knew.

Harry and Hilde lived in a small apartment in a working class neighborhood. I believe he was in business for himself selling notions. They lived modestly, but it was fun to visit them. There was an upright piano, which my uncle played at the slightest request. Much of his playing was from memory and it was always joyous music. I was terribly impressed by him and his abilities. He was my favorite uncle. Their daughter, *Uschi* (Ursula), was a couple of years younger than I and not having any siblings, we developed close bonds.

At all gatherings of my mother's clan, the men would sit down after the meal to play *Skat*, a German card game akin to pinochle. Like bridge it is more a game of thought than chance, and it took me some time to understand the game. Years later, my friends and I would entertain ourselves on cold winter evenings playing this game.

Two or three times during the year, the clan would gather at *Tante* (aunt) Hulda's, my grandmother's sister, and it was always an occasion. She had lost her husband before I was born, and to augment her pension she set herself up in a small business that she operated out of her apartment. She sold yard goods to women who did their own sewing, which was popular among German women. *Tante* Hulda lived in Tegel, which at that time was semi-rural. Her apartment was "modern"; a derogatory term implying that it was not spacious and had relatively low ceilings and electric heating. By comparison, "regular" apartments had larger rooms with high ceilings and steam heat throughout or tile stoves in each room. Tante Hulda's hobby was growing plants in her "greenhouse," which was an enclosed balcony. She seemed to have hundreds of plants, knew each by name and treated them like children. Not having any children of her own, she showered affection on Uschi and me.

A New Year's Day party was a ritual at *Tante* Hulda's. The clan would gather in the morning and inspect the big fish, always a carp, swimming in the bathtub. It would be served for dinner later in the day. There were always lots of chocolates, dried fruits and nuts to fill up on. The women would help Hulda with the meal preparation, and the men would sit in the living room to schmooze. *Uschi* and I would be sent outdoors to play if weather allowed. In bad weather we were entertained by Uncle Kucki. Kucki was quite a character, loved by all. He was the husband of my grandmother's other sister, Aunt Jenny. He was bald and stocky, about sixty years old. He had a checkered career. My parents viewed him as a *Lebenskünstler*, which translates into something like conman. During the time of financial upheaval in the early '20s, he worked for a *Sparkasse* (Savings and Loan) that went under. My parents accused him, behind his back of course, of standing on the bank's front steps reassuring depositors that their money was safe while the bank management carried the bank's assets out the back door for "safe keeping." On that day, Kucki supposedly was almost killed by irate depositors. Nobody knew what he lived on at the moment, and everybody had his own ideas. Kucki was able to fascinate us for hours with card tricks, coin tricks, stories and jokes. He was a great entertainer.

After the meal, when the men sat down to play cards, the women would sit around the table to talk. *Tante* Jenny would take orange peels and fashion them into what looked like a set of teeth that she would slip under her upper lip so the orange teeth would protrude. When she started to talk with these "teeth," she would have us kids in stitches.

Tante Hulda died while the entire family was still in Germany, and it was really a sad day for all. Jenny and Kucki never left Germany and both died during the Holocaust.

When I was about twelve, I spent one summer vacation with Uncle Harry and his family. They had an assigned spot in a tent city to which they returned every year. They owned a spacious tent that had a large sleeping area, a sitting area, and a screened porch. Being knowledgeable about things electrical, my uncle had rigged up electric lighting throughout the tent. He had a large battery, like a car battery, to which he hooked up tiny flashlight bulbs. Even though each individual bulb did not give much light, the totality of them when lit made the inside of the tent quite bright. There was little space between tents, but I remember every tent had a firebreak ditch around it. It was my assigned task to keep the ditch around the tent intact after rains.

The tent city was located in a forest clearing on a large lake. As the summer advanced, the lake would turn progressively greener with algae growth, and one had to rinse oneself off after swimming. I loved swimming with my uncle, who was a very good swimmer, and only once was I really scared swimming with him. That time we swam far out into the lake and must have lost our bearings. I could see my uncle becoming edgy, and although I did not panic, I was quite uncomfortable and glad when we could finally touch ground.

Omi and Eric lived in a three-bedroom apartment in an elevator building. In later years, she became quite ill and had considerable pain. We did not know it then, but she suffered from colon cancer, of which she died after immigrating to South Africa. Throughout she kept her humor, and I remember one of her comments after receiving a mineral oil enema, "*Das war meine letzte Ölung*" (this was my last unction).

All in all, I had a happy childhood. In spite of unstable times, I remember a secure home with loving parents who alternated between setting strict limits for certain activities but often overindulging me, especially during my first ten or so years.

As I entered high school, my mother made it a point to teach me household chores that came in handy much later in life. She insisted I sew lose buttons on clothing, iron my own shirts, polish my own shoes, and even learn some cooking.

My mother's side of the family was our support system; relatives you could turn to when you were in need. When my parents needed moral support, or in later years financial help, Uncle Eric stood ready to help. There were never any questions asked, never judgment, only encouragement.

The same could rarely be said for the Glaser clan, which was one of much bickering and suppressed hostility. Of course the Glaser boys had helped their mother and sisters to some extent but later in life, once they were married, there were frequent periods when someone would be *braügis* (not on speaking terms) with another member. People's sensitivities seemed to be much more in the open and insults, perceived or real, would immediately lead to a rupture of relationships. At no time did I see people trying to resolve their differences through discussion. Time would paper over the wounds, resulting in re-establishment of relationships, always leaving scars ready to break open at the slightest provocation.

I barely remember my paternal grandmother. She died in 1930, aged seventy-one, when I was six years old. As I mentioned earlier, she lived with her daughter and three grandsons, in the district of *Friedenau*. We visited there about once a month. I was told that my mother was not very fond of her mother-in-law, and I believe the feelings were mutual. Emma Glaser was a difficult person, but life had not treated her gently. Losing her husband early on (he was only thirty-seven years old when he died), and being left with five toddlers and no means of support, surely must have been devastating to her. I remember her as having a bad temper and being very egotistical. She ruled the Glaser boys with an iron hand until the day she died.

Tante Hanne's sons, my three cousins, were much older than I and had their own interests. Nor was their relationship to my father an easy one. Since there was no man in the house, the job of being a substitute father fell to my dad, even though he was the youngest of the three uncles. Martin, the eldest, had moved to *Eberswalde* and had distanced himself from his relatives, not only geographically but also by his actions. Max lived relatively close by, but he lost his wife not long after their second son, my cousin Horst (Henry), was born. Max was under terrible stress. His first son, Egon (Eddie), was about the age of Hanne's sons, but with little supervision at home he was off "doing his own thing".

Disciplining and supervising the Cohn boys fell, therefore, to my dad. I believe my two older cousins' relationship with my father vacillated between respect and resentment for the rest of their lives, at least for the older two boys.

Willi and my dad had the best relationship. He was the youngest of Hanne's three sons, and I believe he genuinely loved my parents, a feeling that my parents reciprocated. Willi also loved to help. I was told that, a youngster himself, he wheeled me around in a buggy and helped carry heavy load up to my grandparents' fourth floor apartment on *Pariser Strasse*. One year he played *Weihnachtsmann* (Santa Claus) in our household. Willi always had a sunny disposition and was quite a comedian. In later years, he had a standard routine wherein he would stand facing a corner of the room embracing himself with his arms and feeling his back up and down. It looked like a couple making love in the corner, and he had his audience in stitches. Willy was a *Lagerist* (stock clerk) in a dry goods company.

At get-togethers with the family at the Cohn's, as well as at our house, we would play *Gottes Segen bei Cohn*, (God's blessings at the Cohn's) a card game. The name is a coincidence and has nothing to do with the family. It was a common game played in German Jewish homes and to my knowledge unknown to Gentiles.

In addition to having lost his wife, Max had financial difficulties, and his second marriage to Alice brought some much needed money into the marriage. It would be unfair, though, to presume that Max was only interested in Alice's money. I believe the two genuinely cared for each other, especially in later years. Alice had a difficult situation on her hands. She had to replace a mother whom both boys revered. I know that the shock over the loss of their mother dramatically affected Egon and Horst for the rest of their lives. Nevertheless, Alice gradually gained the respect and love of both boys. Her one great passion in life was playing bridge, and I believe she was a very good card player. She was the perfect match to Max, even tempered vis-a-vis his mercurial moods, and she was willing to be the butt of his often cruel jokes. Even though she often did not seem very bright, she was smart enough to get her way when she wanted to, and she structured her new life to suit her needs.

She also brought about a change within the family. The clan would get- together occasionally at Max's apartment, which was always a unique experience. Soon after lunch, the men would sit in a small gaming room that contained a special table for card games. It was equipped with little fold-down trays for each player to keep coins and a drink. Always the same players playing the same game, draw poker. My cousin Horst and I would kibitz, and it was the custom for players to share a few pennies with us when winning big pots. All the men smoked cigars, so after a while the room was in a smoky blue haze.

By about eight in the evening, the women would come into the room to pry their husbands loose. Invariably Uncle Max would insist on two more rounds, which he always stretched into quite a few more. When we finally got home, I was usually worn out but always a little wealthier.

Tante Paula and her husband, Ludwig, had no children. They lived in a nice, airy apartment of which I remember little except the presence of a piano. My uncle, *Onkel* Ludwig, was short, slightly hunched-over, with a laugh that approached a rooster's crow. He was well educated, having gone to a *Gymnasium,* a high school offering a classic education which included the study of Greek and Latin. He was good in math, occasionally helping me with my homework. He spent the First World War in the newly formed German Air Force and flew on the first Zeppelin airship which dropped bombs on London. By coincidence, he was stationed at an airport not far from Berlin whose name was *Ludwigshafen* (Ludwig's harbor).

As a very young child I loved to play "my compositions" on Weiss's piano. These were, of course, nothing other than a kid's plinking the keys. Invariably, Ludwig would coax me away from the piano with an offer to play chess; a game that intrigued me, and he was very good at. He was able to play with me while participating in conversation with Paula and my parents, winning most of the games (he probably let me win one now and then). I remember being terribly impressed by that. He also played the piano, but, unlike my Uncle Harry, his repertoire tended toward heavy music to which I could barely relate. He came from a well-established German-Jewish family and was a cousin of the well-known writer and satirist Kurt Tucholsky.

Paula was neither a housekeeper nor host. I do not recall ever having a meal at her house, except afternoon coffee with which she served delicious pastries bought at the *Konditorei Schlenkrich,* her favorite fancy bakery nearby.

The family joke was that Paula would mostly visit relatives at mealtime. Invariably she would accept an invitation to stay for dinner with the comment: "*Ich esse aber nur ein kleines Klappstüllchen*" (but I will only eat a very small sandwich).

Although nobody quite understood the symptoms, Aunt Paula showed signs of mental disturbance. Occasionally she would tell stories that indicated paranoia. They usually involved a gypsy fortuneteller who rang her doorbell, told her a story, and then stole something. My aunt would go into great details, which fascinated me and amused my father, who would end her tale with: "*Paula, Du bist ja verrückt*" (but you are crazy, Paula). Unfortunately, many years later she was diagnosed as psychotic.

Like my father, Ludwig worked out of his home. In order to augment their income, my aunt rented a room to a young Jewish lady and thereby hangs an interesting tale. The lady had an affair with a young Japanese diplomat stationed in Berlin. My aunt made friends with them and stayed in touch after the diplomat left Germany. In later years the diplomat (I believe his name was Shigemitzu) became Japan's Foreign Minister and was of some assistance to Paula and Ludwig during their emigration from Germany. He was even in touch with them by mail after the war.

My mother was pre-occupied enforcing dad's diet. On my father's part this became a game. Unsupervised, he took good care of himself, but in my mother's presence he would try to sneak forbidden foods, always making sure my mother would notice so she could stop him. It was his way of being reassured she loved him, and this game went on until he died.

On the Glaser side, I also had a hero, my cousin Fritz. Actually I really did not know him very well, but I heard a lot about his exciting life. The story probably became somewhat embellished over the years, but much of it was true. Fritz, the eldest of *Tante* Hanne's sons, started out as a *Lehrling* (apprentice) to a leather goods manufacturer. He must have been involved in some political activity because he left Germany in a hurry in 1933 upon Hitler's assuming power. He fled without a passport or money.

Somehow Fritz found his way to Lyon in the South of France where a shirt tailor gave him a job as an apprentice. Many months later he started dating the boss's daughter. One Sunday he took her for a drive into the country in the boss's car. As an inexperienced driver he had an accident. Since he was undocumented he expected to be thrown into jail and he fled the scene, making his way to North Africa. In sheer desperation and to gain citizenship, he signed up with the French Foreign Legion. After about eight months of military life, he decided to skip the Legion and somehow made his way to the Canary Islands, a Spanish enclave off the coast of West Africa. Here he slept on park benches, took odd jobs, and lived off bananas that grew wild. Nine months later, he hopped on a Turkish freighter that plied the Mediterranean.

When the ship docked in Istanbul, Turkey, he stayed for a while, again illegally. He wrote home every few months, and his travels and escapades became a good part of the conversations at family get-togethers. Fritz also left a girl friend behind in Berlin. Nadja was a real beauty. I believe that much of my great admiration for Fritz was based on being so impressed by Nadja. If she fell for him, he must really be something.

One day around 1937 (during the Nazi period), our telephone rang and it was Fritz informing my dad that he was at *Anhalter Bahnhof* in Berlin (a key railway station) without a penny, shivering because it was in the middle of winter. *Vati* put a spare overcoat and a scarf into a suitcase and took me along to the station to pick up Fritz; that was, if the police hadn't already done so. On the way, my father explained the situation. Fritz was crazy, he said, and now his foolishness topped everything. It was incomprehensible how he got back into the country without detection. He concluded that Fritz would probably get everyone into trouble. Anyhow, we met Fritz at the station, gave him the coat and scarf and brought him home.

Fritz related his many experiences in great detail, and I must have sat wide-eyed with open mouth taking it all in. It turned out that Fritz came home to see his girl friend, Nadja. The family scraped money together to obtain a visa and boat passage for the two to immigrate to Montevideo, Uruguay, where Nadja had family. Somehow Fritz managed to obtain a passport, thereby being able to exit Germany legally. The two were married in Uruguay, but the marriage did not last very long.

As my mother grew older, and undoubtedly due to the unsettled times we lived in, she became more and more high strung. She always carried a small bottle of *Baldrian* (extract of valerian) to sooth her nerves. Today, such bottles are collector's items because they are rare to find. My mother always carried a few cubes of sugar in her purse onto which she would dispense the valerian. It calmed her down, as it should have, being an alcohol extract of a root, the active chemical being the tranquilizer Valium.

As a remedy against her frequent migraine headaches, my mother would consume vast amounts of "*Eu-Med*", a medication similar to Anacin. Another weapon in her medical arsenal was smelling salts: small glass vials containing some aromatic crystals with dilute liquid ammonia. One sniff would really clear anyone's sinuses. My mother took an occasional sniff to offset the headache pains temporarily, probably trading one irritation for another.

I was prone to tonsillitis. Our pediatrician was Dr. Dinkmann, a vivacious man full of jokes and laughter. I loved going to him because he had a big bowl of chocolate candy in his waiting room. Most of my friends were his patients and their mothers followed his advice meticulously. Since Jewish mothers are known to be overprotective, he would admonish them constantly to "throw away the thermometer" and to "take the kids out of the house for fresh air in any kind of weather".

Mother interpreted this to mean that the windows in our bedrooms should never be closed, no matter how cold it was outside. Of course we used heavy European comforters, so once we were in bed we warmed up pretty quickly, but getting in was another matter. I remember finding a snowball in my bed one time. Probably somebody threw it through the open window and it landed on the bed when the covers were still turned back for airing. Ella, or my mother, probably did not notice the white snowball on the white bed sheet when they made up the bed. It was so cold, that the snowball never melted.

The remedy against tonsillitis involved the application of a foul smelling, very sticky, black tar salve to the neck and jaws. My mother wrapped a woolen stocking around my neck like a scarf, keeping it on for a week. My neck looked brown for days after the stocking came off. I suspect this salve worked by irritating the skin, drawing blood to the general area. When at some other time I had the measles, my mother hung up strips of cloth, dipped in turpentine, all over the room. I have no idea what it was supposed to accomplish, but she swore by its efficacy.

Being sick had its compensations, though. To stay home in bed with a doting mother around, could easily have made me into a hypochondriac. It did not, however to this day I have a feeling of nostalgia when I am forced to go to bed with an illness.

All kids were inoculated against smallpox during the first year of high school. The common practice was for mothers to sew a red cross onto a sleeve to warn other kids not to contact that area for fear that the scab might come off prematurely. Of course, kids being kids, this served only as an invitation to hit somebody on that arm, and I remember telling my mother to sew the cross on the wrong arm to fool them. As could be expected, this did not work either.

Early Childhood

The year before entering first grade, my parents sent me to a kindergarten.

It was run by a lady whom we called *Tante* Hanna. She was Jewish, but it was not a Jewish school. Judging by where it was located, on Kurfürsten Damm, it must have been a relatively expensive school, indicating again that my parents must have been well off financially at that time. I do not remember much about the school, nor do I remember any of the kids pictured in several photographs, one of which is a play-enactment of a country wedding. The boys were done up in paper costumes, top hats, and fancy suits, and I was one of the bridegrooms. The girls wore fancy dresses made out of crepe paper as well. We also had a kindergarten orchestra in which I played a drum. I suspect that *Tante* Hanna put me on it because it was easy to play and I loved to make a lot of noise.

KINDERGARTEN CLASS
About 1928

KINDERGARTEN PARTY
About 1929

The German school year started right after the Easter vacations. Due to my March birth date most of my schoolmates were older than I, so that my level of maturity was often significantly lower.

with *Zuckertüte*

April 15, 1930, was the big day when my mother took me to my first class at the *Volksschule* (grammar school). It was a traumatic experience. Weeks before we bought supplies and the most important item: a *Mappe* – a leather briefcase that was strapped on your back. Now that the day had come, *Mutti* and *Vati* presented me with a *Zuckertüte* before we marched off. A *Zuckertüte* is a nice German custom. (I am sure kids still receive one in Germany today). It is a large papier-mâché cone filled with candy and chocolates. Because school starts around Easter, there is usually a chocolate bunny on top of the cone. In later years, I learned that Orthodox Jewish kids are given some honey together with their first book in Torah study. So trying to associate learning with sweets is apparently a very old custom.

Kids generally attended a *Volksschule* for the first four grades. Upon completion, kids could transfer to institutions of higher learning or continue at the *Volksschule* for another four years. Usually, parents from bluecollar backgrounds expected their children to take up a manual trade, so these kids stayed on until age 14. They then became apprenticed to a master craftsman. As an alternative they went on for two more years at a trade school before being apprenticed in some business. On the other hand, kids from wealthier families had a variety of choices to study at a secondary school, depending on the career path their parents chose for them.

We were about thirty-five kids in grammar school class, all boys, and of these about six or eight were Jewish. This was a high percentage, because Jews constituted less than one percent of Berlin's population. Each incoming class was assigned a teacher, ours was *Herr* List. He was bald, as was my father, and approaching retirement age. He was a "Prussian" through and through. Of course corporal punishment, spankings and beatings, were standard in all German schools, and he made liberal use of his *Rute*, cane, at the slightest provocation. For each infraction there was a specific price to pay. For instance, coming late to class was two strokes, I remember. Yet he was always fair, and I am sure that to his mind he was doing his level best to get his students started "the right way".

He also knew all the tricks kids could dream up. Some of us stuffed heavy cloth into our pants so that the strokes on our rears would not hurt so badly. But List was wise to us and made us take the stuffing out before we leaned over a desk to receive our punishment. None of the parents objected to the harsh treatment; if anything, they encouraged it. It was part of European upbringing, especially in Germany.

I became friends with two Jewish kids in my class: Klaus Peter Wagner (how is that for a Jewish name?) and Gert Knoop. Klaus Peter, who lives in Washington,D.C. today, is still a good friend.

But I had a falling out with Gert shortly before leaving Germany. He had become what I called a "Jewish Nazi." Apparently Gert had changed little in later years. When Peter Wagner (he dropped Klaus when he came to the U.S.) brought us back together again some forty years later, I found Gert to be a right-wing Republican. He passed away since then and true to form asked for a military funeral. Both of them had younger sisters whom they tolerated. Yet, without siblings, I always envied these two fellows for having sisters.

While Klaus Peter was an "A" student throughout, I was a few notches down the ladder, maybe number three or four in class. Actually, the Jewish kids were List's favorites because they paid attention, were generally less rambunctious, and turned their homework in on time. Herr List retired the year I graduated, and I remember all of the Jewish mothers getting together to decide on an appropriate farewell gift for him. They settled on an engraved silver bowl.

The German alphabet differs little from the English except for the *Umlaut* (two dots over a vowel) that change the pronunciation. However, there are two ways of writing the alphabet: the Latin script used in the English system and the German script. The latter method was called *Sütterlin Schrift* and to the untrained eye it looks akin to ancient Celtic. As I recall, this Germanic style of writing was the only one taught in grammar school and it was not until high school that I learned Latin script.

There was no allowance made for left-handed children. I do not know whether it differed from American schools of that time, but in Germany we were not given the option of left handed writing. Since I think of myself as a frustrated lefty, I was sensitive to it. Nevertheless, being forced to write with my right hand contributed to my nearly being ambidextrous, which proved an advantage in later life.

A sign of the times, perhaps, but there was relatively little mingling with non-Jewish kids except, when playing on the street.

Whether this was by choice or because we were being discriminated against, I cannot say. In later years, I became friends with a
non-Jewish fellow who was a few years my senior. We lived in the
same apartment house, and although he was a member of the
Hitler Youth, he had no trouble having me as a friend. Generally,
though, I do not remember ever being invited into a non-Jewish
home or vice versa. For a Jewish youngster like myself, the period
between 1930 and 1934 must have been turbulent, but I recall it as
generally untroubled. There were, of course, anti-Jewish incidents,
as when on our way home from school kids occasionally called us
dirty Jews. But there were no incidents in school that I recall. Kids
can be cruel and in exchange for received insults we used to yell
"*Humpelbein*" at a non-Jewish boy with a birth defect that made him
limp.

During my last year in grammar school there were frequent
drives for money to help the Hitler Youth, to which all kids in
class contributed. I told my parents about being asked to participate in a fundraiser. There was a long discussion with other Jewish
parents. In the end it was decided to let us participate because
"*Man soll sich nicht 'rausstellen*" (one should not set one-self apart);
a phrase I heard throughout my youth. One means of collecting
funds was to sell colored nails, black, red, or white, (the Nazi colors) for five *Pfennig* each. These nails were then hammered into
the appropriate pre-marked places on a board to fill in the design
of the Hitler Youth emblem, with the black Swastika in the middle.
In retrospect, these nails were in the shape of the hobnails used on
Nazi boots. All of us learned the standard Nazi songs, but we did
not really understand their significance.

On the way home from public school I often stopped at a small
cabinet-maker's shop. The man's name was Fürst, and I first met
him when he did some work for my parents. Showing interest in
his work, he invited me to visit his workshop, and for quite a while
I would go there on my way home. He was a bachelor, not very talk-
ative, but friendly. He worked by himself all day long, so he enjoyed

some company. His workshop was a converted corner store, and he displayed his latest furniture creations in the show window.

The store was divided into a front workshop with living quarters in the rear. I still have a picture of the workshop in my mind; a large cabinetmaker's work bench in the center and ordinary benches along the walls, cluttered with pieces of furniture in various stages of completion. Except for a lathe in one corner, he used only hand tools. There were buck saws and rip saws of all sizes and different uses hanging on the walls, cabinets containing planers, not metal ones but the old fashioned wood-bodied ones, and hundreds of chisels, hand drills, hammers and mallets.

A double boiler glue pot on the center workbench, heated by a little alcohol burner, contained melted brown hide glue. The smell of the hot glue permeated the entire shop. It was my job to stir the pot and add a little water occasionally so the glue would not become too thick for spreading uniformly into all the crevices of furniture joints.

I must have asked a million questions, because I became very involved in his work, and my interest in cabinet making surely must stem from those visits. Yet, I cannot recall ever working on anything or handling any tool, but then again I was less than ten years old at the time. He not only constructed the pieces of furniture but also finished them; an art in itself. He seemed to have infinite patience; trying different finishes on scraps of wood to see which would best show the wood grain or polish best for a high-gloss. There were no synthetic finishes, just stains and oil or shellac varnishes, all of which he mixed himself. He tested and re-tested these dozens of times until he was satisfied. Only then would he start finishing the piece of furniture, which in itself took hours, at times days.

On my way home, I often encountered ice being delivered in summer to food stores and residence. Our perishable food was kept in a small wooden chest that had a compartment for a block of ice weighing about fifteen pounds. Ice was delivered by horse-drawn wagons, later in trucks, with canvass covering the back. Inside were large blocks of ice that the deliveryman would cut into smaller blocks. There was always a swarm of kids at each stop waiting to pick up the little pieces of ice that fell off when the large blocks were cut. The trick was getting the biggest piece ahead of the other fellows.

Ice cream was plentiful in the summer, sold from carts by street vendors and in parlors, where it was made often on location. Since there were no electric freezers in apartments, there was no way to keep ice cream at home. On special occasions it would be ordered from the dairy store, which delivered it in a double-walled steel cylinder. It was called *Fürst Pückler* ice cream and only came in a Neapolitan flavor combination, layers of chocolate, vanilla, and strawberry. The deliveryman would come back the following day to pick up the empty container. Obviously, this was a very expensive treat. Dad was a diabetic, so he was not allowed to eat sweets, but my mother and I more than made up for it.

During the week we would stop in a specialty shop during our long afternoon walks to buy chocolate-covered *Spitzkuchen*, a spice-cake in the shape of little wedge, which we demolished long before reaching home. On Sundays, my father would send me to the *Konditorei* (a fancy bakeshop) Möring to buy a *Rehrücken*. It was a chocolate-covered pound cake in the shape of a saddle of venison, laced with slivered almonds to simulate the fat-lacing used on venison meat.

As kids do all over the world, we played a game called *Hopse* (hopscotch.) With a chalk-pattern of squares on the sidewalk, the game was played by throwing an object, mostly house keys, onto one of the squares, then jumping from a base line into the square where the keys landed while touching each of the squares in between with one foot. Girls were much better at this game because they were more nimble.

We had *Reifen* (hoops), but not the Hula Hoop variety. Ours were thin, colored, wooden hoops that rolled in upright position when struck with a short wooden stick. The trick was to maintain these hoops upright while running alongside. The real challenge, though, was to roll them around corners.

For locomotion we had a *Roller* (scooter). It was similar to today's scooter, a steering column with short handles. I used mine so much that I developed a sore hip, and my mother insisted on throwing it out.

Pretend gun fights always appeal to boys. Our favorite game was cowboys and Indians. Some of us had feathered headdresses, others had cowboy outfits. There were specific rules as to how this game was played. Of course, cowboys had pistols and Indians had bows and arrows. Pistols came in different types, all simple and inexpensive. One type was the cap pistol. Behind the firing pin was a reel of *Zündplätzchen* (a red paper strip with small dots of firecracker powder). When the trigger was pulled, the pin would hit the paper strip, making a bang. One other type of pistol was more interesting since I never saw one like it anywhere else. It looked like a regular handgun. The barrel contained a little plunger connected to the trigger. From the front protruded a small, sharp barrel that was stuck into a potato to extract a little plug. When the trigger was pulled, the air pressure would shoot the "bullet" a few feet, making a little pop noise. It was quite realistic yet safe.

A variant was also a spring-loaded pistol and thin wooden dowel tipped with a suction cup to be shot from it. This pistol type was safe as well because the suction cups would stick to a smooth surface like a wall. But being kids, we had other ideas. Once as Indians, my group captured a cowboy. We tied him up against a wall, spread-eagle, and then started shooting at him. Luckily our aim was pretty poor, and his screams brought a mother who proceeded to take all our ammunition away. She then called all the other parents for a pow-wow to discuss the matter. From then on, all activity was restricted to target practice.

As we grew older, a source for neighborhood entertainment was racing little tin automobile models. Every boy had several models, one his favorite. On the outskirts of Berlin was the world famous Avus race track (akin to Sebring or the Indy 500). There, German cars battled it out with Italians–Auto-Union (later AUDI) and Mercedes vs. Alfa Romeo and Bugatti. We chalked our simulated *Avus* track on the pavement and propelled our little models around the track. Each of us became the personality of our favorite race driver. I was the Italian, Caracciola, driving an Alfa Romeo.

The trick was to come in first while staying within the lines. This was not easy because the little rubber wheels did not track straight. In order to correct this, we filled the underside with lead and added paraffin wax in strategic places so the cars ran true. Wheels were lubricated with graphite. Similar to playing golf, you were trading off distance for accuracy. When you hit the curve, however, you had to reverse the process of weighting so that the car would curve by itself. The real pros would play for pennies, but for the rest of us winning was enough of a reward because our standings went up among our peers.

Another outdoor game was marbles. These were small, solid glass balls, often with very interesting colored designs inside them. This game had several aspects to it. The winner was the one who came closest to a designated spot; the rules were related to the Mediterranean bocce ball. Since the winner got to keep the opponents' marbles after each game, skillful players had quite a collection. And this was another aspect of marbles, collecting. Really pretty marbles were not cheap, especially when they were a little larger, and much of the fun was to show off your collection of *Buggers* (pronounced booggers). These were the really large, collectors' items. During the winter, when outdoor entertainment was limited, I would often play Tiddlywinks with friends or parents. It was a great game for a winter's evening, and I am sorry that it is not being played anymore. I am sure, though, that it will have a comeback someday. It is a game of skill, played on the floor or table, preferably on a slightly resilient surface like a wool blanket. The aim is to try to snap little plastic disks into a cup. It develops dexterity and hand-to-eye coordination, and it is a lot of fun.

Another favorite winter activity was playing with my electric train. I received it as a Christmas (sic) present when I was about eight years old and played with it well into my teens. When first given the set, the train circled the Christmas tree in my dad's study. It consisted of a large locomotive with a coal tender, several passenger and freight cars, and a small station. But I accumulated a lot of extras over the years, and it became quite an elaborate system with tunnels, mountains, houses, trees, people, signals, even a freight depot. Many additional tracks allowed me to switch the train to an inside loop for uncoupling cars and other maneuvers.

It was the kind of toy I could enjoy by myself for hours or with friends, who often brought their own engine and cars. We would lie on the floor and dream of all the places we were visiting, the freight we hauled, the people who rode our trains, and the changes we could make in the system if we only had one additional item. As the system grew, it occupied a good part of the floor space in the study and made it impossible for my father to work there. My operations were therefore restricted to weekdays and times like early Sunday mornings when my parents slept in. By March, the system was dismantled and stored in boxes until next fall.

I guess playing with trains appealed to me because it offered an opportunity to combine a manual activity with something kindling my imagination; two facets of my character to this day. Along similar lines, I always enjoyed taking things apart to see how they worked. My first victim was an alarm clock that belonged to Uncle Eric. It was a cheap, large clock that gave up ticking after many years of faithful service. I opened it up very carefully, trying to remember how the parts interacted. But when time came to put it all back together, I had many gears left over. Strangely enough, I did manage to make the clock tell time, which impressed my uncle greatly, but I could not activate the alarm.

This gave me confidence to try bigger items, and as my dexterity grew my rate of success improved as well. But my experience with the alarm clock repeated itself many times in later life. I remember telling my mother how many extra washers and screws my bicycle had, all of them really not necessary because the bike ran very well without them after re-assembly.

Another fond recollection, is the *Leierkasten Mann* (the hurdy-gurdy man) who used to come regularly once a week from spring to fall. He had a peg leg painted black and a very colorful uniform with a blue sailor's cap. He was accompanied by a chimpanzee held on a very long chain, dressed in matching uniform. Musical selections on the piano roll never changed and included the popular song La Paloma. I heard his music so often that I can still hear the song in my mind, and every time I hear the song my hand moves subconsciously to turn the crank on an imaginary hurdy-gurdy.

The Leierkasten Mann appeared in the *Hofgarten* (court yard) behind the apartment building, and I would lean out of one of the rear windows to watch the performance, occasionally dropping a small coin. The little monkey was trained to run after the coins, collect them in his mouth, and then bring the haul to his master. Occasionally, when the mood struck the monkey, he would salute in the direction from which the coins came. The performance would last about five minutes, the man and his monkey would take a bow, and off they would go to the next building.

Even though I was a very good swimmer, I have been cautious of the water all my life. I trace it to the way I was taught. I do not think I was ready when my parents decided I should have swimming lessons. They took me to the *Wellenbad*, which was one of only a few indoor Olympic-size pools with artificial waves. The class consisted of just a few kids. To start our training, the teacher put a leather belt around each kid's waist and hooked a cord onto it. This cord attached to a pole, which the instructor held while walking at the edge of the pool as we swam. This kept us from sinking and allowed the teacher to observe how well we were able to keep above water by ourselves. Once the instructor decided that we did not need the life support, she would let us swim by ourselves for practice. Later, to build stamina, we had to swim when the wave machine was in operation.

That is when my troubles started because I was afraid of the machine, not the waves themselves. Somehow, I thought I would get electrocuted, probably based on someone's offhand remark. At the end of our training course, we were tested by having to swim fifteen minutes without interruption, using only breaststrokes. Receiving the certificate of having successfully completed the test was important since many public swimming areas limited access to swimmers with such a certificate.

During several successive summers we vacationed on Germany's Baltic Sea coast. It was part of my father's sales territory, which allowed him to spend more time with us. Often my grandmother, *Omi,* accompanied us. She kept my mother company, since my father was away during the day and could only be with us night and weekends. We spent the summer of 1931 in Heringsdorf. The next summer we went to Ahlbeck, a neighboring town. As in all other resort areas, one resort town is located next to another and they all pretty much looked alike.

One year we visited Swinemünde, another nearby resort town. An automobile ferry traveled from there to *Bornholm* in Denmark. We had never seen a car- ferry before let alone one big enough to accommodate an entire train in addition to automobiles. My parents decided to take me onboard for a visit. For some reason I became very upset from the minute we got on this boat. I screamed and yelled that I wanted to get off because I did not want to go to Denmark. Much to my parents' chagrin we left the ship before seeing much of it.

The only other memory I have of those vacations is that I was very interested in building sand castles. Every time my relatives came for a visit, I involved them in building sand castles with me. I remember Uncle Harry and family visiting and building the most imaginative castle decorated with Cousin Uschi's name on the front of one.

Some Background on the History of German Jews.

Jews lived in Germany ever since the Roman invasion about two thousand years ago. During that time, their experiences alternated between persecution and acceptance. Not being able to become members of craft guilds or own land, they were forced into occupations that were despised by the church, like money lending and operating pawnshops. Depending on time and location, they were also cattle traders and merchants, often quite successful at these activities.

By the time of the French revolution, Jews were gradually emancipated and finally given full citizenships after eighteen hundred seventy when Germany became a nation. Before that date it consisted of many little kingdoms, Dukedoms, etc. speaking a common language but without any national cohesion. Now German universities accepted Jewish students in all faculties including medicine and law, the latter drawing large Jewish attendances. Before long, Jews were in leading positions not only in finance but also in the media, the arts, sciences and government. A very high percentage of Jews entered the legal and medical professions and many Nobel Prize winners were Jewish, Albert Einstein among them.

Nevertheless, anti-Semitism was rampant under the Kaiser. Practically all bureaucratic positions, as well as those in the military, were closed to Jews. The Nazi era started long before Hitler came to power. Germany was in turmoil ever since the First World War. It culminated in the Nazis' seizure of total power on July 14, 1933, making the Nazi Party the only legal one in Germany. Some of what I will discuss is based on my own experience, some I learned from relatives and friends, and some is based on material I have read. I will try to indicate those facts that I experienced personally.

Germany went into the First World War thinking it was a short excursion. It turned into a four-year standoff with the loss of millions of lives. Having lost the war, Germans were totally demoralized looking for a scapegoat. In addition the economy was in tatters and, being forced to pay exorbitant reparations to the Allied Nations, there appeared little hope for the future. Germans saw themselves as never being able to meet these obligations.

Between 1919 and 1929, Germany went through one traumatic experience after another. Communism had taken over Russia and there was great fear that it would take root in Germany as well. Actually there was a brief Communist takeover in Bavaria. There was a period of terror between 1919 and 1922, during which a Foreign Minister, (Walter Rathenau, a Jew) was assassinated by right wing "freedom fighters". Street fighting was common as these extremists tried to take revenge on those who "stabbed the country in the back," i.e., made peace with the Allied Forces. Germany had gone from a colonial world power, second only to England, to one whose industry was in ruins and whose national pride was deeply hurt. Also, a large part of the country was occupied by France during the nineteen-twenties. Germany was forced to pay for this occupation in addition to paying reparations to the Allies as mentioned, thus its economy was in shambles.

To cope with the economic crisis of 1922, the government started to print money, which created inflation of immense proportions. By 1923, the year my parents married, the inflation had reached staggering heights. This led to a total breakdown of the banking system and the economy as a whole. Money was printed with banknotes up to a billion Marks denomination. The inflation lasted about 9 months.

By 1924, when I was born, the country had entered a period of economic readjustment. Banks were reorganized, and I believe a Central Bank was created. The Mark was stabilized and things started to improve, or so it seemed. Unfortunately, a period of economic instability followed, which hit all of Europe, not only Germany. By 1929 it hit the U.S.

Large segments of the population were out of work in Germany. Homelessness was rampant and there existed an all-pervasive national malaise. There was also a huge discrepancy between the few rich, many of whom were Jewish, and the overwhelming number of poor. The result was that people were looking for any kind of solution, grasping for ways to pull themselves out of their misery and to recreate self- respect. It was a great time for extreme ideologies, and demagogues. Both the left and the right had ready audiences because the government certainly did not come up with any remedies.

Between 1919 and 1933, the Weimar Republic was the only period of democracy in German history. This democratic period lasted until the elections in the fall of 1932. About forty parties were listed on the ballot. At election time, many posters were pasted on walls and windows by each of the forty parties. Sorting out differences between some of the parties was almost impossible for the ordinary citizen.

On one end of the political spectrum were the Communists, whose solution was a proletarian takeover to replace the existing structure with a dictatorship and a totally planned economy. This scared the German middle class. After all, Russia had actually gone through a bloody revolution and instituted that type of a Communist dictatorship. By 1929, Russia had developed a missionary orientation that aimed to export its ideology. The leading theoretician and activist was Leon Trotsky, a Russian of Jewish background. A German-Jewish Communist leader, Rosa Luxemburg, was gunned down and killed by Nazi radicals and, as mentioned, in the early 1920's a Soviet republic had been proclaimed in the State of Bavaria which had been put down by the military with the help of right wing nationalists.

The country was in turmoil! For many Germans, Communism on the left and Nazism on the right were appealing remedies. "Throw the rascals out; we'll do a better job; everybody will be treated equally; you will have a job. We'll take care of you." These were the slogans of the left.

On the right were the Nazis, whose message was: "We will restore pride in Germany, we will plan the economy, we will see to it that everybody has a job. We'll take care of you, we'll give you proper education, health care, etc. Furthermore, we will protect you from the Jewish Communists who want to grab your money and give it to the poor. We will protect you from the Jewish bankers and financiers who plunder you now.

Leadership should again be put into the hands of "real Germans". Of course, this played on the existing prejudice against Jews. "The Jews have sold us down the river; they stabbed us in the back in 1918." "It's all the fault of the Jews." "The Jews brought on the inflation and the depression."

No party achieved a majority at the ballot box, which meant that to govern coalitions had to be formed with smaller parties. The Nazis gained sufficient votes in the election of 1932 to be asked by President Hindenburg to try to form a government, which they did with the help other right wing parties. It should be emphasized that the Hitler regime was elected democratically. How they were able to leverage this election into absolute power is another story.

A word about the history and position of German Jews, which actually did not differ much from that in other parts of Western Europe. Anti-Semitism fluctuated from extreme hatred to toleration depending on location. There was never universal acceptance of Jews.

Historically, Jews were always of political and economic value to their rulers, although for different reasons. Until the beginning of the nineteenth century, Jews were forced to live in ghettos, depending on the area. Segregated from the rest of the German population, they were restricted in their economic contacts with non-Jews. They were only allowed to pursue those professions that benefited the local rulers. As mentioned earlier, after their emancipation in the early eighteen hundreds, Jews were allowed to move out of the ghettos and their occupational status gradually improved. Eventually, the living standard of many Jews equaled, at times even exceeded, that of the general population. The Nazis' initial aim was to reverse this process, which had taken more than a hundred years.

There is always a temptation to contrast the experience of American Negroes to that of German Jews. There were definitely some similarities, but also considerable differences. Blacks were brought to America as slaves to increase the income of their white owners. Even after they were freed, they continued to be the primary source of cheap labor in the U.S.

Not until recently were Negroes given a chance to enter the economic mainstream, and it will be a long time before their occupational status will equal that of the white population. So, from an economic perspective, the two experiences differed enormously. Yet, both peoples were exploited by their oppressors. Exploitation and discrimination go hand in hand. To exploit somebody, one has to be convinced of the other's inferiority. Humanitarian attitudes are based, I believe, on enlightened self- interest, something the Nazis in Germany and Negro haters in the U.S. did not believe in. Thus, Nazis had to downgrade Jews in the eyes of the rest of the Germans to make their economic disenfranchisement acceptable. Negroes, especially Southern Negroes, were labeled inferior for similar reasons.

Until the abrogation of Southern Jim Crow laws, Negroes were never considered fully human. Restrictions against them were harsher than what German Jews experienced under the Nazis until the outbreak of the Second World War. But nevertheless, the shock to the psyche of German Jews was probably more severe because there was an overnight regression from practically full acceptance as German citizens to the status of less than second-class citizenship, a status which Negroes experienced early in life. Without ever accepting it, Black kids gradually learned to come to grips with their lot as they grew up. German Jews, on the other hand, grew up as integrated proud Germans of Jewish religion.

There were isolated killings of Jews by zealous Storm Troopers in Germany, but the treatment of Blacks in the South was much more severe, especially since these atrocities were sanctioned by the State. It was not until laws were promulgated in 1935 (the Nuremberg Laws) that all contacts between Jews and non-Jews were greatly restricted. A small example was the installation of yellow benches in public parks designated "for Jews only", akin to separate drinking fountains etc. for Negroes in the U.S. All this changed after 1940 with the creation of slave labor and death camps, later death camps; the start of the "final solution".

When on *Kristallnacht* (later called "The Night of Broken Glass") on November 9, 1938, German vigilantes burned down synagogues, abused and even killed people, their actions were actually organized by the government. To the individual, it may differ little whether he is being hit over the head by a zealot or by a legal functionary of the government such as a Storm Trooper. But it does make a difference if the zealot knows his action is against the law as in the U.S.A., and the functionary feels virtuous in obeying the law as in Germany. And to that extent, German Jews were really much worse off because there was no real hope for improvement, only fear of further tightening of the screws.

As mentioned earlier, it was true that before Hitler's rise to power there were many of Jews in leading government positions, in the sciences, the media, and in business; not very much different from what one finds here in the U.S. Just as ethnic minorities in the U.S. strive to better their social position, so were German Jews, and they had a perfect right to expect that their German fellow citizens would recognize their abilities.

In general, German Jews of the 1930's voted for center parties and experienced the same frustrations as the rest of the German middle class. Preoccupied with Jewish wrongdoings and paranoid about "Jewish Power", the Nazis conveniently overlooked Jewish contributions to Germany. Their main thrust was pitched toward the frustrated middle class that saw itself wedged between the Communists and labor on the one hand, and bankers and business tycoons on the other. In their view, something was drastically wrong and needed a radical solution. The Nazis offered an easy answer: "It's the Jews' fault. Get rid of them and things will improve".

The Hitler Years

I described the historical context leading up to the election of 1932 that resulted in the Nazi regime gaining power and with it Hitler becoming Chancellor of Germany. Upon his election, he immediately started instituting his programs, which involved controlling the economy, promulgating restrictive laws so that all political freedoms ceased, and, of course, dramatically circumscribing all Jewish activities. A lot of these changes took place behind the scenes, but not for the Jews. Jewish stores were boycotted. Nazi Storm Troopers were placed in front of Jewish-owned stores, warning people not to shop there, often accosting those who nevertheless wanted to enter.

Members of the former opposition, especially Communists and Socialists, were rounded up and put into newly established *Konzentrationslager* (concentration camps). All this had the effect of intimidating the population at large, exactly what the Nazis wanted.

Shortages occurred in staples like eggs, butter, sausage, ham, bacon, etc. Soon strange products like cold storage eggs from

China appeared on store shelves. To strengthen the German currency, German-produced luxury products were earmarked for export and propaganda appealed to people's patriotism, urging reduced consumption even of consumer goods, so that these too could then be exported. The regime instituted meatless meals and *Eintopf* dishes (casseroles). These were actually quite tasty, consisting of combinations of beans, potatoes, vegetables, and a soup bone.

The word *Ersatz* (substitute) became part of the vocabulary. All kinds of substitutes appeared on the market; *Ersatz* cream, butter, and coffee, as well as non-food substitutes for rubber tires and fabrics. Our family did not really suffer from these restrictions. Since my father still traveled to the countryside, he managed to come home with butter, sausages, etc.

Later yet, some foods were rationed and I remember my mother looking down from our apartment balcony to see when the wholesaler had dropped off his deliveries at the dairy store downstairs. She would then immediately send me down to get our assigned weekly ration of six ounces of butter and six eggs.

My parents' basic conservatism now paid off. They had their favorite stores for almost every food category, always shopping at the same location. Furthermore, they had established a relationship with the owner over the years. Since shopkeepers all over the world like to please steady customers, my parents were able to get little extras at these times of stress. I enjoyed the antics shopkeepers would go through, wrapping something under the table for my parents when there were other customers in the store, or when they did not trust their employees. At other times they would tell my parents to come back later. Shops had to keep strict hours, but for people whom the owners knew, the back door would provide access after-hours.

Blue laws, which mandated that stores had to close at specific hours and be closed Sundays, were in effect in Berlin. Storekeepers were fined heavily when they broke these laws. Nevertheless,

I remember my parents knocking on doors, like the florist's on Sundays to pick up a gift of flowers they had forgotten to buy earlier. The florist was a kind, older gentleman who came every spring to plant petunias on our balcony.

Other changes brought about by the Nazis, however, affected us more personally. A policy of *Arisierung* (aryanization) was instituted for all businesses. This meant that all Jewish-owned businesses needed to be transferred to non-Jews, or at least run by party functionaries. This affected my father directly.

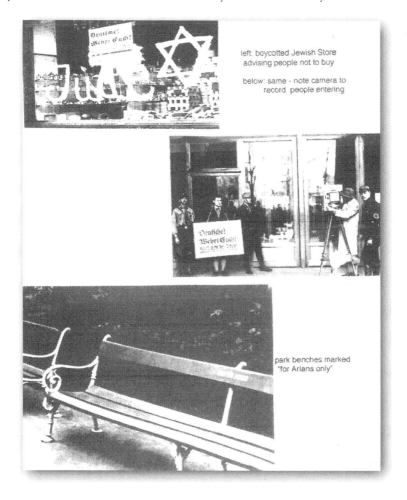

left: boycotted Jewish Store
advising people not to buy

below: same - note camera to
record people entering

park benches marked
"for Arians only"

In 1935, the *Nürnberger Gesetze* (Nuremberg Laws) were instituted. They were designed to "protect German blood, soil, and honor". These laws prohibited new marriages, or even co-habitation, between Jews and non-Jews. They also prohibited the employment of a woman under age forty-five in a Jewish household. Furthermore, these laws abrogated rights of full citizenship for Jews, prohibited any participation in referendums, and forced all Jewish government employees to retire. One would think these laws should have served as a signal to German Jews to leave the country. Some did, but unfortunately most did not. As "good Germans," they refused to see the handwriting on the wall, my parents included.

Our maid Ella had to be discharged, but still she visited us weekly, frequently loaded with goodies from the country. And, when we left Germany in 1939, she accompanied us to the train station to say good-bye for the last time crying her heart out.

On cold winter nights, Nazi big shots would stand on street corners holding canisters to collect money to aid the needy. They instituted a system called *Winter Hilfe* (winter assistance), which distributed free coal and potatoes. Undoubtedly it helped some people in need, but the Nazi's cynicism was to present themselves as egalitarians on the side of the poor when in fact they were neither. In addition, several Nazi leaders used these events as photo opportunities in which they flaunted their anti- Semitic propaganda. One example comes to mind: when Hermann Göring (at that time number two or three in the government) stood on the corner of a main thoroughfare clanking the coins inside the can, hollering,: *"Gibt für die Einbahn Strasse der Juden nach Jerusalem"* (give for a one-way street of the Jews to Jerusalem).

Were there any positive programs instituted by the new regime? Yes, there were, but all seemed to have an ulterior motive. For instance, to reduce the ranks of the unemployed a military draft was instituted. It took the unemployed youth off the streets, which was deemed desirable by the public. However, it also provided the Nazi ideologues with the means by which they trained a new military force (in violation of the Versailles treaty) that was indoctrinated with Nazi ideology.

The new regime also created the *Arbeitsfront* (work front) as an adjunct to the military. It required seventeen year old boys to spend one year in public service before officially entering the military. It was a quasi-military organization, which worked on public work projects such as reforestation, building dikes, fighting forest fires, etc. The emblem of the *Arbeitsfront* was a spade, which every recruit was issued and had to take care of like a soldier's rifle. This system was well accepted because it taught young men discipline and provided useful work in a healthy environment.

Another one of the two-sided programs was *Kraft durch Freude* (strength through joy). It incorporated several aspects that only became evident after Germany entered the Second World War. On the surface, it was a program designed to help workers enjoy their vacations without having to spend a great deal of money, a laudable goal. A system of group vacations was developed, which ranged from staying at a resort to overseas cruises. These vacations were extremely popular, and from a political standpoint the program helped the Nazis immensely.

But there was a darker side to these programs as well. Cruise ships had to be built, which further increased employment. But in reality, these cruise ships were warships and therefore built in circumvention of the German/British naval agreement. These cruise ships were armor-plated for later use as troop carriers.

Furthermore, the itinerary took them to ports that turned out to be strategic targets during World War II. For instance, they called on ports like Bergen in Norway, Tunis in North Africa, and many ports in Greece, just to name a few. In each of these ports, swarms of tourists would go ashore with their cameras, among them a number of intelligence officers who photographed shore installations and other points of strategic interest.

Some of this duplicity was understood by the public. A favorite joke from that time went something like this: a young husband works in a factory making baby carriages. Because his wife was pregnant, she asks him to steal the parts one by one, so that they don't have to buy a buggy. He does just that, and one fine Sunday he tells his wife that he has all the parts and he'll spend the afternoon assembling the buggy. After several hours he comes into the kitchen to tell his wife that he just cannot understand it; no matter how he assembles the pieces, they always result in a machine gun.

From what my parents told me, the public knew it was being hoodwinked but did not mind. After a while it was impossible to tell propaganda from truth. But things were becoming better economically for most and that mattered a great deal. Many people looked the other way or made excuses with such statements as, "I don't agree with all that is being done, but overall things have improved." And aside from the treatment of their Jewish friends (those who had any) there was little to complain about.

Many problems, especially those that bothered the middle class, had been eliminated. Pride had been restored, pride in themselves and their country. Cities had been cleaned up, the homeless were off the streets, and the German pre-occupation with orderliness and cleanliness was given new respect. There was no more pornography on stage and screen, no more graffiti, no more overt homosexuality. Instead, young people were hiking in the forests again and singing patriotic songs, having clean fun. Never mind that these outings were paramilitary, "a little discipline never hurt anybody". Never mind, that the homeless, homosexuals, and some Jews were put into concentration camps and deprived of all their rights, "they probably deserved it".

But there was also a lot to see for those who had an inclination to look. There was a large bookburning ceremony at which Dr. Göbbels, the propaganda minister, presided. All books by Jewish authors were burned, together with any book written by a communist, socialist, or social democrat author. Books by writers who were civil libertarians, free thinkers or anybody who opposed the regime, were tossed into the pyre as well. Many of these books were classics of world literature, and many of these books were not by German authors.

The National Museum for Fine Arts had an exhibition called *Entartete Kunst* (degenerate art), featuring almost entirely modern art. Avant-garde artists, from Picasso to many young painters of the time, were all held up to public ridicule. Their work was shown in juxtaposition to primitive art from Africa as examples of art by "close relatives of monkeys". Of course, the Nazis made sure that these painting were not burned, because they knew very well their value on world markets.

Most people knew of the concentration camps, although the Nazis never mentioned them in their news releases. It was believed that vagrants, gypsies, political troublemakers, and other people with anti-social behavior were being re-educated in these camps. They were not. Through Jewish contacts they must also have learned of Jewish inmates in these camps and about political prisoners. If one remembers that the Communist Party captured a very large share of the German electorate, one is astounded how little opposition the Nazis encountered after they took over. Communist leaders who did not flee the country were rounded up and sent to camps. But the rank and file quietly joined the Nazi party, where they immersed themselves quickly and quietly. We called them "*Hamburgers* –outside brown (the color of the Nazi uniform), inside red". To prove their allegiance, many became more rabid than Nazi party members.

Feelings of apprehension and fear were widespread among the Jews in Berlin. Among our friends, it was commonplace to unplug telephones when talking about sensitive matters. Whether phones were in fact tapped on a mass scale is doubtful, but I recall going to the phone outlet to pull the plug, which created in me a certain conspiratorial feeling for the hushed conversation that followed.

Similarly, my mother would always look for signs of censorship before opening letters from relatives or friends overseas. In fact, there existed a special language used by her when corresponding with Uncle Harry in South Africa, which conveyed messages they hoped the censor would miss.

In conversation among themselves, German Jews had their own vocabulary which dated back to Medieval times. Although some of these words were akin to Yiddish, most were not. Some of the words were taken from the Hebrew. For instance, we identified a fellow Jew as a Barjisroel. The origin of other words I do not know. The word Stieke was used to signal someone to be quiet or to watch out. (The Hebrew Union College in Cincinnati published a little dictionary of German/Jewish expressions).

We did not have a short-wave radio. Not only was it illegal to own one, but these radios were quite expensive before they were prohibited. Some of my friends did, however, have one and I would visit often to listen to Radio Strasbourg in France. This station broadcast the news in German every evening and was really the only source of uncensored information. The broadcasts would start with the station identification: *"Hallo, hallo, ici Radio Strasbourg"*, after which the news would follow in German. The room was hushed, the curtains were drawn, phones unplugged. The adults listened with grave faces, hoping to hear that the world cared about what happened to us in Germany. It did not!

Being a radio operator during the war, it was uncle Harry who gave me a crystal radio set with headphones. Crystal sets were really a forerunner of solid state electrical circuits as we know them today. The crystal was housed in a little glass vial that had one fixed and one moveable contact. The moveable contact consisted of a little handle with a metal filament that allowed the operator to touch different locations on the silicon crystal. We hooked up this little unit in a cigar box, together with the necessary modulator and jacks for earplugs, ground, and antenna. No batteries were required. Under the right conditions, I was able to listen to distant stations.

To make external ground and antenna connections, I experimented with different hook-ups like water pipes, balcony railings and hit on the idea of using the telephone conduit pipe. Suddenly my horizon broadened. I was able to listen in on telephone conversations, not only those of my parents but our neighbors as well. Without realizing it, I built a telephone bug. I played around with this for about a week before my parents found out what I was doing. They made me stop immediately, not only because of the ethics involved, but also out of fear of the authorities. But my ability do this only confirmed their suspicion about telephone calls being monitored.

Two

Emigration

The Gathering Storm

Jewish emigration gradually increased between 1933 and 1936. The first ones to leave were Jews as well as non-Jews who had been politically active or just astute. They were relatively few in numbers. Many of them had close relatives overseas, were familiar with foreign countries, spoke foreign languages, had professions that were easily transferable, and/or had plenty of money. Others, like university professors, often received invitations from institutions overseas to join a faculty, Albert Einstein for instance.

But the bulk of German Jews were convinced that this was a passing phase in German history. Many had fought in World War I and had very strong patriotic feelings. Even though they realized that anti-Semitism was endemic in Germany, many had enough contact with non-Jews to have established friendships. These people felt that they belonged. Often their non-Jewish friends would counsel them not to leave because they too were convinced that this was a passing phase, a bad dream. In other words, the most assimilated German Jews were often the last to leave.

The next phase of emigration started right after the 1936 Olympic Games, held in Berlin. The ambivalence mentioned above continued, but gradually Hitler tightened the screws. Because of the many foreign visitors, there was little evidence of anti-Jewish propaganda prior to and during the games. Göbbels, the Minister of Propaganda, even stated, *"Keinem Juden wird auch nur ein Haar gekrümmt* (not even one hair will be bent on any Jew's head)." But after the Olympic Games, conditions worsened considerably. For example, yellow benches, for Jews only, were installed in all city parks. Many businesses were finally *Arisiert* (aryanized), which meant they were taken over by Nazi functionaries, and the systematic, arbitrary, harassment of Jews began.

Within my family, things had begun to change as well. Uncle Harry was politically more astute than my parents, or perhaps he was better informed through his wife's relatives, some of whom were not Jewish. He actively looked for places to which to emigrate. I believe it was in 1935 that he suggested to my father that our two families should plan to emigrate to South America. He read that Paraguay welcomed immigrants, each family would be given some land and support for the first year. He had investigated the matter and found that the offer was legitimate. Furthermore, he said, he had read Hitler's book, *Mein Kampf*, and had come to the conclusion that there was no hope for Jews in Germany. My father dismissed the idea out of hand saying that he was not cut out to "hunt bears in the forests of South America".

However, this did not deter uncle Harry. He and his wife decided to learn Spanish intensively. Meanwhile, some of their friends emigrated to South Africa. Suddenly the situation changed when these friends suggested to my uncle he should join them there with his family. Uncle Harry came back to my father with the thought that we all go together. Again my father rejected the idea as too drastic a step. Harry decided to go alone with Aunt Hilde and Uschi. They left in 1936.

After 1933, when the Nazi period began, my father's routine changed. It became progressively more difficult for him to travel. Hotels displayed signs in the window that Jews were not desired: "*Juden unerwünscht,*" after an edict came down from the Nazi Party for hotels not to accept Jews. But not all hotels complied. Word got around where it was okay to stay and where it was not. Sometimes hotels had the warning sign in the window, but the inn-keeper would say to people he knew, "It's all right for you to stay here, but we would prefer that you not embarrass us by eating in the restaurant." This was because all the regular customers, mostly salesmen, ate at the table d'hôte (the innkeeper's table). Some of these hotelkeepers were not especially friendly toward Jews, but they did not want to lose the business. Others genuinely wanted to help people whom they had known and respected for years, but they did not want to get into trouble with local party bosses.

Such restrictions made it more and more difficult for my father to travel distances that required overnight stays. He would make day trips with increasing frequency and just make occasional overnight trips. Strangely enough, his customers all knew he was Jewish and he had no trouble selling. But it was obvious that things were getting more difficult month by month.

Why was my father so reluctant to leave? Several factors played a role, foremost among these must have been his business situation. As explained earlier, my father's business was the marketing of agricultural jute and hemp products. There were very few people in that line of business, and everybody involved knew everyone else. My father had known one of his non-Jewish competitors for years and was on very close terms with him. This man was a reserve officer in the German army and had joined the Nazi Party in 1933. Because of his rank as an officer, he quickly rose in the party and attained some position of influence.

Sometime during 1934-35, this man approached my father suggesting that the two businesses merge, in other words my father's business would be aryanized. He thought it would help my father by obtaining non-Jewish cover and would help himself cut down on overhead. The two agreed with a handshake. As travel became more difficult, this man (I forgot his name) suggested that they change their operation; my father would concentrate on inside office activities and handle just a few of his old customers who lived nearby.

The Developing Doom

Around 1932, we moved to a cheaper apartment, reflecting the deteriorating economic condition around the time Hitler took over. It was within walking distance of the other apartment, but it was not as good a neighborhood. Lower cost housing was located across the street; bungalows occupied by retired public service employees.

Niebuhr Straße 64, Charlottenburg
(we lived on the second floor)

While the new apartment was not as big as the older one, it was not small by any means, and we still had four bedrooms. But, with economic conditions worsening, the landlord divided the apartment into two smaller ones about a year or two later. We took the front apartment facing the street, with three bedrooms.

The new apartment was located on the second floor with a balcony, and in the distance one could see the elevated railway tracks. Nights, when the street traffic died down, one could hear the trains running into the early hours. At street level were two shops. One was occupied by a tailor named Wolf, whose wife was the concierge. In later years, the Wolfs saved my father from being sent to a concentration camp. The other shop was a small dairy store. I went there every morning to pick up our breakfast needs.

One day there was a major commotion on the street in front of our house. The street was closed off by police, and storm troopers, the brown-shirted Nazis were all over the place. My grandmother was visiting at the time, and she and I stood on the balcony watching the scene. Suddenly an open, black Horch limousine came down the street together with a hearse. There was no mistaking the car because it was the type always used by Hitler. The procession stopped in front of our house, Hitler got out of the car and walked into one of the bungalows across the street, where he stayed for what seemed a long time. When he emerged, a coffin was carried out and loaded into the hearse. Hitler got back into his car left with its entourage. An old party comrade had died and Hitler had paid his last respects.

That evening, my grandmother kept saying over and over how sorry she was not having dropped a flower pot on Hitler's head, since he stood right under our balcony. My mother's reply was typical. "How do you know that was really him; I heard he never goes anywhere, always sends a double." And yet, I often wondered in later years whether my grandmother could have changed the course of history if, on a sudden impulse, she really would have dropped a pot of petunias on Hitler's head. She was a very determined lady, and it could have been within the realm of the possible.

She hated the Nazis to the extent that I saw her once sitting in the kitchen, peeling potatoes onto a newspaper with Hitler's picture on the front page and stabbing his face every time she finished a potato.

One other incident sticks in my mind. On a Saturday afternoon in 1932, my parents and I went to one of the lakes on the edge of Berlin. We had a great time and it was late afternoon before we started for home. People were lined up to buy tickets for the elevated suburban train that would take them home. My mother waited on a park bench while my father and I walked along the line toward the front to see when the next train would leave. Suddenly, a man stepped out of line and offered his place to my father. Apparently his wife, who waited in another line, signaled that she already bought tickets.

My dad took the man's place. Somebody further up in line started to protest but my father stood his ground. The protester became more belligerent and my father more determined. Before long, fists were flying and the man wound up with a bloody nose. Next thing we knew, there was a policeman on the scene taking both men to the precinct station. Everything was noted down, including the fact that my dad was Jewish. The man did not press charges and the entire matter was dropped. Next year, after Hitler's rise to power, there was a lot of fear in our household that this man might remember the incident, now that justice was in his favor, and seek revenge. Luckily, nothing ever came of it.

I graduated from the *Volksschule* in 1934. This presented my parents with difficult decisions. One concerning the type of school to which I should apply, either a regular *Gymnasium*, or a *Realgymnasium*; the difference between them being in curriculum emphasis (classical vs. modern languages, nine years attendance versus only six). The second question was whether to enroll me in a Jewish school. First they decided that I should apply to the *Leibniz Ober-Realgymnasium* which had an excellent reputation. I was not the academic type, and considering the times it was more practical to know French and English. The school was located within walking distance from where we lived. Acceptance was based on grammar school grades and an examination. There was a Jewish quota, which meant that few, if any, Jewish kids would be admitted. Since individual classes were at most forty students, there was a good chance that, if admitted, I would be the only Jewish kid in class.

I found the exam relatively easy. I even remember the topic of the essay I was asked to write: "I saw a fire engine." I was accepted, but after much soul searching my parents decided to send me to a Jewish school. They consulted our friend, Rabbi Swarsenski, who arranged for me to be accepted in the Lessler Schule. I believe he also arranged for reduced tuition, because this was an expensive school and beyond my parents' means. The school's teaching plan was equivalent to a *Realgymnasium*, and was located about a half-hour ride from my home. My friend Peter Wagner, who was a straight "A" student, applied at the public Gymnasium, was accepted and attended until Kristallnacht. Thereafter he attended a Jewish school located minutes away from mine.

Playing Mandolin at Class Outing
(front row, fourth from right.)

Lessler Schule was located in Grunewald, a suburban area of villas and large mansions. In winter, a streetcar took me there, but in the spring and fall I rode my bicycle. In later years, my parents insisted I commute only by streetcars because traffic had increased a great deal along the route I traveled.

The school was called a *Waldschule* (forest school) because it was located among the trees. It was a large old estate which belonged to Walter Rathenau at one time. He was, as mentioned earlier, the Jewish Minister of Foreign Affairs assassinated by Nazis in 1922. Toni Lessler bought the residence and converted it into a lovely school. There were about fifteen kids in my class. A huge glass arboretum was converted to a gym. The grounds were beautiful, and in one small bare area we were each given a little plot of land to learn how to garden. An ironic aside: last I saw the school housed the embassy of Qatar.

Frau Toni Lessler was a top-notch educator started a private school for girls long before the Nazi period. In 1933 non-Jewish parents were forced to take their kids out of the Jewish school and to make up the lost revenue she and her spinster sister, *Fräulein* (Miss) Heine expanded operations to be co-educational.

School hours were from 8:00 a.m. to 1:00 p.m., with some kids staying all day. One semester of gardening was mandatory for everyone, as was one year of handicrafts. I enjoyed these classes because they allowed for some creativity. I learned bookbinding and remember making a Hanukkah menorah using my mother's spent thread spools.

Even though the students came out of upper middle class homes, the school was very much oriented politically toward Labor Zionism. It was unique in another way, as well. Obviously we lived during very unstable times and had no idea to where we would ultimately emigrate. Therefore, our school participated in a program that prepared students for a high school board examination called the Cambridge matriculation. This accreditation was recognized not only in England, but throughout the English speaking world.

Later, a number of my friends left Germany on *Kindertransporte* (a special children rescue program to England), my friend Klaus Peter among them. Passing the Cambridge exam provided eligibility to enter the English university system, and many of our classes were geared to the English matriculation exam. This meant we were really governed by two school plans: the German school plan mandated by the State, plus a curriculum to the English high school level.

My first class teacher was *Fräulein* (Miss) Heine, a strict disciplinarian. When we completed our first year, *Fräulein* Heine gave each of us a little notebook with her entry on the front page. Mine said: Ernst *Kuck-in-die-Luft* (daydreaming Ernest). Obviously my mind wandered a lot early on, and this trait has stayed with me throughout my life.

In spite of the Cambridge affiliation, French was taught first, followed by English instruction the next year, yet I absorbed far more English because of the teacher. Our French teachers were oriented toward French literature, and much time was spent during the first year learning grammar and vocabulary, followed the second year by French classics. Being dyslexic, I had difficulties reading and my interest lagged.

On the other hand, English was taught by a young, dynamic, teacher. All the girls loved *Herr* Lesser. He was young, good-looking, and charming. His method of teaching was conversational and idiomatic, which was quite unconventional at that time. He saw grammar as a backup rather than the main emphasis, and we learned conversational English, with much memorizing of idiomatic expressions.

Math was another difficult subject for me. Again, being dyslexic, I kept inverting numbers, coming up with wrong results. To make matters worse, regular math was augmented by the English system of measurements and currencies. *Herr* Birnbaum was well intentioned but unable to motivate me. He was jovial, always telling jokes, which he enjoyed more than anyone else. But he was strict and he and I did not get along too well.

The same can be said for the German teacher, *Fräulein* Anker. She had a number of strange mannerisms. She constantly stroked the top of desk nearest her and then wiped her hand on her dress. Of course, we could not resist smearing some ink on the desk, and after noticing the ink stain on her dress she had a screaming fit. The school director rushed to the classroom and punished a number of us. Ultimately, I heard that after the war, fate brought Miss Anker to San Francisco, where she became a saleslady at I. Magnin.

During the last two years in school, the program emphasized English history and literature, especially Shakespeare. Although I was always interested in history, I was so far behind by then that I really did not gain much from these classes. On the other hand science classes motivated me. These were the most interesting, most rewarding, and most important classes during my high school years because they channeled my later career interest.

Chemistry and physics were taught by *Herr* Neufeld, a gentleman in his mid-fifties who met a tragic end. He was arrested on November 9, 1938, *Kristallnacht,* and sent to a concentration camp. A couple of months later he was released but he was a zombie. He came back to school one day, unable to function at all, and shortly thereafter he died. A gentle person, he was a man who was able to teach science through failed experiments; I am sure they were not planned to fail, they just flopped. However, the way he handled their failure was more instructive than if the experiment had been successful. We would discuss these failures at great lengths and by involving us directly in the failed experiment, he effectively taught science. In spite of his clumsiness, or perhaps because of it, he was an outstanding teacher.

Our music teacher, Dr. Misch, looked like a character out of comic opera: tall and skinny, bald with a fringe of gray hair and gold-rimmed glasses. He was totally absorbed in music, but unfortunately he was unable to connect with his students. While he played furiously at the piano, we cut up. Every now and then he would look up over music notes and, realizing what went on, began a screaming tirade. Then, with his anger vented, he immediately found solace again in his music, oblivious to what went on around him.

I should mention one other very important individual, our gym teacher, Herr Mayer. We suspected him to be a Nazi as he looked and acted like a one. Blond, blue-eyed, his hair cropped close to his scalp, he looked like the epitome of an SS officer. He had a scar across one cheek, which indicated he belonged to a *Schlagende Verbindung* (a member of a student dueling society). These were college fraternity organizations, uniquely German, which required settling disputes by saber duels. It should be noted that being Jewish would have prevented him from being a member of a non-Jewish dueling society, but there existed at least two such Jewish organizations. Mayer saw it as his task to make hardy souls out of each of us Jewish boys.

Boxing was a very popular sport at that time, not only in Germany but all over the Western world. Mayer, instituted a system lifted from his fraternity, settling disputes in a boxing ring. Similarly to his fraternity duels, our disputes were called *Ehrensachen* (matters of honor). So whenever a boy felt insulted, accosted, or otherwise threatened, he would request a boxing bout to settle his *Ehrensache*. The class would then form a ring around the two to watch them fight it out with barefists. It was very cruel because it allowed the big kids to pick on the little ones. But then again, this was part of the Nazi philosophy.

To put this in perspective, such aggressive behavior was in direct opposition to my upbringing at home. Not that my father was afraid of a good fight, as evidenced in the story I told earlier, when he got into a fistfight when buying train tickets. He would urge me on occasion to stand up for myself and to stand my ground in disputes with my peers. But it was my mother who, time and again would counsel that *"Der Klügere giebt immer nach,"* which translates "the wiser [person] always gives in".

In Mayer's defense, it must be said that he may not have invented this sport but was required to institute it by order of the Nazi school authorities, and the same system may well have been in effect in all high schools. I hated these matches, and the few times I was involved always resulted in a bloody nose which was fortunate for me because this stopped the fight.

Another example of his Spartan approach was a daily run around a nearby lake irrespective of the weather. I don't know how long these runs took, but I remember them as interminable. After the run, a cold shower was mandatory; in winter that was worse than running in the snow in gym shorts.

In spite of Herr Mayer, I enjoyed gym classes. Not that I was a jock, far from it. I was a klutzy kid, relatively stiff-jointed even at that age. Nevertheless, I enjoyed competitive running, the parallel and horizontal bars, as well as the rings. Probably because of that I have continued working out ever since.

Undoubtedly, aside from my science teacher, I have been most influenced by *Herr* Oppenheim, our history teacher. His teaching abilities left me with a lifelong interest in the subject. He specialized in the Greek and Roman periods, which he was able to bring to life, to make them relevant to events happening around us. Such method of teaching must have been especially difficult and even dangerous considering the all- pervasive dictatorship under which we lived.

The director of the school, Dr. Landsberg, was a well-meaning man who was strict but approachable. Recently I learned that he was not Jewish. I remember one episode that stayed with me the rest of my life. One day he called a general assembly. He wanted to share a traumatic experience with us as an object lesson. It involved a very close friend with whom he had a dispute that resulted in their not speaking to each other for months. When he learned that his friend fell ill, he was too proud to contact him.

Then his friend died, and Dr. Landsberg was devastated. Since one never knows whether, or when, one will see a friend again, the obvious lesson was not to let any opportunity pass to make up after a conflict. Considering the times we lived in, the lesson was well understood by all of us and taken to heart.

As stated, I was a poor student except in subjects that really interested me. Part of my problem started with the adjustment to a co-educational system. Also, mine was a very ritzy school and my parents were on the low end of the income scale at that time. For example, while I bicycled, some kids arrived in chauffeured cars.

As mentioned, I had difficulties with reading. Instead, I liked to observe people at work, watch sport events and go to museums. In the end, I never graduated. My grades had deteriorated to the point where I would have to do a class over again, but by that time we were in the throes of emigration. In a little more than a decade I would receive a Master's degree from Stanford University, but more of this later.

My disinterest in books frustrated my father terribly. Time and again he would admonish me to read. One day he came home with an armful of Karl May books. This changed things. Karl May was a writer whose fame was confined to Germany. He lived around the turn of the twentieth century, and his career spanned about thirty years. In his youth he traveled with a German circus, where he met American cowboys and Indians. He was fascinated by their lore and made it his own. He never saw the Wild West but wrote a lot about it. His books "Old Shatterhand" and "Winnetou" were standard reading fare for all German kids. He was a prolific writer with many dozens of books to his name.

I was so enthralled by these stories that I forgot about not liking books and gradually developed an appetite for reading. As a matter of fact, after a while my father got upset with me for reading too much and not spending enough time out in the fresh air. (Obviously, children can never please their parents) Nor was my reading limited to Wild West stories. My interest in science and history soon channeled me in that direction and books on these subjects had a great influence on my life. Especially two such books come to mind: *"Mikroben Jäger"* (Microbe Hunters) by Paul de Kruif and *"Die Geschichte der Menschheit"* (History of Mankind) by Hendrick van Loon.

A classic German novel, *"Soll und Haben"* (Debit and Credit) by Gustav Freytag, fascinated me as well. I could relate to this book, even though it was written in the previous century. Two of the three main characters were Jewish, one a scholar the other a crook. It was a tale of a young hero, a righteous German businessman being fleeced by the crook but striking up a very close friendship with the scholar. I believe he married the scholar's beautiful sister. I enjoyed the book even though there were definitely anti-semitic undercurrents throughout the book. I read all of these books many, many times.

After-school activities involved homework, play, or a youth group. I belonged to a Jewish boys group headed by *Herr* Preuss. We were about twenty-five boys. *Herr* Preuss was a retired bachelor schoolteacher who constantly smoked smelly cigars. He lived in a little two or three room apartment. He divided us into interest groups. Some played chess while others built model airplanes. He was an avid stamp collector, and through him I developed my interest in collecting stamps. He really enjoyed working with boys, and he was totally dedicated to his activity. As a retired teacher, he drew a pension and the twenty or so parents paid him enough to keep him in cigars.

In a way, it was a boy's club and Herr Preuss really did a fabulous job of motivating us. On some weekends we would go on hikes or to museums, short trips like to nearby Potsdam or to the Pergamon Museum. It was an enrichment program for us all.

During summers and early fall, when not away on vacation, my friends and I spent most of our time at Halensee, a swim resort on one of a chain of lakes in Berlin. It consisted of a large clubhouse, a small gravelly beach, and pontoons with diving boards. Being older now, it was time to obtain my *Fahrtenschwimmer* certification, which meant a demonstrated ability to swim continuously for 45 minutes.

There, I stole my first kiss from a girl–under water. I was so excited about it that I couldn't sleep all night. Her name was Lilly Liepmann. She was a cute little blond who sat in front of me in class. From then on we spent more and more time together to the detriment of our grades.

The winter months provided different entertainment. Many lakes were totally frozen and tennis courts were flooded to create ice skating rinks. I had *Schlittschuhe* (skates), which were clamped onto our hiking boots. Wealthier kids had bootskates and I was especially envious of those owning "racers". We wore knicker-bockers (knickers), which were fashionable about that time, a long scarf, and a woolen hat that rolled over the ears for warmth. Admission was relatively inexpensive and I spent many wonderful hours on the ice.

Loudspeakers usually blared schmaltzy Viennese music, setting the atmosphere. Different areas were roped off for people to prac-tice dancing on the ice, for little kids to get started, and for bigger kids to play ice hockey. The rest of the area was organized bedlam. Groups of kids would form long chains, racing around, alternat-ing between conga and chorus line formations. Racers would dart around the edges, then seeing an opening somewhere, would sud-denly change course to cut through or pick up on a chain.

Time would fly, and even though it was terribly cold, we would spend hours on the ice. We warmed up over hot chocolate in the clubhouse. There was a big iron potbelly stove in the center of the shack with benches all around it. The smell inside was overwhelm-ing, a combination of food, sweat, and wet clothing.

During one of the really cold winters, I stayed on the ice too long and developed frostbite. The doctor prescribed a treatment that seemed worse than the affliction, immersing my feet in very hot and then in very cold water. At the end of about fifteen minutes of this torture, my feet were as red as boiled lobster and itched terribly. My frostbite was never really cured, and to this day it bothers me whenever my feet get very cold in winter.

Another popular winter sport was *rodeln* (sledding). I owned a beautiful wooden sled big enough for two. A streetcar took us to hilly parks at the edge of town. On weekends, my parents would take me to the *Grunewald*, the large forest where my high school was located. I remember when I was about seven sliding down steep hills with my father or mother, and then both of them together pulling me back to the train station on the way home.

Movies were another diversion during the winter months. There was a *Kino*, a small movie house not far from home. Admission was very cheap; I believe it cost fifteen *Pfennig*. Of course Laurel and Hardy were our favorites, but we also enjoyed cowboy movies with Tom Mix and comedies with Buster Keaton. Much of the material came from the U.S. and was dubbed in German. There were also good German movies, one titled *"Lumpazi Vagabundus"*, a story of a vagrant who knew how to live off the land during the hard time of the Depression without losing his dignity.

At times I obtained free tickets to a number of shows. In order to fill the theater and create publicity, show promoters gave free tickets to shopkeepers who were willing to display posters in the window. Since there were a number of stores in the block where I lived and we bought from all of them, I was frequently able to get tickets. I remember seeing Lionel Hampton with his band, probably in 1936, since that was the year of the World Olympics and the regime relaxed its stringent racial regulations. Being black and playing jazz, which the Nazis called *Negermusik* (nigger music), he would not have been allowed to perform before or after that time. I thoroughly enjoyed the performance even though I could not relate to the music. I never saw a performance like it. Hampton was all energy, alternating between playing the xylophone and tap dancing; sometimes doing both simultaneously.

I also remember attending a number of Jewish plays, among them the "*Golem*", "*Shabbtai Tzvi*", and a school performance of "A Midsummer's Night Dream," The "Shabbtai Tzvi" play made a great impression on me because it dealt with a false prophet; a charismatic Jew who took advantage of his uneducated fellow Jews and who finally betrayed them to save his own neck.

I learn only recently did that these plays were performed by an outstanding Jewish professional ensemble, the *Jüdischer Kulturbund*, which consisted of artists who were not permitted by the Nazi regime to perform on public stages.

I had several friends from school. One of them, Bruno Frauenfeld, lived not far from school. His father retired as an investment banker when the firm was taken over by the Nazis. The Frauenfeld's were quite wealthy and owned a beautiful villa on a lake not far from school. I visited Bruno often and we spent many hours on the lake in a wooden canoe. It was a long, narrow lake, houses facing it on both sides, with a number of short, stone bridges crossing the lake.

Once, when passing under one of these bridges, I saw upsetting graffiti covering the walls: "*Juden 'runter vom See!*" (Jews off the lake). I remember that this graffiti upset us more than all the propaganda we saw daily. It was personal and must have been put there by some kids we knew living in one of the villas on the lake. Another experience was more pleasant. One of the houses was occupied by a well-known movie star. On sunny afternoons we could see her practicing her lines on the terrace, and we would make it a point to cruise by as slowly as possible, far enough away to be respectful but close enough to hear her recitations.

One year (probably 1937), there was a citywide Jewish sports festival. All the Jewish schools competed against each other, and it took place in the sports stadium of the Jewish community. I participated on the 200 meter relay team and we came in second place. I also competed in high jumps, but I do not believe I did well. I did a little better in the broad jump.

The only accident in which I was hurt resulted in a broken arm. I played handball with kids in the neighborhood on a playing field not far from home. Contrary to handball as it is known in the U.S., the game was the reverse of soccer, i.e., your foot is not allowed to touch the ball. Also there was a safe area around the goal so that you could not get up close to the goal to score. It was a great game with a lot of running activity. Somehow I managed to trip over the ball, fall on my arm and break it.

My parents took me to a doctor who set the bone. After the cast came off we noticed that there was a very slight impairment in my arm movement. I received a lot of physical therapy that helped in straightening out the arm, but the impairment remained. My parents decided to sue the physician, and I remember having to go to court to show my arm. My mother was called as a witness, and after her testimony the judge complimented her objectivity. My parents won the case.

My parents were very concerned about my learning appropriate social skills. They enrolled me in a Jewish tennis club. Although I received lessons, I never amounted to anything in tennis, but I enjoyed the game very much. My coach's complaint was that I waited for the ball to come to me instead of running after it. Nevertheless, I spent many afternoons on the courts practicing and even playing in tournaments.

I was also given mandolin lessons. Somehow my parents had the idea that being able to play an instrument was a way to instant popularity. As they saw it, the mandolin was a relatively small instrument that could be strapped on ones back when hiking and then entertain friends when sitting around the campfire. My teacher, *Herr* Rudolf, was willing to teach me, but I had difficulty learning. He came twice a week on his motorcycle and made a valiant effort to instill in me a love for the instrument. But it was all to no avail. I learned the basic rudiments, but that was about it.

What amazes me in retrospect is that, aside from seeing my father more often, I do not remember any significant changes in our lifestyle during the Nazi period. Either my parents must have lived off previous savings and/or income from his Gentile partner, probably both. Considering the times they managed well.

For instance, my parents loved to eat out at least once a week, usually on Sunday afternoons. We ate at a different place almost each time we went out. Although there were restaurants in Berlin of almost every ethnicity, I do not remember my parents deviating very much from standard German cooking. Occasionally, we went to a Hungarian restaurant (which was very exotic to me) with strolling gypsy violinists, dark lights and fancy smells.

While heretofore we vacationed on the Baltic Seacoast of Germany, now we went to the mountains for our summer sojourns. Supposedly, the doctor told my parents it would be better to get away from the ocean because the iodine in the air near the ocean was not advisable for some people. This advice was probably directed to both my mother and me, because she was a nervous person all her life and I was a pretty hyperactive kid. But I think it also had to do with the fact that my dad was not traveling into that area anymore. Also, my parents loved to hike. We spent the next four summers in the mountains. For a change of scenery, we started going to the *Riesengebirge* (giant mountains), which is located in the much disputed Sudetenland.

Today the entire area is part of the Czech Republic, populated only by Czechs. At that time German was spoken throughout, and the border between Germany and Czechoslovakia ran right through the middle of that area. It is an attractive mountain range with large forests. The highest peak is about 5,000 feet.

In 1933, we spent our vacation in a mountain resort called Krummhübel. It is located on what was then the German side of the border with Czechoslovakia; the whole area was called the

Böhmerwald in the Sudetenland. I think we went there because it was located right on the border and in case we ran into anti-semitism we could just pack up and move across the border. We stayed at the Pension Hoppe, a place with friendly people and good food. I had a great time.

Since our arrangements were for room and board, *Frau* Hoppe would pack a lunch for us and we would hike all morning. Then we lunched outdoors, with cider for me and beer bought on the trail for my parents. My mother checked off each hike on a trail guide, and the joke was that we could not go home before we did each of them.

We bought our refreshments at mountain rest stops called *Bauden.* Some of these were large mountain chalets with rooms for rent. At higher elevations, where skiing was possible in winter, the Bauden were much larger to accommodate dormitories. When in the restaurant, we usually enjoyed zither music and participated in singing mountain songs. My father usually classified this as *Goyim Naches* (fun for Gentiles), but he enjoyed it nevertheless.

In this regard I should point out that German Jews generally, my parents included, were of two minds when it came to assimilation. They definitely wanted to be one hundred percent German, even more so if that were possible, but they also wanted to preserve some of their identity as a people. Thus they passed on a good deal of the old German/Jewish vocabulary from generation to generation. As mentioned previously, some of the words could be found in the Yiddish language, but some words were uniquely German/Jewish.

It was common for everyone to have a hiking cane, and I was very proud of mine. These canes had a pointed metal tip for solid support. Each Baude sold little metal emblems to nail on the cane to show where you had been. A little picture of the place and its elevation were stamped into the metal. While it was intended as a souvenir, for me these were medals of honor to show my friends back home that I achieved the climb to an out-of-the-world place.

We would spend the whole day outdoors, coming back in the evening for a warm meal. Often we ran into rain and thunderstorms; these mountains were notorious for rain, which is what kept them so green. We always carried raincoats, heavy Loden coats that became heavier as they soaked up the rain. Many a time we arrived in a Baude soaking wet. It would then take hours in front of the fireplace to dry our things sufficiently to walk back. (Loden coats can absorb a fantastic amount of moisture without any of it penetrating.)

Summer vacations were about three months long. As long as we were able to afford it, we spent much of that time away from home. We were able to get away as a family because by that time my father was barely working anymore. In 1935, my parents made arrangements to spend a few weeks at Bad Tölz in Bavaria, but then heard that the town had anti-semitic incidents.

They decided to go back to the Riesengebirge instead, but this time to the Czech side of the border to a village called Spindelmühle. From there we went on to an area called the *Sächsische Schweiz* (Saxon Alps), where we spent part of August in the town of Teplitz/Schönau. This is not far from Chemnitz, close to where my mother grew up. While the Riesengebirge is a typical mountain resort area, the Saxon Alps are less mountainous but unique with sandstone formations, vertical cliffs, and small brooks and rivers. Here for the first time I saw real mountain climbers scaling sheer cliffs on ropes, while we were gliding quietly below them in a rowboat on a narrow river which meandered between the cliffs.

Except for the political scene, there was hardly a difference between the German and the Czechoslovakian areas. People and language were the same. It was called, the *Grüne Grenze*, the green border. Since tourists hiked all over the area, it was difficult to guard this border. To escape in later years, many Jews crossed here to safety in Czechoslovakia. Unfortunately, many were caught when Hitler marched into that country in 1939.

In the spring of 1936 or '37, I had my first adventure away from home. About fifteen of our group accompanied Herr Preuss for a two-week stint to Petzer, a small resort near Spindelmühle in Czechoslovakia. Being with fifteen boys and one adult was very exciting, and we did some crazy things like night hiking. We arrived late one evening at a *Baude* without reservations and they could not accommodate us. There was no choice but to hike to the next place even though the trail was obscured by snow drifts. Fortunately, we had a bright full moon, so it was beautiful and exhilarating. But as time went on, we became tired and scared. To show we were not, we told tall tales about ghosts and goblins.

When we finally arrived at our destination, our shoes were full of snow and we practically fell into the bunks, totally exhausted. The next morning we found it virtually impossible to put our boots back on because they were frozen solid, but, of course, we had no choice.

My Jewish Upbringing

Both sides of my family were at best agnostic, at worst atheist, depending on the individual. This was especially true prior to Hitler's coming to power. My parents went to synagogue on the High Holy Days, primarily out of respect for their parents, but they had no deep religious feelings. Nor was there any involvement in the Jewish community. We did have candleholders, a spice box, a Kiddush cup, and a Menorah, but they were regarded more or less as symbols of a Jewish household.

I do not remember ever seeing a mezuzah at any of our entries, undoubtedly because of not wanting to be readily identified as a Jewish household. I remember celebrating Hanukkah as a little kid, but we also had a Christmas tree in our home until the Hitler years. It needs to be explained, however, that *Weihnachten* (Christmas) in Germany is not identical to Christmas in America. *Weihnachten* predates Christmas in Germanic history and was celebrated as a seasonal holiday – when the winter solstice sun reached its lowest daily arc. It was a national holiday, which was celebrated by all Germans, whether or not they were religious. Similarly, the summer solstice (*Sonnenwende*) was also celebrated in many parts of Germany as a holiday.

We kept a box of Christmas tree ornaments, each of which was wrapped in paper to prevent breakage. I should note, however, that our top ornament was a glass bulb, not an angel. Initially, we used little clip-on candleholders with real wax candles, but these were later replaced by electric lights because of the fire hazard. It was a festive time, especially Christmas Eve, when in the German tradition gifts are opened. We also sang *Weihnacht's Lieder* (Christmas songs), but only those that did not refer to Christian symbols. For instance, only the first stanza of the song "Oh, Tannenbaum" was sung because it only referred to the tree and the season, dating back to pre-Christian tradition.

Starting around 1933, most German Jews changed their attitude. Hanukkah replaced Christmas, and we observed the full eight days. I do not remember gifts, except for Hanukkah *Geld* (chocolate coins). My parents sang Hanukkah songs, and the family would play games with the *Dreidel (spinning top)*. We had a beautiful *Hanukkiah* (candelabra) and only used blue and white candles.

The entire season was a gustatory delight. German Christmas specialties are world famous with *Lebkuchen*, which we bought, and *Stollen*, which my parents baked themselves. My parents took turns kneading the dough by hand. It was hard work because our *Stollen* weighed about five pounds each, and they made several of these at one time to be used as gifts. Of course our kitchen oven was far too small to handle such large loaves, so we took them to a bakery which had a commercial oven. We also enjoyed the universal Hanukkah specialty, which we called *Kartoffelpuffer* (potato pancakes) or latkes. This was also quite a production. My father peeled and grated the potatoes with great care, and my mother mixed and fried. They were only served with sugar, apple sauce, or a jam on the side, and coffee was always served with them.

Purim and Passover we celebrated mainly by eating the holiday specialties. These food rituals were very important to us; *Krepchen:* (also called *Kreplach,* a type of ravioli) were eaten at Purim and matzoth at Passover. Krepchen were only served around the time of Purim and were delicious. I can still see my father getting out the large, round *Nudelbrett,* a board to roll out the noodle dough. The flour and egg mixture would be rolled very thin, then cut into squares. A small amount of a cooked ground meat mixture was placed into the center of a square, another square laid over it and pressed all round. The Krepchen were first cooked in salt water and then served in chicken soup.

Once, probably around the time of my bar mitzvah, my father did go through our entire apartment explaining the Passover tradition of looking for *Chometz* (leavened bread) with a candle and feather. I remember him saying to me: "*das ist wie es die frommen Juden machen*" (this is how the Orthodox Jews do it). However, this was the exception. Passover celebration was limited to the first night's Seder, which was celebrated with *Onkel* Kuckie presiding. He knew all aspects of the celebration, and his readings and rituals seemed to last forever. On the other hand, I do not remember ever attending a Seder celebration with the Glaser side of the family.

We ate matzoth during the entire period of Pesach. My dad was very brand conscious with many of the foods we ate, but he was especially fussy about the matzoth. It had to be from Schönlanke, a small town not far from Berlin. It came in large, round packages. We would buy about twelve pounds, which was a tall stack that was delivered to our home.

My grandmother's favorite story was that of a delivery boy, a Gentile kid of about thirteen, who brought the matzoth up to her apartment, knocked on the door, and greeted her with, "*Heil Hitler, ich bringe Ihre Matze.*" (Hail Hitler, I am bringing your matzoth.) Of course, the kid never understood the humor of that statement, to him Heil Hitler was just an everyday greeting.

The pre-Hitler years were a time of assimilation for many German Jews. With the opening of democracy after the First World War, many put their Jewish identity into the background, making a concerted effort to be as good a German as anybody. The general saying was: "*Wir sind Deutsche Staatsbürger Jüdischen Glaubens*" (we are German citizens of the Jewish faith), even though many did not believe in God. Still they identified with their Jewish heritage, although many tried to pass as non-Jews. When upheavals in Poland and Russia brought Jewish refugees to Germany, there was a real dilemma. As Jews they wanted to help, but as Germans their prejudices against all peoples from Eastern Europe told them otherwise. As a result, help was given grudgingly, and great efforts were made to move these immigrants elsewhere, such as to the U.S.A. In retrospect, it was a shameful period for German Jewry.

As indicated earlier, things changed in 1933, when I was nine years old. With political threats all around people started finding their Jewish identity. Some sooner, some later, but most found their own brand of Judaism. Since there was no choice in the matter anymore, they were Jews by edict, and suddenly many felt more comfortable with being Jewish. They were being discriminated against anyway, so downplaying one's Jewishness did not do much good anymore.

My religious training started at home at about age eleven. Lessler Schule was secular, a school for Jewish kids not a Jewish school. Its orientation was pro-Zionist, which rubbed many of the non-Zionist parents the wrong way. In later years, we received instructions in Jewish history and Hebrew.

My parents hired a tutor to give me religious instructions at home in preparation for my Bar Mitzvah. He was a quiet, unassuming man who suffered through all my inattention and general disinterest. Nevertheless, I learned about our rituals and services, and many of his teachings stayed with me to this day.

My Bar Mitzvah took place on May 29, 1937 (which happened to also be my parent's anniversary and later our son's birthday). The ceremony was held at the Prinz Regenten Strasse synagogue because our friend, Rabbi Swarsensky, had his pulpit there. We were about thirteen kids, and each of us had an *aliyah* (were called to the Torah) and was asked to chant a small segment of that week's Torah portion. I still have a copy of my portion.

All of us wore blue suits with either long or short pants (mine were short) and white, open-collared shirts. There were no speeches or gifts, except that each of us was given a certificate.

There was one very interesting feature about this certificate. It was not issued by the synagogue or the congregation, but by the "Jewish Community of Berlin" without any identification as to which rabbi officiated or in what synagogue the ceremony was performed. This avoided conflict in later years between Liberal and Orthodox rabbis when kids from different backgrounds wanted to get married and needed proof of their Jewish identity.

After the ceremony, family and some friends came to our house for a small party. I remember that we had a cold buffet: roast beef, which was very expensive because beef was not available, many salads, French Sauterne wine, and a lot of cheese, which was also in very short supply. There were about thirty people, *mishpoche* (family) and friends, and Rabbi Swarsensky showed up later for only a few minutes, having to make the rounds to the other celebrants. In the evening, we had dinner for just the closest relatives. That was when I gave my first speech, which, I believe, was as much *Mutti's* work as mine. The following is a translation of that speech, which I kept these many years. I am including it in this biography to contrast it to today's speeches on such occasion.

"Dear Parents, Relatives, and Friends:
   "On this Shabbat I had my Bar Mitzvah at the synagogue. The first segment of my life is behind me. Before starting

on the second segment, I would like to look back at the past and into the future. I know how difficult the last years have been for all of us, especially for you, dear parents; how much effort and care you have expended on my behalf so that I would be able to obtain a good education. And you kept all worries and difficulties away from my young life. To really thank you from my heart can only be done by promising to try to bring you joy, work with all my strength, and go through life with a true conviction of Judaism. The commandments of our religion shall always be my guiding light. It is a special joy for me to have my *Omi* (grandmother) and my Aunt Hulda with me here today to participate in this celebration.

Unfortunately, it was not to be for my other grandmother and my grandfather, whose great desire it was to see this day. In their memory and with gratitude I want to structure my future life.

To you, dear relatives, who have brought joy to this day through your presence here, I wish that you, together with us, will see the better times in health and happiness."

I received a number of treasured gifts that day. Uncle Eric gave me a pigskin (!) suitcase about the size of an overnighter. It was very expensive and it served me well in later years. From my grandmother I received a large travel kit, to match my suitcase. Among the other gifts were a number of beautiful books.

My earliest recollection of the High Holy Days goes back to before the Hitler years. As the season approached my father would go into the closet in his bedroom and bring out a hat box. It contained his top hat, which he wore only on this occasion. With great care, he would take it out of the box and then proceed to stroke it with a special cloth and finish it with a very fine brush. This would lay the nap down smoothly and give the hat its shine.

We attended the Fasanen Strasse synagogue, which was within walking distance of our apartment. It was quite a sight to see the top-hatted men and finely dressed ladies walking to services with their prayer books and *tallith* (prayer shawl) bags under their arms. Of course some people were apprehensive about this obvious show of their Jewish identity. Wanting to look less conspicuous, they did not wear top hats, but carried their paraphernalia in a shopping bag or wrapped in newspapers. Even though this synagogue was Liberal in its service, ladies were seated upstairs.

My dad would take me into the sanctuary where we had seats to the left of the main aisle. It was a huge synagogue, built in the oriental motif, with a dome high above the center aisle. The decorations were quite ornate, especially in the area around the ark containing the Torah scrolls. It was a beautiful ark covered by a heavily brocaded tapestry. The rest of the East wall was covered with huge organ pipes. The choir was hidden from view.

On Yom Kippur the rabbi and cantor wore white robes. Their headdress, also in white satin, had the shape of a Torah crown. A few congregants exchanged their top hats for white satin caps in the shape of folding G.I. caps. Many would also remove their shoes to put on white slippers.

The service was mostly in Hebrew, with the cantor facing the ark, his back toward the congregation. This made it difficult to hear most of the prayers except the cantorial solos. However, the audience was generally knowledgeable and participated in the recitation of all prayers. For those who had trouble following the service, there was always the *Schammes* (sexton) who cruised up and down the aisles. He would help by opening your prayer book to the appropriate page. One of his other functions was to keep down conversation among the men. Nevertheless, there was always a lot of whispered conversation. It always amazed me how conversation would suddenly stop when the service reached one of the more important prayers.

When reciting these important prayers, and especially when the ark was opened, all exits were closed and nobody was allowed to walk around. Cantor Davidson was a trained operatic singer and knew how to pull on one's heartstrings with his music. His *Avinu Malkenu* (the prayer of confession of one's sins during the prior year), bordered on a wail and reverberated throughout the synagogue over the hushed audience. All around me men, including my father, shed tears during its recitation.

I was not Bar Mitzvah as yet and, having a short attention span, was easily bored. At such times I would run up to the balcony to visit my mother. Later, after my Bar Mitzvah this was strictly *verboten* (forbidden). The balcony overlooked the male congregants below, and one had a much better view of all activities. One could also see the choir. Since there was no *Schammes* upstairs, there was quite a bit of conversation going on. But here too the ladies would suddenly become quiet and attentive during important prayers, probably taking their cues from the men below. Toward the end of the service, during the memorial services, all kids would be sent out, and it was always a great mystery to us as to what was going on during that time.

During Yom Kippur services, my mother would frequently reach into her purse to bring out the smelling salts, especially in the afternoon, probably because she had a headache from fasting. My fondest memory of that day was the big spread awaiting us for *Anbeissen*, the Breaking of the Fast, at my grandmother's house.

A few times during the year, we would visit the Weissensee cemetery. It was located in an area at the edge of the city in the eastern part of town reached by first taking the elevated train, then switching to a streetcar. The cemetery covered a very large area. In fact it was so large that my parents stopped into the office occasionally to obtain directions to grave sites of distant relatives they seldom visited. There were corner signs that identified the main paths leading through the cemetery, with lanes branching off which then led to the rows of graves. Because the cemetery was so large, and many older people came to visit, there were benches along the sides for people to rest. We always stopped at the sites of my paternal grandmother, maternal grandfather, and my mother's sister Agnes. Because of the distance between sites, and the time involved in covering them all, we rarely visited the graves of my uncle's first wife, and other relatives and friends.

For me these visits were an uncomfortable experience. I did not quite know how to cope with my parents' grief when *Tante* Hulda died. Also, I found it upsetting that my parents talked to the dead as if they were still alive.

And yet, with these visits I developed a feeling of continuity and belonging. My parents made it a point to talk to me about my relationship with each of them. Even though they brought flowers, they would ask me to leave a small pebble, an Orthodox Jewish tradition, to indicate I had visited.

Although he was not my teacher, I owe a good deal of my religious attitude to Rabbi Swarsensky. As mentioned, he lived with us while attending the seminary. He was a relatively shy person, but I developed a close relationship with him. He and I shared a bathroom, and every morning we would have long philosophical conversations while he shaved. His religiosity was people-oriented. He saw himself as a true *Seelsorger*, (a caretaker of the soul and a collective term used in Germany for clergy). He was a "sociologist for the Jewish people," as he often told me. I once chided him for being a hypocrite, for keeping a kosher salami sausage in his room for his guests while eating non-kosher meat at our table. His answer was that some guests expected him to observe kosher laws, and once they learned he did not, his effectiveness as a rabbi in helping them with their problems would be impaired.

In later years, Dr. Manfred Swarsensky became one of the leading Rabbis in Germany. Recently I was told that his following consisted of people who were basically non-Zionist, while Zionists were followers of Rabbi Joachim Prinz, and there was a certain rivalry between the two.

Swarsensky's service culminated in 1938 when he gave a sermon in which he likened the Jews of Germany to the Moor in Shakespeare's Othello. "The Moor has done his duty, the Moor can go," he quoted, advising his audience to leave Germany. Upon completion of the sermon, he was arrested by the Gestapo and sent to a concentration camp. He showed his true mettle there, assisting his fellow Jews even after he put in a full day at hard labor. He was released after about nine months and emigrated to the U.S., settling in Madison, Wisconsin, as rabbi of a Reform temple and an active leader in the Jewish and non-Jewish communities.

Such was the extent of my Jewish education, but it molded part of my Jewish identity. I became very religious after my Bar Mitzvah. I went to synagogue every Saturday, often schlepping my father with me. I remember little except for the priestly blessings the rabbi extended to the congregation at the end of every service. It was always a solemn moment when he would face the congregants, hold up his arms with the wide sleeves of his *Tallar* (robe) hanging from his arms like a Japanese kimono, reciting the blessing. At a time of instability, when people often dreaded what the next day would bring, this ritual took on a special meaning for all of us. I brought flowers for my mother, and I insisted that *Mutti* light Shabbat candles and we observe the holidays. That phase lasted just about a year.

What followed for me was a period of transition from religious into ethnic involvement. I became active in *Hashomer Hazair*, a Zionist Labor youth movement that based its political philosophy on democratic socialism. As such, it subscribed to the Marxist credo: "Religion is the opiate of the people". As my religious feelings receded, I developed a deep interest in Zionism. My parents saw the possibility of my emigrating separately to Israel, and of course this did not sit well with them. Yet, with such uncertain future no option could be dismissed. Going as a young settler to Palestine, a *Halutz,* was an option open to me but not for them. Even if they wanted to, they would not have been admitted to Palestine because the British demanded proof of assets of at least one thousand English pounds sterling for each person seeking admission. Since it was illegal for Germans to have assets outside Germany, such a requirement could only be met by relatives in foreign countries and our relatives in South Africa could hardly make ends meet for themselves. Children, however, were allowed to enter as part of the youth movement.

Some of my schoolmates joined the *Betar Trumpeldor*, a right wing organization. Their colors were brown shirts with blue epaulettes and blue pants, while we wore blue pants and white shirts. Theirs was a militant organization. The rumor was that the *Betar* had rifle target practice in the basement of a synagogue, and the Nazis were providing them with weapons. The supposed logic was that the Nazis wanted *Betar* to stir up trouble for the British in the Middle East, but I never heard any confirmation of the rumor. In later years, terrorist organizations in Israel like the Stern Gang and the Irgun did recruit from *Betar* for their membership. The right wing of today's Likud Party descended ideologically from these groups.

All these strands of Jewish influence developed in me a certain understanding of what being Jewish really meant. From each I extracted that which I could relate to, and I arrived at a composite that is perhaps difficult to describe. From my religious training and my parents, I obtained a strong feeling of right and wrong as well as a feeling of what is required to be a *Mensch*, a dedicated humanitarian being. It also made me realize the importance of the feeling of "community". Lastly, being discriminated against much of my early life fostered strong feelings toward others in similar position, irrespective of race or creed.

From my father I inherited a strong aversion to sham religiosity, of going through the motions without real belief. From Rabbi Swarsensky I gained an understanding that some ritual is necessary as guideposts through one's life. And from school and the Zionist youth group, came a strong Zionist feeling together with a certain distrust of organized religion. In later years these underpinnings would see many modifications, but in their bare essentials these concepts have not changed in me all that much.

Leaving One's Homeland

By 1937 there was another change in my father's arrangement with his business partner. Because non-Jews were admonished not to employ Jews, it became an embarrassment to his partner, a party member, to have my father show up every day for work. Therefore, he asked my dad to stay home. *Vati* was not to worry about finances as his partner would send him a monthly check as payment for the business. To his credit, he did just that until the day we left the country.

We cut back on our lifestyle, which was never opulent. Probably as insurance against eventualities, my parents started to rent out one room in the apartment. The dining room furniture was sold, and the room converted to a studio. Our first tenant was a young Jewish lady with many boyfriends. Her name was Anita. She used a very pungent perfume, which penetrated everything in her room and which drove me crazy. I fantasized frequently about being intimate with her, but that was as far as it went.

Politically, my parents, as well as everyone else, were getting mixed signals. Events moved very rapidly. On the one hand, Hitler's aggressive foreign policy moved Germany closer to conflict, and his anti-Jewish statements became more vituperative almost daily. Also, the activities of the Gestapo became more and more ominous. On the other hand, some activities went on as usual. For instance, it must be evident by now my parents loved going on vacations. The summer of 1937 was no exception. But where to go?

Again our Nazi friend came to the rescue. He suggested to my dad that if he wanted to vacation in Czechoslovakia, it would be possible for him to arrange for foreign currency, since his son worked for the German Central Bank. Dad took him up on the offer and applied for passports at the ministry. In due course, we received our passports, valid for five years, and went off on vacation.

We visited Prague, a beautiful city with much Jewish history. Visiting the old Ghetto made an unforgettable impression on me. We saw the old *Rathaus* (city hall) where the clock has Hebrew letters; visited the *Alt-Neu Schul*, the old synagogue dating back to the tenth century; and left a note at the grave site of Rabbi Loeb, the creator of the Golem, the first Frankenstein, a mythical humanoid clone. It was the custom to leave a scrap of paper with a wish in the gravestone's cracks, similar to the way notes were left in the Wailing Wall in Jerusalem.

While in Prague, my father read in a local German language newspaper a story about a police action in Germany, wherein many Jews were rounded up by the Gestapo. His comment was typical: these were probably people who had been politically active and this should not be of any concern to us.

By the time we were on the train returning home we had spent practically our last Czech Krona. My parents discussed how they would get home from the station when a lady, a total stranger, offered to share a taxi cab, dropping us off first so that my parents could run up and get the money to pay for the cab.

But over time, things deteriorated drastically. Early one morning my uncle Eric was arrested by the Gestapo and taken to police headquarters. The story as it evolved was crazy. Eric had visited friends the previous week. Some were Jewish, others were not. Sitting on a balcony they discussed the political scene and that anti-aircraft guns had been installed and were in open view. A military officer happened to sit on the adjacent balcony and thought it his duty to report the conversation he overheard.

My uncle was allowed to call my dad, who brought him clothes, a shaving kit, etc. At the police station, Eric and each of his friends were interrogated separately, and it must have been pretty obvious that nothing subversive had happened on that balcony. My uncle stressed the fact several times that he had been a volunteer during the First World War and had been wounded and decorated for bravery. Whether because of this or some other reason, Eric was let go with the proviso that he had to leave Germany within three months.

Earlier, Eric had managed to obtain an affidavit from someone in the United States, a paper necessary to immigrate there. This paper showed the government that the recipient would not become a public burden. With such an affidavit in hand, one could be put on the eligibility list and obtain a quota number that put one on the waiting list. Wanting to emigrate to the U.S., but unable to obtain an entry visa within such a short time, he looked for a refuge outside Germany. Cuba allowed immigrants short-term stays provided they could prove ownership of adequate funds. Over several years, Eric had transferred small amounts of money illegally to a bank in England with the help of a non-Jewish friend. So he was able to provide the Cubans with proof that he would not become a public charge. In October, my dad took Eric to Hamburg to see him off.

Our American Quota Numbers from the American Consulate in Berlin

Disaster struck in November 1938, when a distraught seven-teen-year-old Jewish boy shot and killed a German diplomat in Paris to dramatize the deportation of his parents from Germany to Poland. The Nazis orchestrated a well-thought-out plan, which utilized this event as the trigger to blame the entire Jewish population for the murder. They urged their party members to vent their wrath on Jews by setting all synagogues on fire and destroying all businesses held by Jews. In the days that followed, more than twenty thousand Jewish men were arrested by the Gestapo and sent to concentration camps. The intent was to intimidate, frighten, and demoralize German Jewry so to push them out of the country.

During the night of November 9, 1938 we entered our final phase in Germany. Our telephone rang at about four a.m.; on the line was my father's partner. He advised my father to leave the apartment and to go underground for a few weeks. He counseled we move in with my grandmother, who lived alone by then. More than that he would not say, except to advise my father to stay in touch with him. My grandmother had decided to join her son Harry in South Africa and was in the process of selling her furniture and liquidating her household. We packed a few necessities quickly and moved in with her.

Later that morning, *Omi* and I went for a walk to see what was happening. It was felt that an old lady and a young boy would not be bothered by anybody. As we got to the Kurfürsten Damm, it was obvious what had happened. Jewish-owned stores were in total ruin. The plate glass windows were destroyed, and in front of some of the stores looters were trying on clothing, shoes, etc., or just carting off goods. The police did not stop them.

As we walked further up the street toward the Fasanen Strasse synagogue, we saw fire engines. A mob was running up and down the sidewalks screaming revenge on the Jews. Later we learned that the fire department did not make any effort to save the synagogue and were present only to safeguard neighboring buildings.

My grandmother was a pretty spunky lady, so we just walked on, but it was obvious to me how upset she really was.

A few days, later my mother and I went back to the apartment to check the mail. As we entered, the concierge, *Herr* Wolf, stopped us to tell my mother that two men from the Gestapo had come the previous day asking for my father. He told them that he thought *Herr* Glaser left for France, which was an excellent cover for us. In this way the Gestapo did not bother to leave an arrest warrant. In some instances, when they suspected that the person they wanted to arrest still lived in the area, arrest warrants were issued. This meant that you had to turn yourself in before being able to leave the country legally.

Line-up of arrested Jews at Sachsenhausen Concentration Camp

In retrospect, it was on *Kristallnacht* (The Night of Broken Glass) which started during the night of November 9, that the German population lost its innocence. Up to that point, the discrimination and excesses against the Jews could be rationalized by saying they were based on laws. Admittedly, some of these laws were drastic and harsh, unfair, but legally sanctioned. However, when mob action is encouraged by the police and sanctioned by authorities, then any law-abiding citizen must understand that the mob and the government were one and the same.

To dispose of her furniture my grandmother had placed an advertisement in the local paper before we moved in, so the door-bell would ring often with people wanting to see what was for sale. This meant that my parents and I had to go into a closet every time there were prospective buyers. Nights we slept on the floor because the beds had been sold earlier.

Among my relatives, Uncle Max was arrested and sent to the Sachsenhausen concentration camp. Egon (Eddy) offered to go in his stead but the Gestapo officers refused. My cousin Horst (Henry) was not touched because he was too young. My father's other brother, Martin, had left earlier for the U.S., together with his wife and daughter, Ruth. For some reason, Uncle Ludwig was not bothered, possibly because he had already applied for an exit permit. My two cousins, Kurt and Willi, had left for Shanghai already or were in the process of leaving.

A word about the *Aktion* (operation of the arrests). The entire operation, although planned well in advance of the murder, was initiated on the spur of the moment. As such it differed greatly between locations. In Berlin, the arrests were generally conducted by the Gestapo, (the secret police) in cooperation with the local police. I am only familiar with the situation in Berlin, and much of what I know is second and third hand. Nevertheless, the pattern is interesting.

First of all, the arresting officers always came in pairs. Whenever possible an attempt was made to pair two young Gestapo offi-cers who were ideologically-safe Nazis. Older officers making the arrests, i.e., those in the organization before 1933, often found themselves teamed up with new members of the force. Seldom were two veteran officers of the force working together. Obviously, their superiors did not quite trust older officers. Even so, there were a number of situations in which an officer would try to con-vey certain messages at the time of attempting arrests. In the case of a friend of ours, the doorbell rang, the woman opened the door and the officers identified themselves. They then asked: "Your husband is not home, is he"? Whereupon the woman, who quickly understood, said: "No," and without further ado the pair left. In many other cases it was not so easy. The officers would not take no for an answer but proceeded to ransack the home, trying to find the man they came to arrest.

Gradually the enormity of what was really happening started to sink in. In a planned and coordinated effort, the Nazi regime used the murder in Paris as an excuse to achieve a number of goals. First of all, they wanted to scare the Jewish population into leaving Germany. But they were also after Jewish wealth. As part of the "reparations" for the murder of the consular official, the Jewish community was assessed a huge sum of money. In partial payment, every Jew had to sell his valuables to the state pawnshop.

With heavy heart, my parents took inventory of all the silver and gold they had, as well as precious jewelry. The decree stated that only wedding rings and one piece of jewelry were permitted to be kept. The rest was to be turned in and assessed on a weight basis. We did not have any great treasures, but the silver Shabbat candlesticks were an heirloom of great sentimental value. My mother, who could not tell a lie, insisted that everything they owned be listed. My father did, however, have a jeweler re-arrange a pendant to comply with the order, taking out extra diamonds so he could sell them for cash.

As mention earlier, the Nazis arbitrarily arrested tens of thousands of men and sent them to concentration camps to promote rapid emigration. These camps were not as yet death camps and their purpose was primarily to terrorize the inmates. Long hours at hard labor, starvation diets, physical abuse and beatings, were standard fare. When all the camps were filled, the police called off the *Aktion*. Thereafter, only those inmates were released whose relatives could prove their loved ones had the necessary papers and arrangements to leave the country. Uncle Max came out within a few months. Alice had arranged for them to obtain exit papers and booked passage to Shanghai. Willi and Kurt had left for Shanghai earlier.

Undoubtedly, another aspect of this operation was to test world reaction to a *Pogrom* in Germany. *Kristallnacht* underscored the lack of moral indignation and outrage on the part of the Western world. The West could not say that it did not know. It was there for the whole world to see. It was reported by the world press, and the French and American ambassadors were seen taking movies at the height of the mob's action with the police standing by. The Western world wrung its hands and then sat on them.

Three

Refuge of Last Resort

*T*he question which always comes up is why Shanghai was picked as a destination. As in the case of Cuba, Shanghai was seen as only a stopover place. By the end of 1938, people began to realize time was running out. For almost anyone, the U.S. was the preferred place to relocate.

We had our U.S. quota numbers and even though the German quota was quite large compared to other nationalities, it was not adequate to allow such large numbers of people to enter the country all at once. The idea was, therefore, to spread this wave of immigration over a few years. Also, the U.S. was barely coming out of the Great Depression and did not welcome people who competed for scarce jobs.

By the end of 1938, there were practically no havens for a temporary refuge and Shanghai, as I will explain later, was an exception. First I need to digress and explain the process of immigration as we experienced it. Almost every Jew in Germany seemed to have contacts in the U.S. These were either direct relatives or strangers who were approached through Jewish organizations. Just as recently with the American Council for Soviet Jewry, there were generous, caring people who would open their financial records and do all the paper work required to document their ability to take care of those for whom they issued the necessary affidavits. These guaranties were often only a pro forma arrangement because *HIAS*, the Hebrew Immigrant Aid Service, took care of most of immigrants. Nevertheless it was a great act of kindness. In general, many American relatives stepped forward to help while many others just sat on their hands.

I want to interject here that the events of the late thirties molded my character and shaped many of my attitudes. Only fourteen years old in 1938, I had been exposed to a lifetime of experience which sped my maturation. All around me I saw well-to-do people lose everything, saw people disappeared overnight or returned from concentration camps broken in spirit and body. It became obvious to me that security was a sometime thing; that personal discipline was necessary to survive, and that survival in adversity depended on one's wits and health.

The latter point was especially poignant. People who were overweight and suffered from diseases associated with prosperity had much more difficulty surviving the camps then those who were called "*Sportler*," meaning people who practiced any type of sport. As could be expected, concentration camp guards were rougher on people who matched the stereotype "*Stürmer Figur*," the caricature of the fat Jewish banker depicted in the Party newspaper. Also, overweight people had much greater difficulty adjusting to the hardships of physical activity and camp labor. Of course, those who survived lost excess weight quickly and often seemed physically healthier after their ordeal. Uncle Max was an example. For me the lesson was clear, stay slim and exercise. This was totally at odds with the way I was brought up. Not only was obesity considered a sign of prosperity, but doctors told their patients that nerves needed to be imbedded in fat or else one would become "nervous." In general, the prevailing European attitude considered excess fat good insurance against adverse times.

Returning to the decision to leave Germany. What finally prompted my father to decide on emigration? Again, his Nazi friend came through. A few days after the *Aktion* was over, i.e. the concentration camps were filled, he advised my dad that it was time to leave Germany. He told him that from what he could see there was no future for Jews in Germany and the time to get out was now.

People were frantically searching for relatives in America who might be able to provide the required guarantees. My father's first cousin, Rudolf Arndt, left Germany in the early nineteen hundreds under very clouded circumstances. Apparently he ran into trouble with the law, and even though there was little money, the family scraped a few *Marks* together and shipped Rudolf off to the U.S. He prospered and after the First World War returned for a visit as the rich relative from America. Within the family, everyone except my dad extended a warm welcome to Rudolf.

Now my dad was too proud to contact Rudolf for the necessary affidavit. Instead he obtained the guaranty through Uncle Eric's relatives in the U.S. Max, on the other hand, contacted Rudolf, who did provide the necessary papers, but by then Max was already in the camp and Shanghai was the only quick temporary refuge.

Leaving Germany

As fate would have it, Uncle Eric Uncle met the love of his life, married and was able emigrate from Cuba to the United States with the help of his new, wealthy in-laws in New York.

Once there, he persuaded them to provide my family with the required affidavits as well and in January 1939 the U.S. Consulate in Berlin contacted my parents and gave each of us a quota number which, when called up, would allow us to emigrate to the U.S. Because of the urgency, the consular official suggested we go to an intermediate location, contact the American Consulate there and wait for our quota numbers to be called to complete our journey to America. At least we would be safe.

Shanghai offered such a temporary haven. Actually, it was the only remaining safe haven. This city was unique as politically it was not part of China. Instead, it had international legal status, its security guaranteed by troops stationed there from a number of countries. It was an open city, which meant visas or permits were not demanded. All one needed was the transportation to get there.

That was the difficulty. There were relatively few passenger ships going from Europe to the Far East. Aside from several Japanese cargo carriers that had some passenger cabins, there was an Italian luxury cruise line, the Lloyd Tristino, which regularly plied the route from Italy to the Far East. I believe there were four ships making this run, the *S.S. Conte Biancamano*, the *S.S. Conte Rosso*, the *S.S. Conte Verde* and the *S.S. Conte Vittoria*. The first two were the larger ships. The ships would leave alternately from Genoa or Trieste. They were able to carry between 800 and 1200 passengers at a time. These four ships became the conduit for almost all of the 18,000 immigrants who arrived in Shanghai between 1937 and 1939, and their names played an important role in our collective memory. During a brief period in 1940 to 1941 some people escaped via Russia through the port of Vladivostok to Shanghai on Japanese freighters, but their numbers were small. My cousin Horst (Henry) was among these latecomers.

Aside from the long lines of people in front of the U.S. consulate, there was now another long line in front of the Berlin offices of the Lloyd Triestino. People were desperate for a ticket to get out of the country. Luckily, my parents were able to obtain passage on the *S.S. Conte Rosso,* leaving June 16th, 1939. The only accommodations available were in first class.

Although these ships accommodated a relatively large number of people, they were really small. Cabins were tiny and they had a steerage level below deck in which people were packed like sardines, dormitory style.

Little did we know how close to the end we came before all exits from Germany by this route were closed. Hitler marched into Poland during the first week of September of that same year, 1939. Thereafter, everything changed.

Holding confirmed bookings and with signs the *Kristallnacht* pogrom was over, my parents hoped that imminent danger had passed. We moved back to the apartment and began the task of preparing to emigrate.

People who met each other waiting in line at the steamship offices formed friendships and built networks. After all, they were going to spend time together on a boat and share new experiences, so they had a lot in common. They all had to cope with apprehensions about the future. Many lifelong friendships started in those waiting lines.

My parents met distant relatives, the Berwins, and brought them to our apartment after the day's ordeal at the shipping line. Bruno Berwin was very handy and had a carpenter friend who offered to build unique shipping crates that could serve double duty. Not only would they be sturdy crates for our belongings, but they could be easily converted into clothes closets and chests of drawers. As it turned out, this was a smart move because most who arrived in Shanghai had no furniture. This meant they had to spend money on furniture, dipping into the financial aid they received or doing without.

Many things needed to be done in the intervening seven months. In order to obtain passports and exit visas, we needed certificates of disclaimer from the finance ministry stating that all taxes were paid. In addition, the Jewish community had to certify that we met our obligation to pay part of the assessment the Nazis leveled against all Jews for "having killed the consular official in Paris." We also needed certificates of good conduct from the police, and I recall going with my parents to the police station nearby, full of apprehension.

By law, anyone who had at least one Jewish grandparent was considered Jewish. It required that the name "Israel" be added for men and "Sarah" for women to immediately identify them as being Jewish. Now my full name was Ernst Adolf Berthold Israel Glaser.

I imagine many police stations around the world are built to intimidate, but Germans were experts at it. There were vaulted hallways with polished stone floors, and our footsteps reverberated throughout making us feel self-conscious and insignificant. Inside the office, the official sat behind a high wooden desk looking on us.

Passport Photo 1939
(note Israel as part of my name)

When it came time for me to sign the exit application, I had trouble getting my full new name on the signature line and I so told the officer. He told me to do the best I could. We were lucky; he did not give us any trouble and we were dismissed within a few minutes, but others had frightening experiences.

I do not remember much about the actual dissolution of our household except for the process of packing up our belongings. Until *Kristallnacht* one could obtain lift vans for shipment of household goods. These were large wooden containers, shipped as deck cargo, similar to today's cargo containers. Considerable restrictions were instituted after the ninth of November, which included the elimination of such containers. From then on, only a limited number of crates (I believe seven) were permissible.

We had seven crates, and the packing had to be supervised by Customs representatives. The two customs officers who came to our apartment were young and very hostile. They made us take apart almost every item before allowing the packers to stow things away. My bicycle, which had already been disassembled for easier storage, was the special focus of their attention. Apparently they suspected my parents of trying to smuggle valuables inside the tires or the body of the bike. I had to remove the tires and they felt every inch of the rubber tubing. Finding nothing their hostility increased, and when they came upon two dozen new washcloths, one of them objected that this was a commercial quantity for which we needed an export permit. The issue was resolved by giving all but three washcloths to one of the moving men, but it showed the official's harsh attitude.

Since we were going to the Orient, we had to be inoculated against tropical diseases. Friends recommended we go to the Robert Koch Institute, which specialized in tropical medicine. I mention it because for me, having read DeKruif's book, *Microbe Hunters,* I felt on familiar ground. Because of it, I was less fearful than my parents about the shots, and I could act an "expert". The actual inoculations were uneventful but painful afterward. I suffered them without complaint, remembering how Dr. Robert Koch had experimented with serums on himself. Actually, I remember the physician being very nice, inquiring about our voyage and wishing us well.

Each of us was allowed to take only ten German Marks out of the country. It amounted to US$12 for the three of us. We received our passports, which had a fat, red letter "J" stamped over a third of the first page, indicating we were Jewish.

Finally, it was June 14, 1939 and we were all set. Ella, our former maid, and a few friends, among them Peter Wagner, came to see us off at the train station. I remember Ella being very upset, insisting still that we were making a big mistake. With the last few Marks my father upgraded our train tickets to first class, which meant a compartment of four. At first, we had the compartment to ourselves, but by late evening we arrived in Munich, where a middle-aged lady joined us in our compartment. Suspecting that we were Jewish, she did not try to make any conversation; neither did my parents.

About midnight the trained stopped at the German/Italian border near the Brenner Pass. A border patrol officer entered our compartment requesting to see our passports. He took one look at ours, marked with the "J", and the lady's regular passport, and jumped to the conclusion that we might have asked her to smuggle something for us. He requested to inspect her purse and found a 100 Mark bill hidden behind a mirror. She had to get off the train and accompany him to the station office. As we found out later, many Jewish passengers had to open their suitcases for inspection, some were taken off the train to be searched and never made it back onto the train. But nobody bothered us.

Shortly before the train started to move again, the lady reappeared in our compartment. She was visibly shaken and then started to open up. Yes, they suspected her of smuggling when in fact the money was meant for emergencies and she actually forgot about it. To prove her innocence, she had to call a Nazi party official out of bed to personally vouch for her. With all this going on, they seemed to have forgotten about us.

A little later, the Italian train conductor appeared to check our tickets. He told us that the first class up-charge, paid for in Germany, was only good to the border and we needed to now pay the Italian up-charge. My father explained that we did not have any money, but the conductor insisted or else we had to transfer to coach. To our surprise, my father produced some German money to pay the difference. My mother was flabbergasted, knowing what we just went through at the border. My father insisted he had been told in Berlin that aside from the 10 Marks we changed into dollars, each of us was also permitted to carry 10 Marks in change. Much later we learned that my father's information was incorrect, and the little money could have jeopardized our leaving Germany. We were very lucky indeed!

In Trieste, all Jewish passengers were met at the train by a representative of the American Jewish Joint Distribution Committee (which everybody called the Joint) and assigned a hotel room. It was early morning when we arrived, and after the experiences during the night everyone was exhausted. We rested and then went sightseeing. Trieste was exciting. I remember being most impressed by Italian ice cream parlors, the *gelatèrias*. They were colorful, with beaded curtains at the entrance, a fascinating aroma in the air, and a huge assortment of flavors. Later, we checked in with the Joint. Hundreds of people were milling around in a small, very hot office. We were given embarkation instructions and told to come back the next morning.

We went to bed early, totally exhausted. I woke up early the next day and, not wanting to wake up my parents, dressed quietly and then went for a walk to explore the town. The hotel was located on a street near the harbor, and within a few minutes I was in the midst of port activities. I became intrigued by the fishing boats coming in to drop their catch and all the hustle and bustle going on around me. After a couple of hours I decided it was time to return to the hotel. I remembered its name but not the address, nor did I remember the path I took to get to the waterfront. I was lost.

Asking people at the wharf was fruitless. Finally, I came across a policeman who took pity and accompanied me part of the way back. It was a frightening experience.

An Exciting Adventure

Later that morning, we went to the offices of Lloyd Triestino, where we received our cabin assignment, then to offices of the Joint, where we were given a ticket for a luncheon meal. Having been told that embarkation would probably be late and we should not expect any dinner on board ship, we filled up at the restaurant. Back at the hotel, we picked up our suitcases and then made our way to the pier. The waiting room was stifling hot and noisy with passengers waiting to get on board. After what seemed like hours we finally walked up the gangplank and were greeted by ship's officers in crisp white uniforms. Sailors in blue took our luggage and showed us to our cabin.

The *S.S. Conte Rosso* was a luxury cruise ship and our cabin was on the top deck, with big windows opening directly onto the promenade deck. This was in the days before air conditioning, so there were several oscillating fans pushing the hot air around the cabin. The cabin steward introduced himself, and Giovanni and I became fast friends. After the day's excitement, which for me started very early that day, we started to get ready to go to bed. Suddenly the ships gong came on over the intercom, informing everyone that dinner would be served within fifteen minutes. Obviously we had been misinformed about not expecting any dinner, but we were not about to pass up the first meal on board even though we had eaten a big meal earlier.

In the dining room, we were assigned a table and the fun started. The room was very ornate, but what really impressed me was the size of the printed menu. It offered a fantastic variety, the likes of which I had never seen. Also, there were a number of foods offered which were totally strange to me. The next few weeks promised to be quite an eating experience for everyone.

On Board the S.S.Conte Rosso

Vati had deposited some money with the shipping company in Germany to be used as "board money." This was legal because fascist Italy was an economic partner of Germany. Of course we were not allowed to take any of this money off the ship at the end of the voyage, so we could only spend it on tips and extras on board.

My father immediately tipped the table captain, waiters and room steward, and from then on we received the best service imaginable. I was seated next to a middle-aged bachelor, an emigrant from Austria. He was a forester by profession, and he was used to country cooking. After a few days, he started to complain about all the fancy foods, yearning for the simple cooking he was used to from home. I couldn't understand his attitude because I was having a great time. I discovered spring chicken on the menu and started ordering this dish every dinner. It was crispy and served with fresh potato chips, something I had never eaten before.

After about a week of this, Mutti put her foot down and told me to order something else. Being headstrong and spoiled, I insisted on spring chicken, whereupon my parents sent me back to the cabin without a meal. On my way back I ran into Giovanni and told him my tale of woe. He did not say anything, but about twenty minutes later there was a knock on the door. When I opened, there was my friend Giovanni with a big plate of chicken and potato chips.

Aside from potato chips there were other foods I had never seen before. Green and black olives, avocados, artichokes, passion fruit, guava and mangoes, several varieties of cheeses and desserts were all new to my parents and me.

The first morning aboard, I started to explore the ship. As a first class passenger, I was allowed to visit throughout the ship. Being a young kid, the officers seemed to enjoy showing me things on the bridge, in the radio room, etc. It was to be the best of times for me.

We arrived in Venice the first morning and were allowed off the boat to see the sights. The three of us tagged along with some others, really having no idea where to go and what to see. People were so overwhelmed with the thought of leaving Germany and preparing for emigration that few had any inclination toward sightseeing. My memory of that visit to Venice was totally overshadowed by revulsion against the dirt and debris I saw in the canals, the stench in the side streets, and the leaky roofs in churches we visited. It was not until forty-five years later that I was able to see the real beauty of Venice.

On board ship, there were a swimming pool, a gym, facilities for skeet shooting, and of course the inevitable shuffle board. I did them all. My parents and most everyone else spent a good deal of their time lounging on deck, trying to learn English by reading self-teaching texts. A favorite one, called "Basic English in 800 Words," promised that knowledge of these words and some idiomatic phrases would allow anyone to communicate adequately in English. This turned out to a vastly exaggerated claim, but it did get people started in their future language. For my mother, this turned out to be much easier than for dad because she could build on her high school education and experiences at work. *Vati,* on the other hand, had never gone beyond grammar school and found learning English extremely difficult.

About two days later, we arrived at the port of Brindisi. It is located almost at the southeastern tip of the Italian peninsula, a rocky, very poor city with crooked streets and more poverty than I had ever seen. It was very upsetting for me, coming from a comparatively affluent background, to see children in rags, begging. I was glad to get back on board ship into a safe and familiar environment. But it gave me an inkling of what I would experience later.

Our next stop was Port Said, Egypt. At the time, Egypt was under British political suzerainty. Palestine, sharing a border with Egypt and under British rule, did not want to see any refugees entering the country through Egypt, so they prevailed on the Egyptians not to let us off the ship. That was a disappointment, because I had looked forward to seeing Egypt, especially after seeing the smart looking Egyptian police officers stationed on board who wore fancy uniforms and red fezzes.

We had a nice surprise waiting for us though: a delegation of Egyptian Jews came on board offering help and presents. Simon Artz, the largest department store in Port Said, was Jewish-owned. They presented each of us with tropical clothing, shorts, hats etc., and armloads of cigarettes. Considering that nearly eighteen thousand preceded us here, we marveled at the generosity of this Jewish community. We were to experience this over and over again during our voyage and later.

Port Said is located at the Mediterranean entry to the Suez Canal, and after setting sail again, I stood at the railing for a few hours watching the actual transit through the canal. I was fascinated. A British pilot came on board to supervise the passage through the narrow channel; barely wide enough to accommodate our ship. Since they could not use the ship's propellers, we had to be pulled through the canal by a little steam engine that ran on tracks parallel to the canal.

Along the route of the canal, we saw sand dunes like the ones I had seen in movies, camel caravans, and palm trees. It was quite hot and got hotter as the day progressed. But this did not bother me; I had to see everything. I do not remember how long the passage took, but it must have been many hours. Finally, we entered the Red Sea, the pilot left the ship, and we were under our own steam again.

As we moved further south, the heat in our cabin became unbearable during the day; nor did it cool off much at night. *Mutti* suffered terribly. The fans seemed useless. We gave up some of our privacy by opening the window facing the deck and the door that opened to the corridor to create some cross ventilation; all to no avail.

The next day we steamed into Massawa, a thriving port on the east coast of Africa. I believe it was part of the Italian colony of *Eritrea* at the time. A lot of cargo was taken off the boat by betel nut chewing stevedores. They were really the first black people I had seen close up. Their teeth and tongues were crimson red, and occasionally they would spit betel juice, which looked revolting. The other memorable experience about this stop was the heat. I believe that the thermometer read 120 degrees Fahrenheit in the shade, and it was the hottest weather I had ever experienced.

Our journey continued across the Red Sea to Aden, the key port of Yemen. It was not much of a port in that there were no docking facilities. We were allowed off the boat and a lighter ferried people back and forth to town. However, my parents decided to stay on board because of the heat. Some people did visit Aden, but from what I recall they were quite disappointed by what they saw. However, their main motivation for going ashore seemed to be just to get off the boat and touch solid ground again.

For those of us who stayed aboard, there was a spectacular show in the harbor. We first saw kids diving for coins in Port Said, where they asked people to throw coins into the water for which they would dive. But here in Aden, out in the open harbor, our ship was totally surrounded not only by these young divers but boats of all sorts offering merchandise, souvenirs, old weapons, etc. The scene was a floating bazaar. There were even performers doing their acts, including snake charmers. I was so fascinated by all this that I had trouble tearing myself away from the railing to have something to eat. Some time later we hoisted anchor and steamed out of the harbor into the Indian Ocean heading for Bombay.

Now for the first time we experienced rough seas. It was a new experience for most passengers. The storm tossed our boat as if it were a toy. My parents were hit hard. They stayed in bed and did not want to go near food. I prided myself on being untouched by the storm. I made my way to the dining room to have something to eat and found it almost empty.

The storm lasted only a day or so, and for me it was a great adventure. Once the sea calmed down, I spent a lot of time standing at the prow watching flying fish jump out of the water and at the stern watching sharks following in our wake. These sharks seemed to know that every few hours the kitchen boy would dump a pail of garbage overboard. As soon as that happened, there was immense thrashing and fighting for food in the water. It was a real spectacle!

Our arrival in Bombay was a spectacle of a different sort. As we pulled alongside the dock, there were hundreds of women in colorful saris waiting and waving. A large part of our crew was Indian, and their wives, girlfriends, etc., were there, obviously dressed in their finest clothing to greet them. For some reason, again the British authorities did not allow us to leave the ship. My father was quite disappointed. Through business contacts in Germany, he had been in touch with an Indian exporter of hemp and jute, who promised to be on hand when we arrived at Bombay to show us around. Instead we were stuck on board, having to eat more fancy food to console ourselves.

By now we had developed quite a routine. It was a good thing that our stomachs were well trained in Germany. As on all cruise ships, in addition to three solid meals a day there was teatime in the afternoon with lots of pastries. To make sure we did not get hungry during the night, coffee and pastries were served again at nine o'clock in the evening.

We soon learned that the board money my father deposited in Germany with the shipping company was really of very limited value. On previous voyages, passengers were able to buy cameras, watches, etc. But when the Nazis learned that people were buying these for subsequent sale in Shanghai, they prevailed on the shipping company not to allow board money to be used for such purchases. Consequently, my father was "forced" to spend the money on champagne and similar luxuries.

Our next port was Colombo, Ceylon, now Sri Lanka. We arrived about nine o'clock in the evening and our entrance into the harbor was an unforgettable sight. The harbor was surrounded by a high breakwater on top of which was a huge electric sign reading "Drink Lipton Tea." One could read the sign out at sea long before the city lights appeared, and it was eerie to see a huge lit-up sign floating above the water. The next morning we were allowed to get off the ship for the day.

After breakfast, the chief steward came over to tell my father that two Indian gentlemen were waiting for us in the lobby. One of them was a business associate of the man we were to see in Bombay. We were overwhelmed and eager to see Colombo. A car was waiting and we were off. What impressed me most were the beautiful beaches that surround much of the island. They appeared to be a mile wide, spotless white sand. I never saw beaches like these before or since; it seemed like my idea of paradise. The architecture downtown was typically colonial British and I was thrilled by the ambiance. Every passenger had been given a little lapel pin onboard ship. This turned out to be an item much in demand by local kids, who offered to trade mangoes and pineapples for the pin. After many offers, I decided to give mine to one of the kids, who promptly ran off with it, probably afraid that another kid would steal it from him.

For lunch our new friends drove us into the jungle far outside town. The road seemed to be cut through a wall of green with only an occasional clearing where there were little stands along the road. After about forty-five minutes, we arrived at a lodge that seemed out of a Kipling novel.

It turned out, during the lunch discussion, that our hosts were quite wealthy. Among other businesses they were partners in mining of semi-precious stones which are plentiful in Ceylon. I cannot remember other details, but I recall that we were introduced to the governor of Ceylon who happened to visit the lodge. He wore shorts, which struck me as very funny, and he smoked a pipe filled with aromatic herbs and spices. To me that entire scene seemed absolutely incredible. Here we were, refugees with less than ten dollars in our pockets, being entertained by millionaires and meeting the governor of the island.

On the way back, we stopped to purchase a soft drink, and I noticed that our friend paid with a bank note he tore out of a checkbook. He explained that this was common in Ceylon. We arrived back at dockside in the nick of time, since the ship was almost ready to leave. I would have loved to stay longer, and to this day I have the urge to visit Sri Lanka again. Unfortunately, the country is strife-torn, none too safe for foreigners.

Several British couples had come on board ship in Colombo. They spent their vacations in Ceylon and were on their way home to Singapore. All were young and loved to dance and suddenly things changed on board. After dinner, the band entertained the passengers with dance music. When we first came on board in Trieste, people were not in a mood to dance, and after we left the Mediterranean Sea it seemed too hot to do so, even if one wanted to. But the verve and stamina of these British seemed to be infectious. Even my parents danced despite the tremendous heat. Mostly, though, we just sat and watched. The British couples dressed in evening clothes and, because of the heat, the men would go back to their cabins after a couple hours' dancing, change into a second tuxedo, then come back and dance some more. This went on night after night; we were exhausted just watching them.

Before briefly crossing the equator into the Southern hemisphere, the lounge was decorated and paper hats were offered to celebrate the event but I do not remember any celebration. The ship docked in Singapore somewhat distant from downtown in a warehouse area. Since we stopped for only a few hours we decided to limit our visit to the area surrounding the wharf. Some more enterprising friends went into the city, riding in a *pedicab*, a three-wheeled bicycle-rickshaw. They came back with fabulous tales of a modern city.

The British couples left the ship in Singapore, and with their leaving some of the spirit of abandon left as well. We were now in the Far East, going into the final leg of our voyage. Within a few days we would put into Hong Kong harbor, the last stop before Shanghai, and the mood on board became more pensive. Almost everyone on board had direct or indirect contact with people who preceded us. In some instances they reported horror stories, and at the very least they counseled to be prepared for a culture shock.

In Hong Kong, the British were up to their old tricks again and did not let us off the boat. Arrival in that port, however, was spectacular. I believe Hong Kong is one of the prettiest harbors in the world and arriving there early in the morning was unforgettable. Thanks to British bureaucracy here and in most previous stops, we felt like Moses looking into the Promised Land, but not allowed to visit. Our stops became routine. Not being able to leave the ship, we would lean over the ship's railing, and below us would be an armada of small boats offering wares of all descriptions.

A sign of their apprehension was that people began to squirrel away food in their cabins to take along when they left the boat in Shanghai. My folks, too, began to accumulate oranges, etc., and our cabin began to smell like a produce store. It was not surprising then that the captain pleaded over the loudspeaker system with passengers not to take food into their cabins because this would attract vermin. When nobody listened, he instituted a cabin search which turned up immense quantities of food.

Another sign of the voyage coming to an end was that people looked around for ways to use up their unspent board money. The only goods my dad was able to buy were a few cases of Curacao Triple Sec liqueur. It was stock the bartender wanted to get rid of. About a year later in Shanghai, when my mother had an upset stomach, she suggested my father open a bottle to give her a sip. My dad told her he would be glad to give her some, but she should not expect too much from it. He had tried the liqueur on board ship and found that it had little flavor. To her surprise it tasted wonderful. The bartender must have diluted it for a little extra income when serving it by the glass.

Actually, *Vati* was a good bar customer. We joked that if his liver held out he would even gargle with champagne in the morning for breakfast. The bar was the place where men met every afternoon to play cards and have a few beers. How people were able to cope with so much food and drink is beyond me, but they managed. Undoubtedly, they compensated for their apprehensions by eating and drinking a lot.

Arrival in Shanghai

Very early on the morning of July 9, 1939, we arrived at the mouth of the *Yangtze* river, and a pilot came on board. For the next few hours we steamed up the Yangtze and then up one of its tributaries, the *Whangpoo*. There were a lot of Chinese junks in the river, breaking up the otherwise monotonous view. The *Yangtze* River was wide enough so that both shorelines were too distant to make out in detail, and they looked a monochromatic olive green. As we entered the *Whangpoo*, activity on the river picked up, and after some time the city came into view. We noticed a number of warships anchored in the middle of the river. Finally we pulled alongside a pier and dropped anchor.

A gangplank was lowered and as we made our way down, we were greeted by my cousin Willi. The scene around us was truly

Arrival in Shanghai

overwhelming. A wide dock in front of the warehouses, locally called *godowns*, stretched in either direction as far as the eye could see. Several other ships were unloading cargoes in front and behind our liner. Coolies passed us carrying heavy loads on their backs or in tandem with a bamboo pole between them from which hung immensely heavy cargoes. All of them screamed in sing-song at the top of their lungs to help them in their work; the heavier the load, the louder their screams.

On the dock were thousands, not only the passengers, but at least an equal number of friends and relatives who came to greet them. Mixed among the crowd were customs officers in crisp white uniforms, police, ship's cargo officers, hawkers and an assortment of thieves and beggars. The police consisted of Caucasian officers in khaki uniforms carrying swagger sticks, Chinese clad in blue, and enormous Indian Sikhs, also in blue uniforms but with khaki turbans. The Chinese and Sikhs carried wooden nightsticks in addition to revolvers, and they kept some order by extensive use of these sticks.

We had to stand around and wait until our luggage and crates came out of the cargo holds and were lowered over the ship's side in large nets. Willi was an expert in how to get our stuff together, get perfunctory custom's clearance, and find transportation. Being among the early arrivals in Shanghai, he had the opportunity to go through this routine several times before when picking up friends and distant relatives. After a long wait, we had our things together, and arrangements were made with Herr Nachemstein to have them brought to our new home.

Herr Nachemstein was an institution. Shortly after his own arrival, he realized that local shipping agents were ill prepared to cope with the massive influx of immigrants. He set himself up in business to help newcomers with their belongings. During the remaining years of our China odyssey, it was a foregone conclusion that Herr Nachemstein would handle our moves. He knew all the immigrants, or so it seemed, knew where people lived, and where there was available housing. He was a tall man, who stuck out in a crowd, which made it easier for him to signal his helpers and to spot what or who he was looking for. He was also a very nice man whom I got to know a little better in later years. After the war he emigrated to Australia.

Other than a cursory inspection of our luggage and crates by a customs officer, there was no passport check or any other form of governmental control. As we emerged from the dockyard, we were immediately surrounded by Chinese rickshaw coolies. Since I will use the term coolie frequently, I want to explain that it is not a derogatory term but simply one that defines unskilled laborers in the Orient. Rickshaws, which are outlawed in China today, were the standard mode of transportation for short and intermediate distances.

Rickshaws carried one passenger, were pulled by a coolie, and were quite inexpensive. There were tens of thousands of them all over Shanghai. At first we felt squeamish about being pulled by another human being, but for several reasons we soon became accustomed to using rickshaws. First of all, the city was geared for their use. All over town there were rickshaw stands within easy walking distance, where coolies waited for their next customer, or you could hail an empty one passing by. Secondly, the Chinese did not see anything wrong with the practice, nor did the coolies seem to resent their work; they needed the income.

We were surrounded by coolies, each man trying to earn our fare. Willi, showing that he was almost a native, explained to them where we were headed and started to bargain with them for the price. Finally, we were off on my first rickshaw ride; it was a strange experience. The coolies would run two abreast, which allowed them and us to talk to each other. The axle of the carriage was suspended on two strong springs, which reduced shocks from the many holes in the road. Nevertheless, one was bounced around quite a bit. But who cared, it was a new adventure.

The street along the wharf area in the Hongkew district was called Broadway. Much of the area later became the ghetto. As one would expect from its name, it was a wide, main artery, with rows of warehouses fronting it, as well as many semi-destroyed buildings, large and small. In 1932 and again in 1937, this area had experienced massive bombings during the Japanese-Chinese conflicts.

The rickshaws turned into the 1166 East Broadway Lane off the main street and dropped us off in front of a dilapidated one-story building. Lanes were commonplace all over town. Essentially they were cul-de-sacs with side streets. Some were quite large. Lanes were gated communities with a large wooden front gate through which all traffic had to pass. At night and at times of unrest, these front gates would be shut and bolted, and individuals were only allowed in or out through a small door inside the large gate.

It is impossible to describe the shock my parents must have felt when seeing our new abode. It consisted of a single room with peeling pink paint, three iron bedsteads, and a creaky wooden cupboard. As we learned later, it also had a leaky roof. There were no bathroom facilities, instead there was a wash stand in the corner and a "honey bucket." Honey buckets were quite common:

wooden pails, some polished on the outside, with a wooden lid. One would use them, inside the room to "do one's business," obviously, privacy was non-existant. Early each morning, these buckets would be placed in front of the house to be picked up and emptied into a pushcart. Ultimately, this "night soil" found its way to farm fields as highly prized manure.

Honey Bucket

Our lane was primarily occupied by Chinese and Koreans. Being located close to the ships, there were several whorehouses catering to sailors. There were also several hole-in-the-wall eating places, most of them pick-up joints. Poor sanitary conditions and high humidity created incredible odors and made vermin control impossible. Furthermore, during early fall, when we arrived, the mosquito season was in full swing. Between our fear of roaches and mosquitoes buzzing around, we barely slept the first night.

I think Willi lived nearby; he showed up early the following day to accompany us downtown to check in with Jewish aid organizations. The way into town led across the Garden Bridge, which played a key role of delineating the military jurisdiction of one section of town from another. It crossed *Soochow* Creek almost where it flowed into the Whangpoo River. As one crossed the bridge which divided two districts, British and Japanese soldiers stood guard at their respective dividing lines on both sides of the street.

Garden Bridge Crossing required I.D below

The British Scots Highlanders were dressed in tartan kilts and black leather boots covered with white spats, and smart black berets with a red tassel. The Scotsmen would rarely be inside them. They would parade in very slow and deliberate steps to the right and left of the guardhouse, turning around snappily almost in slow motion. The soldier on each side of the street timed his motions to coincide with the other. After a while they would stop in front of the guardhouse and come at ease there, feet spread apart, rifle butt next to the right boot, left hand behind their back.

Nobody seemed to pay any attention to this performance. Busses, trucks, rickshaws, pedicabs and thousands and thousands of bicyclists and pedestrians went by daily without ever looking at the soldiers as if they were animated statues that were part of the bridge itself. I often wondered what these soldiers must have been thinking about as they did their duty. Obviously they represented the British Crown, and they knew it. But to go through this routine day in day out must have been mind-numbing.

As one entered the British controlled sector, the scenery changed. To the left was a small public park; only it was not public. A sign read: DOGS & CHINESE NOT PERMITTED. This sign, probably more than anything else, epitomized the society in which we now lived. For us, coming from Nazi Germany with its yellow park benches, this seemed familiar. Only this time we were accepted; but I do not believe any us ever felt comfortable with it. Along the opposite side of the street, facing a wide boulevard called the Bund, was the British consulate. It was a huge piece of real estate with sprawling gardens, many buildings and residences, and, of course, a Highlander Guard in front.

The Bund in 1939

The Bund extended several miles, curving with the banks of the river. The waterfront was mostly occupied by docks for thousands of sampans bobbing in the water, small boats which served as water taxis, stores, and barges. Families were created, born and raised on these tiny boats; it was their livelihood and abode, where people spent their entire life. The Bund was lined with very impressive office buildings and hotels. These buildings were as modern as any seen in Europe, often much more luxurious. Some rose thirty or forty stories. Major banks and merchant houses had their headquarters and offices there.

We turned off the Bund into Nanking Road, another main thoroughfare. The entrance to Nanking Road was flanked by two Shanghai landmarks: the Palace Hotel on one side and the Cathay Hotel with the adjacent *Sassoon* office tower on the other. The two were not only on opposite sides of the street, they represented social and business opposites as well. The Palace Hotel was a staid old hotel, five stories high, with a colonial flavor preferred by British businessmen. There was a relaxed, British atmosphere about the place.

The Cathay Hotel across the street was a modern highrise with ten floors. It was owned by *Sir Victor Sassoon* and his family, leaders in the Shanghai Jewish Community. Despite its British ownership, the hotel had an American atmosphere and, as would be expected, was mostly frequented by American, Australian and Canadian businessmen. There was a sense of urgency about the place; the action was here. The adjacent *Sassoon* office tower was one of the most prestigious locations in Shanghai.

A little further on we turned into Central Road and visited the offices of *HIAS* (the Hebrew Immigrant Aid Society). Here, I believe, we received a check for fifty pounds, which Uncle Harry had deposited for us in South Africa with the Jewish Welfare Society. My parents also inquired about what was best for me to do, and arrangements were made for me to enroll in an ORT school.

Our next stop was the IC (the International Committee) to register. The IC, also called the *Komor* Committee, was created by local Jewish residents. Paul Komor was a Hungarian Jew who had lived in Shanghai a long time and prospered as a businessman. The Committee saw its mission as limited to making grants and loans to people wanting to start a small business. But the IC had many other very important functions. It worked with the Shanghai Municipal Council (the city administration) to register the new-comers for statistical purposes, etc., and to issue a local certificate of registration.

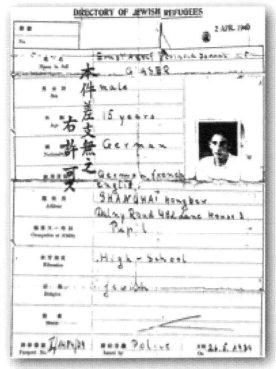

Registration with Authorities

The IC provided services to the refugees which were vital in other ways as well. Since most immigrants lived by selling some of their valuables, the IC established a thrift shop. They also set up check cashing facilities because our financial resources were too small to allow us to deal directly with banks.

The familiar Joint, the American Jewish Joint Distribution Committee, was the other organization helping Jewish refugees. It concerned itself with the broader picture. I believe HIAS cared for the newcomers' immediate needs while the Joint dealt with the creation of institutions such as schools, hospitals, and *Heime*. The latter were essentially shelters for the homeless and indigent and served as interim absorption centers for people who, less fortunate than we, did not have relatives to look after them upon arrival.

After walking around downtown for a while, I remember my father making the remark: *"Na ja, hier sieht es etwas besser aus als in Hongkew"* (well, it looks a little better here than in Hongkew). He did not speak the language, he was almost broke, he found himself in a totally strange environment, yet he saw opportunities. His old entrepreneurial spirit and optimism made him view all this as a new challenge. He had started from scratch several times before, and he could do it again, even though as yet he did not know how.

The First Year

For the next few days, my parents and I looked for more suitable housing. We thought we found it at Dalny Road Lane 483, House 3; a place I barely remember. It was cleaner and in a better neighborhood, though located in a bombed out area. At least we were away from the wharf area with its seamy life. Once we moved in, however, we found the place full of bedbugs. I remember taking our furniture out into the lane to pour boiling water on it to temporarily get rid of the bugs.

Shortly thereafter we moved again. This time to Point Road into a place that had miraculously survived the bombings. It was an old Chinese mansion converted by an immigrant owner into a rooming house. It was built like a square fortress, with only small windows to the outside while all rooms faced an atrium. There were floor-to-ceiling glass doors in each room that opened to a balcony-walkway overlooking the atrium. A very large wooden door connected the atrium to the street. In the middle of the courtyard stood a dilapidated ping pong table; the sun shining on the table attracted a lot of flies. The owner, an old man, would sit next to the table swatting flies for hours and piling them up in heaps. Swatting flies was a never-ending task in Shanghai.

Besides flies, mosquitoes were a constant nuisance in summer, especially at night. Mosquito nets were available, but the high humidity, coupled with the lack of air movement, made the nets unbearable. We used mosquito candles made from aromatic insecticides compressed into coils. While lit, they kept bugs reasonably under control. But life in the tropics was difficult, especially for we newcomers.

We were given information as to how to minimize our exposure to infectious diseases. Coming from Central Europe, where sanitary conditions were generally excellent, we were totally unprepared for dealing with this constant threat of disease. Because human wastes were used in fertilizing the fields, all fruits and vegetables had to be cooked or peeled. When this was not possible, we were told to dip the produce into a solution of potassium permanganate. Crystals of this germicide were available from pharmacies and when dissolved in water would turn it a deep purple.

Of course, we had to boil water before drinking it. Nevertheless, even with all precautions, a number of refugees came down with intestinal diseases, our family included. On the other hand, all of us must have developed some immunity simply by being exposed to so many different organisms. Picking up germs was unavoidable. For example, the bread we ate was handled by several people who may have been carriers. Similarly, dairy products, even though pasteurized, would be re-contaminated by people unfamiliar with the rudiments of sanitation.

Some old Shanghailanders who had lived in the Orient most of their lives claimed not to bother with all these precautions; some even drank water right out of the faucet. They claimed the solution was to drink a lot of whiskey every day, but that turned out to very be bad advice, as many refugees found out.

Cholera and typhoid were commonplace during the summer months and inoculations against them were mandatory. At such times, the municipal health authorities would do public inoculations. Key bridges, like Garden Bridge mentioned earlier, would be controlled, and only people who had proof of inoculation were allowed to pass. Those without proof were inoculated on the spot. Of course, some enterprising coolies would sell their certificate to somebody waiting to cross; then go through the line again to receive another shot and certificate. After repeating the process several times, I imagine they did not feel too well that evening.

About a week after our arrival, I went to the Pingliang Heim to enroll in the ORT school. The Heim was located quite a distance from where we lived, and I had to take a bus to get there. The location was a converted warehouse and the front section of the complex was occupied by immigrants, mostly bachelors. The ORT shops were located in the rear and consisted of several simple one-story buildings, all of which had corrugated steel roofs. Tools, equipment and supplies were sparse, but the teachers, also immigrants, were very knowledgeable and knew how to improvise.

I enrolled in a course on the fundamentals of electric services, covering basic circuitry, installation, and problem solving. The courses also included instructions on motors and use of the smithy. I believe two of the three instructors were graduate engineers, thus really overqualified, but they were good teachers. Part of the day we did practical applications, the rest of the time we learned electric theory. In the forge we were taught how to make some of our own tools, such as chisels, screwdrivers, and hammers, and we learned the fundamentals of hardening steels as well. I enjoyed the program a great deal and it all came very handy later in life.

About thirty fellows were enrolled in the course, all of us about the same age, which gave the opportunity to make new friends. One friendship came about by coincidence. We were teamed up in pairs to string some electric lines along the side of a building; one doing the installation, the other holding the ladder and assisting with tools, wires etc. My teammate asked where I was from, and when he learned I was from Berlin he wanted to know whether I was familiar with *Landschulheim* Caputh (a boarding school near Berlin). I told him that I was familiar with it because I knew a girl who went to that school and later transferred to my school, the Lessler Schule. As it turned out, we both had a crush on the same girl. From this coincidence my lifelong friendship with Walter developed.

Vati had started to explore various possibilities of making a living. He dropped the idea of going into the business he had carried on in Germany. There was just no market for cordage, etc., because the local merchants made such things themselves from local fibers.

Somehow he found somebody who made metal telephone directories; the ones that flipped open after one choose the desired alphabet letter on a sliding indicator. They were a real novelty at the time. Dad went downtown, from one office building to the next, peddling this item door to door. Not knowing any English was a serious handicap, but somehow he managed. He sold a few but not enough to make a living. One day, though, he hit it lucky.

A small import/export firm was interested in buying one hundred of these as a Christmas present for its customers. They wanted to have their name imprinted on the cover, and things got a little beyond my father's ability to handle in English, so I was involved. I took a few days off from school and accompanied him to the call. I believe the man was English, and even though my language ability was worse than my sales abilities, we made the sale.

The logistics of having boxes made for the directories, getting them imprinted and boxed, and then delivered required all the skills my father had acquired over the years. Then there was always the gnawing fear that I misunderstood something the customer wanted. Also there was the possibility that after going through all this work and expense, they might be rejected and we would be stuck with the registers. In the end it all worked out, and our first major transaction in Shanghai was a success.

In going door-to-door, my father learned there were actually quite a number of foreigners in Shanghai who spoke German. Of course, many of these were German businessmen who had lived in Shanghai for many years. But there were also many Swiss, Danish, Swedish, Hungarian, and Austrian nationals with whom my dad could communicate easily. Some of them were Nazis and anti-Semitic, but many were friendly and willing to deal with my dad. He wracked his brain trying to come up with something he could either make or buy to sell to these people. He hit on the idea of manufacturing liqueurs.

Actually the idea originated when my mother had an upset stomach and sipped some of the liqueur we had bought on board ship. This gave my dad the thought that he might be able to find customers for such a product among the businessmen he met. The next day my father took a couple of bottles to peddle into town. They were snapped up immediately with the balance sold the following day. Quickly recognizing the market potential, he decided to go into manufacturing liqueurs.

He knew nothing about making the stuff, but that did not stop him. Dad bought pure drinking alcohol, which was easily available in Shanghai. He mixed this with some dried fruit and sugar then steeped the fruits in alcohol for a couple of weeks. The fruit was then discarded. He made a sugar syrup that he added to the fruit extract, and presto, the product was ready to bottle. He also managed to get bottles, corks, and caps, and have some labels printed. The entire operation was handled on a little enclosed porch in front of the room the three of us shared. He made his sales calls carrying a briefcase with open sample bottles for customers to try, then he took the orders and delivered the liqueur next day.

After his business expanded, my father used a young fellow, Werner Michael Blumenthal, who did package deliveries of products on his bicycle. About thirty years later this same young fellow became the Secretary of the Treasury of the United States during the Carter Administration.

I left the ORT school when I was offered a job by a soft drink manufacturer. It was a well-established company which was originally established by an expatriate German. Trade was mostly direct to private homes, primarily those of German-speaking businessmen. The soft drink plant was managed by a father and son team, immigrants from Germany, who had the technical know-how. My job was that of a bill collector and to work around the plant in my spare time. This brought me in contact with a lot of customers, all of whom were potential consumers for my father's liqueurs. Since I called on homes, my contact was often with the wives of men my father met at their offices, but occasionally I was able to steer him to some new contacts.

Gradually, Dad expanded this business to wines and any merchandise in which his customers were interested. This included items such as crystal, oriental carpets, and similar items of value which other immigrants had brought along and now had to sell to survive. Every other day he would travel into the International Settlement or the French Concession, as the two main areas of Shanghai were named.

Although the civil administration of the entire International Settlement came under the jurisdiction of the Shanghai Municipal Council, composed of nationals from fourteen nations, certain areas were designated as British, American and Japanese sectors and patrolled by their military forces. Actually, the area of *Hongkew*, where we lived, was also part of the International Settlement and was safeguarded by the Japanese.

The area had experienced extensive bombing during the Sino-Japanese War in 1936-7 and was largely destroyed before we arrived.

The French Concession, slightly smaller in size than the International Settlement, was France's presence in China. French troops guarded the district, which was run like a French city. It had its own police force, run by French officers, with Chinese and Annamite rank and file (Annam was a province in Viet Nam, which at that time was called French Indo-China.) It also had its own electric, water, and public transportation companies. Street names were French, as were the building style of private and public buildings, giving the entire area a French ambiance. It was the best residential area in Shanghai.

My parents wanted to get out of *Hongkew* as soon as possible and since my father's travels frequently took him into the French Concession, he decided we should move there. Of course, housing was unaffordable, but he had an idea. Shanghai had a system by which one could lease a residence for thirty years at a fixed monthly fee. To compensate the owner for the possible risk of inflation, the tenant was required to pay a large sum up front; this was called "key money".

Aside from the fifty pounds sent by Uncle Harry, we received US$250 from Uncle *Eric,* which was a lot of money at that time. With this money, my father acquired a thirty-year lease on a new, six-room house in a very nice neighborhood in the French Concession. The aim was to rent out five of the six rooms so that we could live free.

In retrospect, I am still astounded that my father went through with this transaction. First, because our aim was to complete our journey to America as soon as our quota number came up which meant a long lease might pose a problem. Then there was the business transaction itself. The real estate broker, also an immigrant, my parents, and I went to a very small office in the downtown area. The builder, who leased the house to us, was Chinese and did not speak English, but he had a translator on hand to help. My father and the agent signed a contract, written in Chinese, without really any knowledge of the contract. After the builder put his seal on the document, there was a lot of handshaking and tea drinking and we were the proud tenants of a house in the French Concession. For somebody as suspicious as my father, to put nearly all of his assets on the line must have been a traumatic experience, but he was sure he did the right thing and he did.

In February 1940, we moved to our new address: Passage 80, Maison 30, Rue Kaufman, right off Rue Cohen. (the Jewish names of the streets was a coincidence). It was a nice, three-story house with a bathroom on each floor and a small kitchen on the first and second floors. The top floor had two small mansard rooms and a little storage area. The baths had flush toilets, a sink, and a bathtub. The water heater, however, was only large enough to serve the kitchen and bathroom sinks, totally insufficient to heat enough water for even a half of one tub. As it turned out, this was common in Shanghai, and it did not present a problem.

Hot water was a precious commodity in Shanghai, and every few blocks throughout town there were shops selling hot water, from filling a thermos to a bathtub. For a bath, the water would be delivered to your house, taken upstairs and poured into the bathtub. A coolie carried about fifteen gallons of boiling water in two wooden buckets suspended from a bamboo pole on his shoulders. By his moans and groans, he indicated he expected a fat tip for his hard work.

We did not have any difficulty renting the five rooms. On the ground floor, an elderly refugee couple from Hamburg moved into the room behind ours. They owned a little retail leather goods store nearby. Above us lived a fine arts painter from Berlin who converted the front room into a studio. His mother and aunt shared the back room. On the top floor, we rented one room to a former stockbroker and his wife, the other room to a young couple of nurses.

Aside from trading a room in a bombed-out neighborhood for one in the best part of town, the venture also turned out to be lucrative. While our monthly lease was eighty Shanghai dollars, my parents took in about six hundred Shanghai dollars each month in rentals. This sounds like quite a mark-up, but we had invested quite a lot of money up front that needed to be amortized and paid back to Harry and Eric. Nevertheless, as inflation gradually accelerated, we were in the fortunate position of being able to raise rents to keep up with inflation, while the cost of our lease was fixed.

Renting rooms in this neighborhood also required the services of a houseboy. One has to remember that Shanghai was still a colonial city. An employment agency referred a man who turned out to be a unique individual. He introduced himself in German, *"Ich heisse Fritz"* (my name is Fritz), which turned out to suit him to a tee.

He was probably in his early fifties, very neatly dressed in a traditional Chinese outfit, with a crew cut. He explained that he hailed from Tsingtao in the North, which had been a German colony before World War I. He had learned German in his youth and then went to work for German expatriates. His last employer was "Master" Hartmann for whom he worked for many years. Fritz came highly recommended and his qualifications were far beyond our needs. Why did he want to come to work for us? Not being able to speak English, he was essentially unemployable except to a German- speaking household.

My parents hired him on the spot, and he stayed with us throughout the time we lived in that location. He was a jewel: hard working, knowledgeable, and very bright. He soon made himself indispensable, not only for my parents, but also for all our tenants.

The first day he came to work, he brought his paraphernalia, which consisted of galoshes, white aprons and a white working suit. He always carried his prized possession on him, a pocket railroad watch given to him by Master Hartmann before he left. His first words that day stuck in my mind forever because they were so incongruous: *"Na, da wollen wir mal sehen was zu machen ist"* (well, let's see what's to be done).

He was extremely conservative and set in his ways. For instance, he would not have his picture taken because he believed in the traditional Chinese adage that doing so would make one ill. Once, when we took a family picture in front of the house, he warned against it, and when months later I happened to catch a cold he immediately related it to the taking of my picture. All in all, he led a pretty miserable existence, but he was always cheerful. His wife lived in Tsingtao, so he was practically alone. My parents recognized that and tried to make him part of our activities, but he would always decline, keeping a certain distance.

Since we now lived in a totally different part of town, I started looking for employment closer to home. Somehow I managed to obtain a job close by as an apprentice in a small necktie factory. The owner was a miserable, old, Russian immigrant who started his business shortly after he came to Shanghai in the late '20s. His junior partner, a much younger man by the name of Katz, also had constant troubles with his associate. Whenever possible, I dealt with Katz because he was much easier to get along with. They paid me very little, and since I had to put in long hours I felt terribly exploited. Nevertheless, the old man knew his business and I learned a lot from him.

By the end of the first year, we had settled into a routine. We were making a living and life was actually quite good. Hitler had marched into Poland and Europe was at war. Although we were still hoping that our U.S. quota number would be called up so that we could complete our voyage, there was also the sense of relief for being in a safe haven while the war lasted.

Shanghai before Pearl Harbor

Shanghai was an exciting city! What made it so was an unusual confluence of circumstances. At the time it was not quite 100 years old. After Commodore Perry opened Japan, the British "negotiated" a deal with the Chinese Emperor. They established several treaty ports in which British nationals had special privileges. Later Germany ruled *Tsingtao from* 1897 to 1918 and, like the British and French,imbued their concession with their national character and architecture. The Americans were included in the British agreement in exchange, I believe, for rights elsewhere.

The British, and later the Americans, saw China and its large population as a huge, untapped, market for their manufactured goods. The British began to monopolize the opium trade. When the Chinese government resisted, they enforced their philosophy of "might is right" by sailing gunboats up the Yangtze River. Around 1900, the foreigners had their first big scare when a reformist underground society, the Boxer Rebellion, tried to drive the "Foreign Devils" from China. The British prevailed at that time, but after the First World War the administration of some treaty ports was expanded to include other nations. In the case of the International Settlement in Shanghai, thirteen nations guaranteed its security.

Foreigners in Shanghai came from all corners of the world. Each nationality retained its own identity, created its own social clubs, but also intermingled with the others. Since the British were the oldest and largest foreign segment, they set the tone for the social scene. The Shanghai Race Club was the center of social activity. The Lyceum Theater, located in the French Concession on Rue Cardinal Mercier, provided the community with culture and good professional entertainment.

But for day to day entertainment, Shanghai was unrivaled in the Orient and probably in much of the world. Innumerable ultramodern, air-conditioned movie theaters provided the latest shows. Nightclubs offered nonstop dancing to the music of excellent big bands, most of them Filipino. Several of these nightclubs had huge dance floors on springs for extra enjoyment. Beautiful Chinese taxi dancers offered their services, which often extended to a full night's entertainment. The city was wide open, with legal gambling ranging from storefront operations to full service casinos. Just walking along some of the main arteries, one could see literally thousands of prostitutes with their *amahs* (a term used for nursemaids or housekeepers) who would pimp for them.

The age of these prostitutes ranged from early teens well up into middle age. All of them were dolled up, some were demure, others aggressive with passersby. Men strolled the sidewalks, eyeing the merchandise, joking with them, some finally walking off with a girl after a lot of haggling.

For a young fellow like me, coming from a sheltered background, this environment was mind-blowing. I would ride my bicycle through these districts on the way home from work, fantasizing about all the girls I could have. But I never had the guts to approach one of them. It just did not feel right, and I was scared as well. During the time I attended ORT, a young fellow was brought back to the *Heim* early one morning unconscious and terribly beaten up. It turned out that he had been with a prostitute during the night. I remember a teacher saying to us: "The idiot should have known better." That was a better lesson than any preaching I heard from my parents.

My major preoccupation was learning English. I had a good background in colloquial English from high school, but understanding the language spoken in rapid conversation was something else. To get the ear acquainted with the sound and cadence of the language, all of us spent long hours listening to news broadcasts on the radio. One announcer, whose name escapes me, patterned his style after Walter Winchell, who was popular in America at the time. His fast, staccato delivery was especially hard for us to understand, and it took a long time before we were able to follow him.

My ORT friend, Walter, and his parents moved to the French Concession before us. They rented a room from a White Russian landlady on *Rue Mercier*. It was a nice building with some interesting tenants. One of these was a young Russian doll who had all kinds of male visitors, day and night. Walter's parents were very hospitable to me, and I ate many a meal with them. His mother had found employment at HIAS and his father, who had been in the coal business in Hamburg, tried to establish himself again in the same line.

Through Walter I was introduced into the life of ordinary young people my age, i.e., non-refugee foreigners. Walt was in a unique situation. A branch of his father's family lived in England, one of whom was married to a business tycoon in Shanghai. Charley Arnold and his wife, Winnie, neither of them Jewish, extended themselves to their distant immigrant relatives from Germany. Through their connections, Walt joined the Union Church Boy Scout troop and obtained a job in a stock brokerage company. The job involved night work in which he learned to handle overseas' telegraphic stock market transactions.

With my Shanghai Friends

Walter introduced me to his Aunt Winnie at the Arnolds' home in the French concession. They lived in a mansion across the street from the Lyceum *Theater*. She was an imposing lady, almost twice as heavy as her husband, and she ran the household with an iron fist. The house was typically British on the inside, with dark wood paneling throughout the downstairs rooms. There was a garden behind the house, in which she put both of us to work. Of course, there was a staff of servants who would normally have taken care of such things, but she probably felt that the work would do us good.

Walt also introduced me to his Union Church Boy Scout troop. Soon after Jewish refugees from central Europe arrived in Shanghai, a Jewish troop was formed by young fellows from Austria, where the Boy Scouts had been legal until 1938. By contrast, in Germany Hitler outlawed the Boy Scouts after coming to power and replaced them with the Hitler Youth, which excluded Jewish boys.

The Union Church troop was made up of a variety of nationalities, but Walter and I were the only Jews. Our scoutmaster was a British businessman, Mr. Gordon. His assistant was a half-caste whose father was Danish and mother Chinese. A couple of outings stick in my mind. One Saturday during the summer of 1940, we were invited by the American President Line to visit their foreign employee living area. APL was the largest American shipping company, and all their foreign personnel were assigned company housing in a large compound across the river from Shanghai.

We went there by motor launch. When we arrived, the manager greeted us at the dock and showed us around the place. Afterward we had a weenie roast with lots of soft drinks and ice cream and then spent the afternoon playing baseball. All of this was new to Walter and me, never having experienced an outdoor barbecue or baseball in Europe. Nor did we know the rules of the game or how to hit the ball. I felt like a real outsider, even though the other kids tried to teach us the game and make us feel welcome. I remember coming home from this outing quite depressed because I suddenly realized how much I had to learn before I could become "one of them."

Another adventure involved an outing on Mr. Gordon's house-boat. It was a beautiful old motor yacht anchored in the *Whangpoo* River near a sawmill. To get to it though, we had to cross large logs lashed together in the water along the pier, bobbing up and down with the waves. All of us lost our footing on the slippery logs and fell into the water several times. This would have been all right under normal circumstances since it was a hot day, but the river was badly polluted. It was a wonder that we did not get sick. Once we were on board, we had a great time picnicking, singing songs, and telling tall tales.

Once Aunt Winnie gave Walter tickets to see a play at the Lyceum Theater. He took me along and it was a wonderful experience. The play was "Charley's Aunt," and even though I was not able to follow the dialogue completely, I understood the play sufficiently to tell my parents about it. They had seen it in Berlin in transla-tion, so the explanation was relatively easy.

The area surrounding the International Settlement and French Concession was occupied by the Japanese. Although we were per-mitted to visit, we rarely, if ever, did. One day Walter and I decided to take a chance and explore *Pootung*, across the river. We took a *sampan*, a small water taxi, and were dropped off at the dock with our bicycles. As we cycled inland, we got further and further away from Western influence. We went through the city and then into the open countryside where people were working the fields. Since there were no roads, we took little farm paths. What struck us were the large ceramic pots buried at the corner of the fields. Workers as well as passersby were expected to use the pots when nature called, so that this valuable "night soil" commodity could be used as fertilizer.

As we came close to a village, we first heard dogs barking, then met up with the village idiot (or so it seemed), and then were followed by the kids into the center. Houses were close together, and bamboo arches covered with vines extended over the narrow alleys for shade in summer and to protect against the rain. It took a while for our eyes to adjust to the darkness underneath the covering, but it was a relief to be sheltered from the intense summer heat.

English was practically unknown here, but people were extremely friendly. I remember being quite concerned when one of us had a flat tire, and we were not too sure how soon we could get the thing fixed. But the kids found somebody who spoke English, and he helped get us back on our way before dark. All in all, that day was quite an adventure.

I mentioned this adventure in detail because Pootung is an ultra-modern part of Shanghai today. Shanghai's airport is located there and connected to the other parts of town by a *Maglev* train: a high speed electric train magnetically lifted above the tracks to reduce rail friction; one of the very few in the world today.

The move to the French Concession brought other changes into my life. Walter made a number of contacts with young people our age who had lived in Shanghai for a long time and they included us in their circle. There was Paul, whose father was in the import-export business. Born in Hong Kong, he was a British subject and a product of the Shanghai public school system. Paul was a very polished individual with a charming laugh. He would have made an excellent politician. He lived with his parents in an apartment in the International Settlement. His parents were welcoming, and their friendly cocker spaniel complemented the family beautifully.

Another new friend was Richard. Richard was Paul's opposite in many ways. He studied electrical engineering at the French l'Aurore University in Shanghai. He was somewhat withdrawn and introspective, especially in contrast to Paul's outgoing personality. Richard was Jewish, Paul devoutly Greek Orthodox. Richard's parents left Germany shortly before Hitler's rise to power, so they were part of the European expatriate community; well-to-do, well-connected and relatively isolated from the events in Europe. Richard's father exported animal products such as hides and bristles. His mother was part owner of a bookstore. They lived in a house in the French Concession, not far from where I lived.

A third fellow was Tsung Lo, who was something of an enigma. Chinese, with an excellent command of English, he appeared to come from a wealthy background. But nobody really knew much about him. He was very pleasant and fit well into the group. I believe he was a student at St. John's University located in the International Settlement. Nobody ever saw his home. I remember Tsung Lo giving a party for which he hired a professional photographer whose pictures were published on the society page of the *North China Daily News*. Sure enough our group's picture was picked up by the paper.

Aside from Walter and myself, there was another young refugee in our group. We met Franz (Frank) at the ORT school, and throughout our Shanghai years we were a close-knit trio. Frank lived with his mother and elder brother, Robert, in Hongkew. They came from a wealthy background in Germany. Robert and a cousin came to Shanghai very early in 1938. Through his father's association with the Freemasons in Germany, the cousin had an introduction to the German manager of an aluminum mill in Shanghai. The man gave both of them a job immediately. The company was Swiss owned, and Robert stayed with them the entire time he lived in Shanghai, ultimately being named plant manager.

Franz was the only one I knew who immediately put his ORT training to good use. He went to work for an immigrant engineer who set up a business rewinding electric motors. Franz stayed with his job the entire time he spent in Shanghai. When he came to the U.S., he studied electrical engineering and went to work for a large defense supplier. His mother was a charming lady who had a regal air about her.

The group also included a number of girls. There was Lilly who was born in Shanghai of Yeminite Jewish parents. She was a dark-haired beauty with a cheerful personality. She lived near St. John's University, and I cannot remember whether she worked or was still a student. She had grown up with another girl, Eva Hess, who brought her into our group. For a while, Walt and Lilly were very interested in each other, but it did not seem to lead anywhere.

Eva was vivacious girl, always on the go, she was a lot of fun to be with. She knew all the latest jokes, most of them dirty. She lived with her younger brother, mother, and stepfather. Eva's mother and father were Jewish and came to Shanghai in the early thirties. They did very well financially, but the marriage fell apart. Her mother then married a non-Jewish German Communist, who also did very well in Shanghai. The family went back to East Germany immediately after the Second World War.

Then there was Helga. She also was one of Eva's friends. Her father was a Jewish pediatrician who came to Shanghai in the early thirties in anticipation of things to come. Why he took his family to Shanghai, I do not know, but he did very well there. They lived in a beautiful apartment near the Race Course on Bubbling Well Road, one of the main arteries of the International Settlement. Helga was about five foot one, and prematurely grey about nineteen. Although she came from a wealthy background, she was down-to-earth, with a great deal of sensitivity.

Later on, another girl joined our little group. Her name was Lotte, the only girl who was also a refugee. She came from Austria and had a lot of the Austrian charm. As I recall there was something sexy about her. For a while she and Richard were inseparable. Things fell apart after we had to move to Hongkew, and later Walter picked up where Richard left off with Lotte.

This was the core group and for a while we spent practically every weekend together. There were others who drifted in and out on the fringe, and there were some of us who saw each other more often, but for the most part we all stuck together. Whenever the weather allowed we would take our bicycles for an outing; otherwise we met at someone's home.

Of course, the financial discrepancy between the four of us refugees and the rest was obvious, but it never seemed to interfere with our relationships, nor did we ever feel left out because of it. Except for Richard and Lotte, there were also no really close relationships between the boys and girls. Even though there was some pairing up, no long term romances seemed to evolve.

I dwell on my social life in some detail to describe the wide variety of backgrounds of the young people I encountered and how much it all differed from my German upbringing.

As mentioned earlier, exercise was part of my life ever since I entered high school. Since our arrival in Shanghai, however, there was little opportunity to continue workouts. After we moved into the French Concession, I tried to improvise a little, using bricks for weights, but I was looking for something better. So when Walt joined Stambo's gym, I decided to give it a try. It was located in the International Settlement in a private residence. Mr. Stambo was a Russian immigrant, and his clientele was a racial and ethnic slice of Shanghai. He was a bald man of about fifty with a stern demeanor who ran a tight ship. His instructions as to how to use weights and what exercises to do were very strict. I remember not being able to pull up my pants after the first lesson; I was absolutely exhausted. Nevertheless, or because of it, his method of working out set a pattern that stuck with me to this day.

When I last described my job, I was learning to make neckties in a small shop owned by a couple of Russians. When I realized that there was no future with them, I started looking around for something better. A German immigrant, a recent arrival like me, had started a necktie business that competed successfully with my employers, so I contacted him and switched jobs. Walter ran the shop together with his female cousin. It was an interesting arrangement in that he was gay and she a spinster. They had three Chinese employees, and I came in as assistant manager. It was a fancy title for a utility man, but I enjoyed the freer atmosphere and the better pay.

This man brought a whole new dimension of making neckties in Shanghai. He was an expert in textile manufacturing, totally familiar with the entire process from the dyeing of silk yarns to the designing of special patterns for French Jacquard looms. Instead of importing expensive silks for neckties from Italy and Switzerland, Walter worked with little local shops that wove Chinese brocade fabrics, and he taught them the production of his patterns. He was a perfectionist who only made silk ties of the highest quality, and he was able to capture a good share of the market.

As far as I knew, I had never met a homosexual, so this was a new experience. Walter had a steady boyfriend who visited him once in a while, but there were a number of other characters coming and going through the little offices, and I could not figure out what was going on. Most of them were older men who looked pretty shabby and it appeared they came for a handout. Nobody bothered me, but it was uncomfortable at times to be part of the scene.

I was, therefore, not unhappy when a change in my career came out of the blue. A Swiss businessman, who knew me from my days at the soda water factory and bought from my father, told him that he wanted to talk to me. He offered me yet another apprenticeship, this time learning the import-export business. He owned a relatively new firm, which represented some famous Swiss brand names, such as Rolex watches, and he wanted me to learn the business. I started with W. Schetelig during 1941 at age seventeen, and I have to thank him for setting me on a business career. I liked the work, taught myself how to use the typewriter, and went to evening school to learn shorthand.

Mr. Schetelig's personal story was typical of many expatriates. As a young fellow fresh out of school, he joined the Swiss firm of Lieberman-Wälchli in Kobe, Japan. The firm had offices all over the Orient. Over the next thirty years, he worked himself up to managing partner. He learned to speak Japanese fluently, albeit the female version, indicating how he learned the language.

Every five years he went back to Switzerland for six months, at the end of that period itching to get back to the Orient. On one of these trips home he married. He and his young bride settled in Kobe, but before their first baby was due she went back to Switzerland to assure the baby's Swiss citizenship. As the boy came of school age, he was sent back to a Swiss boarding school, perhaps seeing his parents once a year. So, while expatriates lived a life of much comfort and leisure, there were heavy penalties to pay as well.

When Mr. Schetelig was to be transferred to another location, he decided to go it alone and set up shop in Shanghai, the business hub of the Far East at the time. His new firm consisted of about ten people, most of whom were immigrants he hired away from Lieberman's offices in Shanghai. His chief assistant was Ernst who was my immediate supervisor. He was an unusual individual of about forty, a Jewish immigrant from Stuttgart, Germany. He spent several years in a Nazi concentration camp because he had been a functionary in the Communist party. Although he told me that he was still a convinced Communist, he was an excellent businessman who seemed to know every trick of the trade. Professionally he was an accountant, but his inclination was wheeling and dealing. Within a few years Schetelig made him a partner of the firm.

Another Lieberman alumnus was the sales vice president. He had been a pharmacist in Germany but he could not find work in Shanghai so he became a salesman. Being a jolly fellow, he was very good and was always full of the latest jokes. Since his desk was next to mine, we spent a good deal of time together. Being a bachelor with an eye for ladies, he shared stories of his escapades with all who were willing to listen, mostly me. I did not know whether all of his stories were true; no matter, I enjoyed it all and lived vicariously through them.

Shanghai was a city of extremes: great wealth and luxury on the one hand and extreme poverty on the other. Aside from ubiquitous and rampant vice, living in Shanghai exposed us to many dehumanizing experiences. Starvation was commonplace among the Chinese and many died in the streets. Each morning city workers on tricycles would pick up the bodies of people who had died during the night. Human life, especially of Chinese coolies, was worth very little. Police had no patience, especially with coolies. Small infractions of rules, either out of ignorance or neglect, prompted traffic cops to swing their wooden clubs, and rarely did I see an offender talk back.

This was especially true for the Sikh policemen. They were brought to Shanghai by the British and did police duty all over the Orient. Well over six feet tall and heavily overweight, they dwarfed the Chinese. To look even fiercer, or out of personal preference, they all carried large six-shot revolvers, which hung threateningly from their sides. In their blue uniforms and khaki turbans, they stood well above the crowds. The Sikh families lived in apartment complexes next to the police stations to which they were assigned, and it was a colorful scene to behold the throngs of their wives and children in native costumes.

The International Settlement harbored many functionaries of various Chinese political parties, which would occasionally get into each other's hair, resulting in frequent shootouts. These took place in areas foreigners seldom frequented, so we read about them in the morning papers. There was considerable gang warfare as well, not unlike what happened in Chicago at about the same time, which gave Shanghai the dubious reputation of the "Chicago of the Far East".

The French Concession seemed more orderly. It was said that the French appointed the head of the largest Chinese gang, the Green Gang, as assistant chief of police, which accounted for the orderliness. But it certainly did not make the police any kinder to the man in the street.

Because political as well as non-political kidnappings were frequent, bodyguards protected many Chinese who could afford this luxury.

I joined the foreign YMCA to be able to swim, but before long I participated in many of their other non-religious activities. At the Y, I met an unforgettable individual, Trebitsch-Lincoln. When I met him, he was dressed in robes of a Buddhist monk. He was a tall, intense man with white hair and penetrating eyes. He lectured on some obscure religious subject, but he was such an unusual person that I started asking others about him.

I learned that his original name was Ignácz Trebitsch and later changed to Trebitsch–Lincoln. He was born in Romania or Hungary of Jewish parents. He went to Vienna as a young man, attended the university there, and converted to Christianity. He then migrated to England, where he switched to the Church of England. Before long he was a Member of Parliament. He later became a spy for the Germans and became active in the very early Nazi movement. Then he fled to China where he became a Buddhist monk

An exceedingly intelligent man, he supposedly spoke about ten languages fluently. I also learned that he was still in the espionage trade, spying for the Chinese in Japanese occupied territories. A few years later it was announced that he had died in the Shanghai General Hospital. This may all have been a tall tale had it not been for an interesting postscripts. A letter to the editor appeared in the North China Daily News after the war, datelined Lhasa, Tibet. It was short and stated: "My friends, if the Japanese thought they killed me, they killed the wrong man because I am very much alive in Lhasa". It was signed: Trebitsch-Lincoln. That letter could have been a hoax, but in 1988, the New York Times reviewed a book about the life of Trebitsch-Lincoln that corroborated some of my story, and recently I saw a write-up of his life on Wikipedia that corroborated his life story.

The Japanese Take-Over

I was on my way to work the morning of Monday, December 8, 1941, when I thought to myself things just did not look right. There were more policemen out the streets in the French Concession, and a tank rumbled in front of the bus, something I had not seen before.

Japanese Takeover, December 7, 1941

As I entered the International Settlement, I saw Japanese gendarmes checking some Chinese for identity papers where regular police used to be stationed, but nobody bothered me. Our offices were located in the Continental Bank Building. When I reached the sixth floor, I heard blaring Japanese language radio broadcasts emanating from Japanese offices on our floor. It was usually quiet at that time of day.

Our boss, Mr. Schetelig, told us that he had been informed by phone at his home that Japan had attacked the United States. We also heard there had been some shooting during the night between a Japanese battleship, docked at a wharf in Hongkew, and a British patrol boat. Also, that an American frigate had surrendered to the Japanese. Later we learned the British boat had been sunk.

It was a day full of rumors, and none of us got much work done that fateful day. Mr. Schetelig received an urgent telephone call from the manager of the Hong Kong and Shanghai Bank, (today HSBC), who asked him for a meeting that afternoon. The bank was the most important and largest in the Far East, being partly owned by the Bank of England at that time.

Since we were in the import-export business, we had frequent contacts with the bank, and my boss had cultivated a personal relationship with top management. Having opened his own business within the last couple of years, he used the bank as a reference when trying to obtain representation of European manufacturers. He also used the bank's overseas offices to establish contacts with prospective customers. Of course, all our banking was done with the Hong Kong & Shanghai bank, and we were considered an up-and-coming company.

This time, though, the bank manager approached Mr. Schetelig with a request for help. He told him that he assumed British nationals would probably be interned by the Japanese affecting all the bank officers and their families. He wanted Mr. Schetelig's agreement to transfer bank funds to a Swiss bank in his own name so at some later date Mr. Schetelig could draw on these funds as a Swiss citizen. The aim was to set up, if possible, a support operation to help those interned. Mr. Schetelig agreed immediately. It turned out to be an important decision for him, since it cemented the relationship between the bank employees and Mr. Schetelig after the war. For me, it was also a very important decision because I was put in charge of the aid operation that evolved within a few months.

Within days, the Japanese rounded up all British and American business and political leaders for internment. Among these were the bank's manager and Walter's relative. The Japanese authorities catalogued all assets belonging to enemy nationals. This meant not only businesses but private assets as well, such as residences etc.

In this regard, a tragic comedy which happened at home of Walt's relatives is an example of at least one spunky Britisher's experience. After the executive was interned, several members of the Japanese gendarmerie visited his wife. They were of a special arm of the military that dealt with police matters, security, etc. Members of this organization wore regular soldiers' uniforms with armbands that identified them as gendarmes. One has to picture the scene to appreciate the situation. The Chinese servant ushered the soldiers into the house and asked them to wait in the living room while he fetched Mrs. Arnold. She was about twice the size of each of the officials, and as she entered the room one of them was sprawled on the couch with his rawhide boots on the polished coffee table. He did not bother to get up as she greeted them, whereupon she turned to her Chinese servant and asked him to bring some newspapers. With those in hand, she walked over to the young soldier, lifted his boots and placed the newspapers under them. The young fellow was probably fresh off the farm, and this was probably his first contact with the stiff upper lip British. The soldier got the message.

After the gendarmes inventoried everything, a notice was pasted on the front door advising everyone that the house and all property within it was under the jurisdiction of the gendarmerie and nothing could be removed without permission. All British and American nationals not interned were issued red armbands with a letter "B" or "A" identifying them as such. For the next few months, life went on pretty much as usual, but a lot was going on behind the scenes that we did not know about.

Our little group kept getting together on weekends, and although there was some apprehension as to what would ultimately happen to some of our friends, there was little personal concern. One weekend our group had an interesting experience. As usual, we bicycled to a park at the boundary of the International Settlement when we ran into a group of Japanese soldiers camped along the roadside. Suddenly we heard someone shout, "Hey, guys," but there was no American in sight. As we looked around, one of the soldiers came over and introduced himself in perfect English. He told us that he was from the States visiting relatives in Japan when the war broke out. Between the pressure of his relatives and his fear of what might happen to him, he opted to accept being drafted. Now he was stuck in the army with people who did not trust him, miserable and homesick; an unlikely soldier fighting for the Emperor.

Food was still plentiful but prices, especially on imported items, went up. There was, of course, a lack of reliable news. *The North China Daily News*, the establishment paper in Shanghai, was of course taken over and printed only what passed the censors.

What we read and heard on the radio seemed incomprehensible. That Japan should be able to capture Hong Kong and Singapore and stand on the doorsteps of India; that the Dutch East Indies should be overrun and Australia threatened, sounded like a fairy tale. But within a few days, news filtered through from people who owned short-wave radios that most of what we heard and read was really true, and we began to realize that the Orient might be altered permanently.

Things began to change in the latter part of 1942. All enemy aliens were given time to wind up their affairs before internment. The war began to affect us directly as well. The authorities picked up some of my friends, those with British passports. Food and fuel became less plentiful. The most noticeable change was in street traffic. Since gasoline was rationed or unavailable, private cars all but disappeared and rickshaws did tremendous business. Bicycles were at a premium.

Most interesting was how trucking firms coped. Enterprising engineers developed wood-burning converters to fuel trucks. Every morning, one could see truck drivers starting a fire in a contraption attached to the side of the vehicle. It consisted mainly of a large bin, about the size of a residential hot water heater, which contained either charcoal or just small chunks of wood. The fire would smolder all day, releasing the gas that drove the trucks. It was an ingenious system, which worked well, even though it polluted the air terribly.

Although most of Shanghai was flat, there were bridge approaches and a few hills that trucks had difficulty managing with the new fuel system. Unemployed coolies soon figured out that here was a way to make a few cents. They would gather at the foot of these hills and wait for trucks to stall so they could pitch in to shove them up the hill. Trucks carrying rice were especially welcome because it gave the coolies an opportunity to slash some of the bags and steal some rice. Police, if they were around, were pretty helpless in such situations because they were vastly outnumbered and people were desperate.

An important permanent change occurred on Friday, January 1, 1943. Shanghai's traffic changed from the left (British) to the right side of the street. Bedlam ensued, but it could have been much worse had there been more automobiles. The shift was advertised well in advance, but it seemed as if Martians had landed. The police were out in full force, swinging clubs at unsuspecting rickshaw coolies, who by force of habit, kept drifting back onto the left side of the street. Things improved by Monday, with most everyone obeying the new rules.

It is the custom in China to pay one's debts before the Chinese New Year begins. Because of pervasive poverty, thefts and break-ins were commonplace, but they multiplied manifold around the time of Chinese New Year. Holdups were frequent, although foreigners were bothered less than Chinese. Some people carried defensive weapons like brass knuckles or even small blackjacks, but I never heard of anybody actually using them. Similarly, Mr. Schetelig always carried a small Browning automatic pistol in his hip pocket and one of my jobs was to take it apart once a month and oil the parts. He never had occasion to use it, but I suppose it made him feel more secure.

Gradually, the war directly affected Shanghai and its people. The presence of Japanese troops was all pervasive in the International Settlement. Bridges, which used to be manned by British troops, became checkpoints controlled by Japanese sentries. Thousands of Chinese shuffled passed the sentries daily and were closely scrutinized. Everyone had to exit busses, rickshaws and automobiles at the head of the bridge, walk across while the driver alone was allowed to stay with the vehicle. Everyone had to show identification papers.

Inspection was mostly perfunctory, but occasionally a soldier would break the monotony of his duty by picking out a passerby to detain or subject to physical abuse. A favorite punishment for some obscure infraction, like holding the passport upside down (because the coolie was illiterate), would be to force the man to half-squat for as much as half an hour. When the man sunk down too low in this position, the soldier would poke him with his bayonet to force him up to a position that was difficult to hold. These actions were totally arbitrary, and no Chinese seemed to be immune. However, I never saw any foreigners subjected to this punishment, not even enemy aliens with their identifying armbands.

Occasionally an area would be cordoned off after some terrorist action, everyone searched and identification papers closely inspected. Hit-and-run resistance by Chinese was frequent. The Japanese reaction was swift and often cruel. One comical episode comes to mind that involved a Jewish refugee. He wanted to have his portable typewriter repaired downtown. As he walked down Nanking Road, he ran into a friend, set the typewriter down, and stopped to schmooze a bit. Then, saying their goodbyes, they went on their way. The man was upset by what his friend had told him, so he walked in deep thought not noticing that he left the typewriter on the sidewalk.

The "black box" sat on the sidewalk in front of the Sassoon Hotel, the doorman noticed it and called the police, who roped the area off to a safe distance. Meanwhile, our friend noticed his error and turned to retrieve the typewriter. As he got close to the scene, he was stopped by a throng of people who had gathered at the scene. Fighting his way through the crowd, he walked up to a soldier to tell him that it was all a mistake. By the time one was found who spoke English, an armored truck arrived. Everyone was convinced that the typewriter was really a bomb, so they threw a net over it and gently lifted it onto the truck. By now the Japanese understood the man's story and they took him along with the "bomb."

At the police station, they unloaded the box into a bunker, put our friend in with it and watched through a thick window as he opened it up and started to type on it. Everyone broke up laughing, followed by a lot bowing and handshaking. Now our friend wanted to leave with his treasure. "Not so fast. First you have to pay our expenses before you get your bomb back." I do not know what he finally paid, but I am sure this was an experience he would not forget.

Aside from the pleasant, relatively safe neighborhood, living in the French Concession gave its residents less exposure to the Japanese occupation. From all appearances, it was still "a little piece of France in the Orient." This was so because after its defeat the remnant French government had created a right wing regime in the South of France, with the capitol located in Vichy. The Japanese recognized this government as long as the commander of the French troops in Shanghai indicated his allegiance to the Vichy.

Those of us living in the French Concession had to register with the French police in July, 1942, undoubtedly at the behest of the Japanese. It was not long after the last enemy nationals had been ordered to report for internment that things began to change for us.

Gradually the clouds of war were coming closer to us. Very high flying bombers flew over the area and dropped their bombs on outlying areas. The usual sequence was that we first heard the bomb explosions, followed by air raid sirens and anti-aircraft fire. Actually, ground batteries did the only damage seen at that time. Mr. Schetelig brought several green steel helmets to the office which were hung on the wall for eventualities.

I happened to be working at the office one Sunday and heard the start of another bombing raid. The electricity went off, leaving the office dark, with only light from a large window facing the light shaft. Unable to work, I decided to walk up to the roof of the building to see what was going on. I took a helmet and started up the stairs. There were groups of Chinese on every landing, cowering in the corners, away from the windows. For them such raids were nothing new, having gone through them many times during the Japanese air raids in the thirties.

It took me some time to climb to the roof. The view from there was spectacular. The raid took place across the river over Pootung, a couple of miles away. I could see warehouses on fire. Several other people were watching from the roof, but I felt very important because I was the only one with a helmet. We heard anti-aircraft fire all around us. Suddenly, shrapnel hit someone in the leg. He was carried inside immediately and the rest of us scrambled to get off the roof as quickly as possible.

As I found out the next day, I had had a close call. I took a coworker up to the roof, this time by the elevator, to show him what I witnessed, and we saw a large number of pieces shrapnel lying around. These must have fallen down shortly after I got off the roof.

Food shortages began to appear. Sugar was in short supply as was rice. As usual, people with money did not suffer because there was a healthy black market for everything. At one time, the police became suspicious when the number of funeral processions increased beyond the number of deaths. As suspected, black market rice and sugar were transported by this ingenious method until a stop was put to it.

Our business began to change as shipments from overseas dried up. Historically, most of China's pharmaceuticals and dye-stuffs were imported. The war offered entrepreneurial opportunities to immigrants with technical know-how. Two chemists started their own manufacturing operation of fine chemicals. A pharmacist, whose name I cannot recall, produced saline and glucose injections. Another, chemist started a soap factory. Mr. Schetelig traded with all of them and established manufacturing partnerships with others.

One item much in demand was caffeine. For a long time it was a mystery as to who used such large quantities of caffeine. Finally, word got out that the ultimate buyer was a German trading company and that all of it was shipped by submarines to Germany to pep up German troops. One could always tell when a German submarine was expected because the price of caffeine skyrocketed.

Mr. Schetelig set up a manufacturing operation to produce caffeine employing a refugee chemist as operations manager. This man had never made caffeine before but he talked a good line. The source for the chemical was black tea and the trick was to separate the caffeine from the tannins and impurities. His process used lye to precipitate the impurities. Unfortunately the end results were aggregates that looked like gallstones. They were totally insoluble and the valuable caffeine was trapped in them.

The next plant manager was more inventive. He used cheap rice wine for its alcohol content to extract the caffeine from the tea and our product became the standard of the industry. Then, as quickly as the market developed for the product, it evaporated, practically from one day to the next. Apparently the German submarines could no longer penetrate the British blockades, and Mr. Schetelig was stuck with thousands of pounds of caffeine and a useless plant. Nobody felt sorry for him, though, because he made a fortune while demand lasted.

My job also changed drastically. After about a year with Schetelig & Co. I was given the responsibility of managing the operation to prepare and ship foodstuffs for those British internees who had been with the Hong Kong & Shanghai Bank. Each family was allotted a ten-pound package monthly, which was forwarded through the Red Cross to the camps. We supplied about sixty families. High energy foods like cheese, powdered milk, dried fruits, dried salami sausage, etc., were the most sought after items, but we also shipped other products liked jams, canned butter, canned sardines, powdered eggs, flour, and cereals. Occasionally we would also ship medications, especially toward the end of the war when conditions in the camps deteriorated and people suffered hardships.

We leased a section of a warehouse with its own access to the street. I became the receiving clerk, order processor, packer, and shipping coordinator. It was a great job. As long as I got the packages out in time, kept my records straight and had orderly inventories, nobody bothered me. The added fringe benefit was the little *cumshaw* I took home, using a Chinese term for a "freebee." This helped my family a lot, especially when things got tough later on.

Procurement of scarce items became quite a challenge. Mr. Josephson did most of that work, which entailed dealing with many middlemen. Because Shanghai supplied much of China before the war, warehouses were well stocked when the war interrupted trade. Consequently, there was quite a reservoir upon which to draw, but because of adverse storage conditions much of these valuable foodstuffs spoiled.

So-called "warehouse receipts" were issued for the products in storage. These papers were traded on the market, mostly between speculators who waited for prices to rise. Often such receipts would have twenty or more endorsements on their back, indicating how often ownership had changed hands.

When taking delivery of the goods, we often found them to be spoiled. For example, sardines in tomato sauce, a highly prized item, frequently had raised can lids indicating spoilage. A memorable comment by one broker who sold the merchandise best explains the business environment: "This is not eating merchandise – it is trading merchandise". Shortages caused inflation which added to the peculiar political situation. The Japanese had installed a puppet regime in Nanking under a turncoat former member of the Chinese Nationalist's inner circle. This government issued a new currency, changing the name from Sh$ (Shanghai dollar) to CRB$ (Central Reserve Bank dollar). Of course, it was more than a change in name.

Historically, the currency had the confidence of the people, but then things changed. Although many adherents of the new regime saw themselves as pragmatic patriots, the new Wang Ching-wei government had few friends. One of its leaders lived in our immediate neighborhood, and his house was protected round the clock by guards armed with submachine guns.

In spite of the ongoing war against the U.S., the Yankee dollar was traded more or less openly on the black market. To give some understanding of the scope of inflation, here are some figures for comparison. When we arrived in Shanghai in 1939 it took six Sh$ to buy one US$. By the middle of 1942, six months after Pearl Harbor it took fifty CRB$ to buy one US$, and shortly before the end of the war the same dollar cost CRB$3,000.

Probably because the printing presses could not keep up with the demand for currency, the central bank held back on the issuance of paper money. This created a preposterous situation. Banks started to ration the amount of cash a depositor could withdraw daily and long lines formed in front of banks each morning. In order to maximize the amount of cash one could obtain, people opened checking accounts all over town, sending their servants and wives each morning to stand in line for their quota of cash. Of course, the banks were suddenly swamped with mountains of checks and processing these checks delayed accurate accounting for weeks. Merchants worked on the "float" by not covering checks immediately, which exacerbated the situation. They also instituted a two-tier pricing for their merchandise depending on whether the customer paid in cash or by check. At times cash commanded a 20% discount.

Needless to say, all schemes backfired for the government, actually fuelling inflation and ultimately forcing the Central Reserve Bank to flood the market with even more currency. Toward the end of the war, notes were issued without serial numbers, and at one point the printers were in such a hurry that currency was printed on one side only.

A number of currency exchange shops were located around the corner from where I worked. They were storefront operations facing the sidewalk. Tellers sat behind iron-barred windows, handling several telephones, talking to other shops, traders, and the customer standing in front of the window, at the same time. They would deal primarily in gold and the US$. The Chinese had always treasured gold, the ultimate yardstick of stability and security. Gold was sold in one and ten-ounce bars, each bar marked with a little red sticker indicating its exact weight. But buying or selling gold is cumbersome, so for the less conservative Chinese as well as for us foreigners, the US$ was the currency of choice for storing assets.

Dealing with these traders was an experience in itself. They would offer several quotes depending on what was in demand at any particular time. For instance, at one time bills larger than US$5 were discounted, supposedly because there were too many large counterfeit bills floating around. At another time small US$ bills were discounted because they were too bulky to handle in quantity. At yet another time all US$ bills with the overprint HAWAII were discounted because they were not "real US$" while the same bills were at a premium at another time because counterfeiters would not bother with such notes.

While on the topic of money, I should discuss how needy Jewish refugees were taken care of. Approximately twenty-five hundred of the eighteen thousand refugees lived in the *Heime*, totally dependent on welfare, and another five to six thousand received either free or low cost meals. In addition, there was a clinic and a hospital and other institutions requiring support. Until the outbreak of war between Japan and the U.S., there was a steady flow of funds administered by the local representative of the American Jewish Joint Distribution Committee.

Of course Pearl Harbor changed all that. With the knowledge and approval of the Japanese, a group of well-known Jewish businessmen, old Shanghailanders, was authorized by the *Joint* to raise funds locally, issuing promissory notes denominated in US$ and Swiss Francs to come due after the war. Wealthy Chinese and foreign businessmen welcomed the idea of buying such notes because the terms were very attractive. In spite of this unique arrangement, services to the needy had to be curtailed, but without this help we would have had an even greater disaster than already existed.

We tried to stay in touch with Uncle Eric through the Red Cross. We were allowed to write a twenty five word message that went off on May 11, 1942. It was returned on November 15, 1942, with an answer that all was well with him. Our next opportunity for such a message was on May 5, 1944, to which we never received an answer until after the war ended.

The Shanghai Ghetto

On February 18, 1943, the Japanese administration issued a proclamation notifying all "stateless refugees" to move to a "designated area" in Hongkew. Note that the words "Jew" and "ghetto" never appeared in the proclamation. Nevertheless, everyone knew what this proclamation really meant. We were given three months to wind up our affairs and find housing in the ghetto.

What none of us knew at the time was this order was instigated by "the long arm" of the German Gestapo. Not until after the war and the Nuremberg trials did we learn that the original plan of the Germans had been to exterminate all Jewish refugees in Shanghai. They even offered to run the gas chambers. When the Japanese

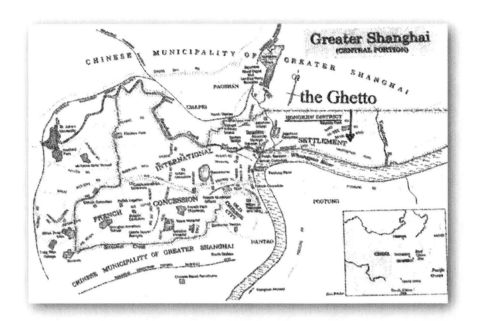

refused, the proposal was amended to use us as hostages, reasoning that American Jews would influence the U.S. military not to bomb vital installations close to the ghetto.

In the beginning, it seemed impossible to comply with this edict because of the housing shortage in the ghetto, but after some extensions everyone complied. To get a picture of the scope of the problem, the ghetto was about one square mile in area with an indigenous population of about 100,000 Chinese, some Japanese, and 8,000 Jewish refugees. Now, approximately 8,000 more people needed to be housed there.

Through a real estate broker, of which there were suddenly quite a few, my parents found a Chinese partner willing to exchange his house in the ghetto with ours in the French Concession. Although it was centrally located, across from the Muirhead Road police station, the house was a throwback to what we had left when we moved out of the area the first time. It was located in a small, squalid lane, without indoor plumbing, cooking or bathing facilities. It did have about the same number of rooms as the one we lived in, allowing my parents to continue to have some income by renting rooms. As

Our "Home" in the Ghetto. Second Door on the Right.

I recall, most of our tenants moved with us, some only temporarily until they could find something better.

The move into the ghetto brought many changes. Only people with jobs outside the ghetto were permitted to go back and forth to work. For those who could prove secure jobs, a blue three-month pass was usually issued, accompanied by a blue lapel button to be worn at all times. For those judged to be in less secure positions, a pink thirty-day pass was usually issued, along with a pink lapel button. Everyone else had to prove to the authorities that they had legitimate reasons for wanting to leave the ghetto before they were issued day passes.

Rules for the issuance of passes were applied arbitrarily by the two Japanese administrators of the ghetto, Messrs. Okura and Goya. Goya was a totally unpredictable dictator, whose behavior would have been very amusing had it not been so tragic for the people involved.

Line-up in front of Goya's Office

Goya issuing Passes for leaving Ghetto temporarily.

Goya was very short in stature, with a Hitler mustache. He had advanced through the ranks in the consular service, which had exposed him to some Western culture. His facility with English was quite good. But he was a megalomaniac who called himself "King of the Jews". Okura was a former police officer who was much more predictable but, unfortunately, calculated and sadistic. Both would punish people for minor infractions, slapping them or worse. To have to appear in front of either of these men was always a nerve-wracking experience.

There were also some Jewish refugees employed in the office. One man was able to become an officer with the Shanghai Municipal police before the war as he was Czechoslovakian. His name was Morris Feder and he acted as Goya's secretary; no easy job. There were also several women typists, all of whom had to constantly witness the indignities endured by their fellow Jews.

The tragi-comedy which played out every day was based on Goya's prejudice against certain types of people. Being short, he hated all who were tall. He also hated people with beards as well as those who were untidy or disrespectful. Rarely would these people obtain a pass on their first try or even at a second try, which meant that they had no income over a period of weeks, thereby losing their livelihood. Goya liked to slap people who he felt offended him, perhaps just by being too tall. For the latter, he would stand on a chair so he could reach their faces to slap them. He would insult others and scream at them before physically throwing them out. At rare times, when the mood struck him, he would look out the window, see the long lines, and issue passes to everybody without asking questions.

In his private life, he continued this role. He played the violin, had a refugee teacher, and insisted on accompanying a refugee chamber music ensemble. He would visit Kadoorie School, so named after a prominent Jewish family that had paid for its construction. At the school, he would play with the kids, but on his way home he might pick on some unsuspecting passerby whose lapel button indicated that he had permission to leave the ghetto, rip it off, and tell him to turn in his pass the next day, just because the man did not greet him.

There were innumerable anecdotes about Goya, but the one I like best concerned a Catholic missionary. One of the refugees worked for the French Catholic mission. When applying for a pass, Goya told him to bring in his boss to verify his employment. A few days later when the two appeared in front of him, Goya took one look at the tall priest's long beard, black cassock and black hat, then jumped out of his chair screaming at the priest that he did not like Polish Jews. When his assistant explained that this man was a priest, Goya broke up laughing, calling people in line into his office and issued passes to everyone.

Compared to Okura, Goya was not a evil person just crazy, but because of the fear and anxiety he instilled in people he was the more hated. Goya was beaten when the war was over and repatriated to Japan, where I understand he lived out his years in isolation. I do not know what happened to Okura.

My own experiences with Goya varied. Being young, only 19 at the time, and having a permanent job, seemed to carry the day even though I was relatively tall. Nevertheless, I had to appear before him every three months, and I had a great deal of apprehension each time. Later on, because of my own doing, I ran into problems and my pass was changed to the 30-day pink variety. Here is how that came about. Soon after the Pearl Harbor attack, the Japanese authorities instituted a self-policing system all over Shanghai called *Pao Chia*. The system was rooted in Chinese history whereby the country was divided into small *Chias* (districts), each being responsible for its own internal security. The head of each *Chia* was held responsible for the actions of all residents. The Japanese revived this system for their own ends. Neighborhoods all over Shanghai were charged with the responsibility for what happened in their areas. Primarily it was aimed at combating terrorism.

Pao Chia Members

With the establishment of the ghetto, the *Pao Chia* there was given additional responsibility. Beyond the standard duty of providing for collective security, it now also had to police refugee traffic in and out of the ghetto. All men between 20 and 45 had to report for guard duty for several hours each week. This involved being stationed at crossing points leading in and out of the ghetto, checking individual passes, or manning the guard houses located all over the ghetto itself. Duty was scheduled around the clock, days as well as nights. People hated to do guard duty at border crossings because it meant turning in pass violators to the Japanese, who would then punish offenders by either confiscating passes or beatings or both. Violators were those who stayed out of the district longer than permitted, used expired or someone else's pass, or tried to sneak out without one.

With my twentieth birthday, I reported for duty and was made an officer, probably because I volunteered for night duty and owned a bicycle. My identification armband had a blue stripe on the top indicating that I was an officer with an official seal of the Japanese gendarmerie. My duty was to travel from post to post, checking whether people manned them properly. It was relatively easy duty except during inclement weather or during air raids. Taking the night shift allowed me to work days without interruptions and had the added advantage of being on duty during quiet hours with little traffic.

One morning, while running a business errand to the general post office in the International Settlement, I encountered a blockade. The street was roped off by the police with pedestrians waiting behind the rope. Having run into this situation before on several occasions, I put on my *Pao Chia* armband, even though I was off-duty, and walked into the roped off area. Several policemen saluted and things went fine until a detective came up to me asking to see my identification papers. He took one look at them and sent me into the paddy wagon. Inside I found a number of other refugees. Since I had no business wearing my armband outside the ghetto, I quickly took it off and put it into my pocket. It turned out that this time the blockade was intended to round up black marketers, especially refugees who illegally dealt in US$. I explained at the police station that I was on a business errand and that I had nothing to do with the black market. I had no proof to back me up other than to give my boss's telephone number for the police to check. I was slapped into a cell with a number of other people and waited for things to happen.

After about two hours a guard, called my name and I was sent up for further interrogation. My boss appeared before too long and began to talk to the officer in Japanese. He identified himself as being Swiss and the officer was very courteous to him. Then, suddenly, the officer became very agitated, finally throwing my boss out of his office.

Apparently what happened was that my boss misled the officer to thinking he was a consular official, but when the man learned he was only a businessman who happened to speak Japanese, he felt insulted. I was sent into police station's yard with the others after the interrogation. In looking around, I noticed one refugee leaving through a side gate without being stopped, so I decided to follow suit.

There were no immediate repercussions, but when I applied for renewal of my pass, the record showed I had been picked up and Goya gave me a very bad time. I was not issued a pass for about three weeks which meant that I could not work. When I finally managed to get one, it was of the pink 30-day variety. Fortunately, the war ended a few months after that episode.

Ghetto Life

The ghetto was under Japanese control from May 1943 to August 1945, but it seemed like decades. It is extremely difficult to describe the life we lived and things we experienced, to convey a sense of the times and our feelings. It was a period of great deprivation and uncertainty.

By 1943, having lived in China for about four years, we had become accustomed to boil all drinking water, to wash all fruits and vegetables in a solution of potassium permanganate, to not eat uncooked foods, and to be properly inoculated against tropical diseases. Our immune system must have adapted to the constant barrage of diseases all around us. As long as our food intake was adequate our health was good, but with the onset of food shortages our susceptibility to disease increased.

This was especially true for those who relied on public assistance, as usual the first to suffer. One of the most virulent diseases directly related to hunger was called the sprue. Its symptoms were nausea, diarrhea, and, in severe cases, vomiting. It only attacked the weak and seemed to be related to vitamin deficiencies. Almost all of us came down with sprue sooner or later. Sanitation, or the lack of it, seemed to have nothing to do with sprue. Some of the older or very weak died from complications brought on by the disease. My mother came down with a pretty severe bout of it and it took a long time for her to recuperate.

To combat vitamin deficiencies, refugee doctors came upon an ingenious idea. They recommended everyone keep a large bottle of a light sugar solution on a shelf to which a cake of fresh yeast was added. A glass of this concoction each day provided most vitamins, especially the B-group, once the yeast became active. To replenish the fluid, a glass of water plus a teaspoon of sugar were added each day.

Markets were usually empty of staples. Flour, rice, sugar, and cooking oils were in very short supply. Rice shops would open daily for only a few hours and long lines formed in front of them. Sugar was rationed. Fish seemed to be more plentiful, but often of very poor quality and always very high priced. Trying to purchase meat was hopeless. Aside from being outrageously expensive, it was marketed under very unsanitary conditions. Chinese merchants found many ingenious ways of lining their pockets. Watermelons, for instance, would be injected with water to make them heavier, thereby also making them a source for possible infections. Beans and lentils were usually mixed with small chips of stones to increase their weight. I remember sitting with my parents for hours picking out the stone chips.

All of us lost a lot of weight during that time, which speaks more eloquently about the conditions than I can. By the end of the war, I weighed 125 pounds and my parents were equally thin. Keep in mind that our family was relatively fortunate as I could bring home some extras occasionally and we could afford to buy some items on the black market from time to time. Still, many a night I went to bed hungry only to go to work next morning without breakfast.

Switching back to "honey buckets" from the luxury of our previous home with flush toilets was our first shock after moving to Hongkew. Also, the place was full of roaches; fighting them was a never ending battle. Cooking was done on electric hot plates, but since the wiring was inadequate, we could only use one hotplate at a time. Consequently, other means of cooking had to be used. The most common system involved use of charcoal briquettes.

There was a little open-air patio in front of our ground floor room where we placed two small Chinese coal stoves. These consisted a five-gallon tin can lined with baked clay. A small metal grating inside held the coals, and a cut-out in front allowed for the removal of ashes. One bought either ready-made briquettes or mixed coal dust with some clay, forming little balls that were then dried in the sun. Lighting these stoves and keeping them going by use of a Chinese palm fan was a constant chore. Coal smoke penetrated the neighborhood throughout the day.

As mentioned earlier, our new abode did not have bathrooms. Consequently, we had to use a public bath located in one of the *Heims* on occasion. The bath consisted of a changing area and one long shower room which accommodated about thirty people. Two long perforated pipes hung suspended below the ceiling and warm water dripped onto the people below. Only when the room was filled to capacity would the water be turned on and then only for a few minutes. In between the first and second rinse there was a lot of jumping around to keep warm. During the summer months this was not a hardship, but in winter it became quite an experience. It left such an impression on me that to this day I rarely take a shower without thinking of those days.

By the time we returned from the French Concession, much had changed in Hongkew. Some of the streets had undergone a metamorphosis. Refugee builders refurbished whole lanes from bombed-out shells to relatively nice housing. Chusan Road, a short thoroughfare, became a stylish shopping street with living quarters above the shops. There were coffeehouses, restaurants and nightclubs in the area, which were not only frequented by refugees but also by some Japanese, wealthy Chinese, and foreigners.

My circle of friends shrunk considerably. Frank lived not far from me with his mother and brother. They had leased one of the newly refurbished houses; one of the nicest developments. Their place was every bit as nice as the one we just moved out of, with flush toilets, bathrooms, and kitchens. Their one tenant was a young couple. By contrast, Walter and his parents had to move into the *SACRA* compound (Shanghai Ashkenazi Collaboration Relief Association), which was essentially public housing. It was a sprawling complex of inter-connected buildings with long hallways, home to about 2700 people. Walter and his family had a room at the outer periphery of the compound near a high stone wall.

For a while Frank, Walter, and I spent a lot of time together. We would prowl around the neighborhood or just sit some place and talk. One day one of us came up with the idea that we all go to a Chinese whorehouse. I was terribly frightened, remembering horror stories about victims of such places, but I did not let on. I believe Walter had been there before, but it was a first for Frank and me. None of the girls there spoke any English so there was only non-verbal communication. After we paid the madam there was a small parade of girls, and I picked the one I thought would be most understanding.

What followed seemed to be over so quickly that I felt I did not get my money's worth, nor was I in the mood for more even though the girl started to make further advances. I just wanted to get out of there, but neither of my buddies was ready, so I had to bide my time for what seemed like hours but was probably just a few minutes. All in all, not the greatest introduction to sex.

I believe Walter was at loose ends. After his British employer was forced to cease operations he was out of a job and without a job he could not leave the ghetto. So he started to repair bicycles and in my free time I joined him. With many bicycles around, and tremendous wear and tear due to poor roads etc., there was plenty of work for both of us. Of course we had to compete with the Chinese repair shop down the road, but as I recall we did all right.

We worked in the hallway in front of Walter's room, so evenings we had to pack up and move everything into the crowded room which accommodated him and his family.

We obtained our tools from flea markets where vendors, Chinese as well as refugees, displayed their merchandise. The kinds of items on sale were an indication of prevailing conditions. Rusty nails were sold by the piece, as were old screws, nuts and bolts. Each item was lined up by size, like little soldiers. European tools were rare; most tools were made in China and needed some repair. But there were a large number of personal items on display, from kitchenware to wearing apparel, from crystal wine gobblets to Persian rugs. It almost seemed like everybody either needed something or had something to sell, often both.

My cousin Willi was one of those street vendors. He and his wife Carole had their stand not far from where we lived. It was hard work and there was lot of competition, but somehow they muddled through and managed to survive on their own.

My cousin Kurt's story is different. He was married to a woman named Gerda who was very pleasant and friendly. But Kurt had personal problems. He loved to gamble and seemed to have little understanding of the value of money. He was either "in the money" and lived in grand style, or he was flat broke. When he ran out of money, he "borrowed" from his brother, my father, or anybody. Finally, Gerda could not take it anymore and left him for another man.

Unfortunately, Kurt was unable to pull himself together and started going downhill. He had to move into one of the *Heime*, where he spent most of his time gambling for pennies. Before long, he was down and out, totally separated from his relatives. I ran into him one day on the street. When he noticed me he crossed the street to avoid me in the crowd, but I saw the condition he was in. He was barefoot in tatters and filthy. When the war was over, he made a turn-around. I believe his second wife helped him work his way out his compulsion to gamble and got him back on his feet. My uncle Max and his family also lived in the ghetto, but I do not recall ever getting together with them.

My cousin Horst was younger by two years, which at that age was a large gap. Also, he traveled with a faster crowd than I did. Max continued in the paper business, supplying stores with paper bags, wrapping paper, etc., and Horst worked with him. Horst had undergone a number of traumatic experiences. Instead of leaving with his father and stepmother for Shanghai, he was left behind in an orphanage in Germany at age fourteen. Horst was expected to be part of a children's transport (*Kindertransport*) to England, which never materialized. Max and his wife were able to book only two passages to China because he was under orders to leave the country.

Understandably, Horst felt abandoned, as would anybody under the circumstances. Somehow he wound up in a concentration camp, even though he was considerably underage. In 1940, Max arranged for a trans-Siberian railway ticket for him which took him Vladivostok and from there to Shanghai on a Japanese freighter. This all happened during the short period of the Hitler-Stalin Non-Aggression Pact, and it was literally the last opportunity to escape from Germany. It was not until many years later when both of us were in the U.S. that Henry (Horst) and I became close.

I want to say a word about language. Europeans, except the English, have a somewhat different attitude toward foreign languages than do Americans. Some facility to handle a foreign language is expected of anyone with a high school education. Perhaps the close proximity of one country to another in Europe accounts for this attitude. Perhaps also Europe's constantly shifting borders forced people to adopt, or at least understand, the neighbor's language?

Not having gone to a high school, my father did not learn a foreign language until he came to the U.S., and he always considered this his greatest handicap. I was brought up to believe in the importance of knowing at least one foreign language.

As pointed out earlier, I was fortunate in having a capable English teacher in high school who taught English in a way that stimulated his students. In Shanghai, I spoke German at home, German and English at work and Chinese on the street. My ability to communicate in Chinese was limited to what I would call coolie language.

Like almost all refugees, I saw our stay in China as temporary and made no real effort to learn Chinese. That was a great mistake and in retrospect I am very sorry for not having made the effort. Chinese language classes were given at the YMCA in Shanghai, but to my recollection none were offered by refugee organizations. Yet there was a Sinologist among the refugees who gave occasional lectures on Chinese history and culture. Nor did we make any attempt to learn Japanese, which certainly would have been expedient.

We spoke German among ourselves, *Pidgin English* (a Far Eastern *lingua franca*) or Chinese with the natives, and English with the Japanese. Pidgin English is like an oriental Yiddish, a mixture of English, Chinese, Indian, and Portuguese. Since some of us were German and others were Austrian, there was a lot good-natured, and some not so good-natured, bantering between us. My girl friend, Fritzi, was from Austria and often tried to score off me by ridiculing my German pronunciation of some words. To get acclimatized to English, Fritzi and I tried to speak as much English as possible. This worked fine as long as the conversation did not get serious, but whenever we got personal we would revert to speaking German.

I met Fritzi at a seminar and quickly fell in love. Fritzi was about a foot shorter than I, with dark brown hair and a very pretty face. She was as Viennese as I was German. She was bright and vivacious, as are most Viennese girls, but she was also moody. She lived with her mother in a studio apartment above one of the shops on Chusan Road. By profession she was a designer, but she earned her living as a seamstress. Her mother was widowed, an expert at acting helpless and dishing out guilt. Fritzi, having lost her father early in life, was devoted to her mother who hated being left alone. I resented this situation but decided early on I would not get between the two. Before long, I spent most of my waking hours at Fritzi's home.

After the war her mother decided to return to Austria to claim her rightful pension since her husband had been a director at the state railroad. Of course Fritzi went with her, which was the end of our romance. A few years later, the two resettled in San Francisco, but by that time I was otherwise pre-occupied. Fritzi never married; perhaps her mother served as an excuse for not wanting to face marriage, perhaps her mother would not let her get married. She met a tragic death years later when she drowned off Stinson Beach in California. A number of her friends and I thought Fritzi committed suicide.

In spite of the dire circumstances in the ghetto there were lots of activities for young people. There were a large number of professional people among the refugees who were frustrated at being unable to work in their chosen field. Many of these welcomed an opportunity to share their knowledge and stretch their minds giving lectures, seminars, and what the Germans call *Kulturabende* (evenings of culture) for young people.

In retrospect, it was incongruent to have cultural events, such as a series of lectures on *Beethoven's* symphonies, the German philosophers, and modern economics under the prevailing conditions. Many were held outdoors among bombed out buildings, often in between air raids. One such event stuck in my mind because I realized at the time how insane it really was. Here we were, about two dozen young people, sitting on ruins under the summer stars listening to an economist expound on the subject of: "Should America be on the Gold Standard"?

But it was not all heavy stuff. There were several soccer teams and their games were well attended. There were also boxing matches, bridge tournaments, and evenings of dancing to live music. In European style, there were many outdoor cafés, serving mostly soft drinks and tea, where people of all ages schmoozed, mostly just to get out of their depressing and overcrowded housing.

At that time, I was a heavy smoker. It was an expensive habit and local cigarettes, the only ones I could afford, were very strong. I cannot remember when I really started to smoke, but it probably dated back to Germany, where I experimented with it in the bathroom. Smoking was "smart" and you just were not "in" if you did not smoke. Of course, this was long before anyone knew the connection between smoking and lung cancer, but we all knew that it was not "good" for you. I had an inkling as to how bad it was for my health when I passed out one time sitting with my friends in one of these cafés. The doctor, who examined me, later told me that I had nicotine poisoning, which I then bragged about as if it was a badge of honor.

Fritzi

I cut back for a short time, but, with Fritzi and everyone else smoking, I was soon back to puffing nearly two packs a day. Of

course, the times were extremely stressful which undoubtedly contributed to my habit. A second fainting spell left me with a tobacco allergy, which helped me stop smoking. To this day I get slight chills every time I put an unlit cigarette into my mouth.

I mentioned air raids and I want to try to describe these experiences. As I recall, serious air raids started about a year after Pearl Harbor. At first the planes would fly so high that we could not distinguish them. The Japanese had installed listening devices that triggered air raid sirens. These did not seem to work too well. We would usually first hear the bombs explode, followed by air raid alarms and then anti-aircraft fire.

When these raids took place at night, they were really spectacular. Anti-aircraft batteries would shoot tracer bullets to check their trajectory and bomb explosions would light up the night sky. Damage done was mostly at quite a distance from where we were, but by the time we moved into the ghetto the war had moved much closer to us. By then, we saw occasional daytime raids when planes dropped their bombs only miles from the ghetto. It was eerie to see these bombs being dropped, then hear the thud at a distance and later see the clouds of smoke over the horizon.

Night bombing raids came with greater frequency. Air raid shelters were practically unavailable in the ghetto, except for the Ward Road jail near our residence. It was an old British jail built of concrete and brick. The basement was opened as a shelter, but few people bothered to go there. We needed rest, if not sleep, and hoped that the Allies would not bomb us directly. Besides, a jail was not an inviting location. After the war we learned that the military had stored bombs in the subbasement of the jail. A direct hit could perhaps have blown everyone to kingdom come.

Residents were ordered to dig holes in the sidewalks so that people could jump into them during an air raid to avoid the air pressure from the bombs. These holes were about 3 feet deep and presented a constant hazard, especially for people coming home after dark. Nor could we really understand the value of these holes until raids hit the ghetto directly.

That started to happen at noon on July 17, 1945, when U.S. bombers hit in broad daylight. I was at work and it was a short, sudden raid. It sounded as if it was not very far away, so I ran up onto the roof again to see.

The smoke seemed to rise close to where I knew Walter lived, so I ran down, told my boss about it, jumped on a bicycle and started peddling in the general direction of the SACRA compound. After I entered the ghetto I needed my trusted *Pao Chia* armband to get through the roadblocks. The closer I got to the SACRA buildings, the more evidence of the raid was all around me. The air pressure from the explosions had pressed people flat as pancakes against walls. It was an unforgettable sight with hundreds of people dead and wounded all around me. Only those who took the advice and jumped into the holes on the sidewalks were spared, but the lack of any warning prevented most from doing so.

I was sure that the SACRA buildings had been hit directly and I feared for Walter. As I entered the area where he lived, he came toward me, dazed and pitch black. He was very fortunate living close to the wall surrounding the entire compound. Several bombs fell on the other side of the wall which deflected the air pressure upward away from him. Nevertheless, the dirt particles had imbedded themselves so deep in his skin that he could not wash them off, and over the next few weeks he broke out in eczema all over his body. In all, over thirty refugees lost their lives in this one raid, several hundred were wounded, and more than twice that number was made homeless.

After leaving Walter, I joined some people in rescue operations, then decided to go home to check on my folks. They were frantic because they heard about the raid at the SACRA location and worried about all the people we knew there. Luckily, none of our friends and acquaintances were killed, although a large number lost their shelter. I was called out for *Pao Chia* duty during the next few nights because people feared looting might take place.

From then on, we saw many more bombings with a lot more people getting killed, but none came as close to me personally as the one I just described. While all of us were deathly afraid of air raids, we also realized that each brought us closer to the end of the war. Although ownership of short wave radios was strictly forbidden, some people hid a set and the news was disseminated through the grapevine.

When we learned about the invasion of Europe in June 1944, it was the first news that gave us hope of an ultimate collapse of the Axispowers. When the Allies won the war in Europe, we learned of it within a day of the surrender their full our attention now being directed toward Japan's defeat. What we feared was saturation bombing of the type that hit Europe. We also feared that the Japanese would vent their anger and frustration on us, or that open warfare would break out between the Chinese and Japanese within the populated areas. Each and all of these events were possible, even likely. For civilians the last few days of any conflict are usually the most dangerous.

There was more good news! Goya had been removed from office and replaced by a Mr. Harada, who turned out to be a reasonable person. Obtaining permission to leave the ghetto was now a matter of bringing sufficient evidence of employment or proof that one's livelihood depended on it. On occasion passes were also issued for medical reasons.

Interned enemy civilians were also up-to-date on current events since, some had smuggled short wave radios into the camps. A Japanese dentist, located around the corner from our offices, visited the camps occasionally. He was trained in the U.S., spoke English fluently and was willing to smuggle messages out of the camps. Occasionally he would arrange for an internee to be sent downtown under guard for special treatments in his offices. He would then contact my boss to come over and visit. Unauthorized mail got into the camps by this route.

War's End and a New Beginning

There were a number of indications that the war was coming to an end. One of these was an interesting story. Mr. Schetelig was contacted by a foreign lady. She came up to our offices, and since my desk was close to his I was able to observe her without being too obvious. She was very good looking, in her early forties, tall with bleached blond hair, very smartly dressed, with a manner about her that reinforced the strong impression she made on men.

Her husband was a well-connected Swedish businessman in Shanghai. The purpose of her visit was, so she, said, to see what connection could be established between the two firms. However, at a second meeting she had a different proposal. She was interested in moving large amounts of cash to Switzerland for safekeeping. She thought that the war was coming to an end and she wanted to make sure she would not lose her assets. In answer to a question as to why she did not move funds through Sweden, she volunteered that these were her own personal funds, implying that her husband was unaware of her wealth. She was willing to pay a good commission for assistance.

Never averse to making money, Mr. Schetelig stalled with his answer to find out more about this person. His inquiries yielded some stunning information. She was born in Austria where as a young art student she fell in love with a Japanese diplomat. He brought her to the Orient and she traveled with him throughout Korea, Manchuria and North China.

When he tired of her, she was stuck in Manchuria and finally landed in a local brothel. There she met several high ranking officers and developed a side business of spying for the Chinese. She later expanded her business by becoming a double agent, working for the Japanese as well. With the center of action shifting South, she came to Shanghai where she acted in her various capacities, working for the Japanese and the Chinese. She spoke a number of Oriental languages fluently, as well as several dialects. Along the way she had also become an opium addict.

Her husband probably did not know her past and need for some neutral cover. She aslso but kept her own apartment. She had accumulated a tidy nest egg which she wanted to protect from possible confiscation after the war by either the Americans, or the Nationalist Chinese. With this much information about her, Mr. Schetelig decided not to pursue the offer. That should have been the end of the story, but it was not.

She had been right that the war would be over quickly. A few months later, after the Japanese surrender, Shanghai was swarming with American military personnel. I happened to walk down Nanking Street past the Palace Hotel. A black American limousine was parked in front and I noticed the two flags on the sides of the fenders. One was a gold braided Stars and Stripes the other a silver braided blue flag with four stars. I stopped, never having seen such a car, and suddenly a marine snapped to attention as an admiral exited the hotel arm in arm with her. I looked, she smiled, and they were off. Perhaps she spied for the Americans as well.

There were more indications that things were reaching a climax. Through short wave broadcasts we learned that the Philippines had been liberated, then Okinawa. The Allies were now moving in the right direction. I could also see the difference in the demeanor of the Japanese business people who had offices on our floor. As in the beginning of the war, they were again glued to their little radios, only now their faces were glum. Red Cross letters from our British friends in the camps carried coded messages stating that they expected to see us again soon.

Mr. Schetelig, privy to more information and unwilling to part with it, started to concentrate on the direction the business should take after the war. The funds deposited for him in Switzerland by the Hong Kong and Shanghai Bank had been depleted, and he had to dip into his own pocket to continue to supply Red Cross parcels. Now he asked the bookkeeper to prepare statements and documentation, so that he could collect the debt the bank owed him as soon as it reopened.

Bombing activities intensified around Shanghai, and we worried about the kind of war ending we would experience. By July, rumors were flying and the Japanese authorities reacted with stricter enforcement of all rules. Japanese air raid wardens had been supervising nightly blackouts very strictly, but now they began their enforcement in the late afternoons. These wardens were Japanese paramilitary civilians who lived throughout the ghetto area. They wore civilian garb except for a military olive drab cap and an armband that identified their position. Usually they stationed themselves in the middle of intersections. These fellows would have shot their own wives had they disobeyed orders.

The day after the atomic bomb was dropped on Hiroshima on August 5, 1945, the *North China Daily News,* which was censored, carried the headline that the Americans exploded an atomic bomb. But there were no details, as I recall, and none of us really understood the significance of the headline. But things changed within days. By the August 9, it ew the war was over. Yet there was no evidence, and those who celebrated by filling in the dreaded air raid holes in the sidewalks were made to dig them up again by the police.

Actually, the next couple of weeks were more like a bad dream. Rumors kept flying the war was over but there just was no evidence and we now began to fear that the Japanese might become trigger happy. Finally, on August 15, I learned from a Chinese neighbor that the Lung Hua military airport outside Shanghai was all lit up. We congratulated each other and went to bed. I was awakened a while later by loud banging at our front door. Here was Fritzi, all exited and aglow to bring us the news. I told her that we already knew before we went to bed and advised her to do the same. She looked at me like I was crazy, then started screaming at me for not immediately coming over to her place with the news. Finally she left in a huff. Next day I learned that she and many others danced in the streets until the wee hours of the morning.

As I passed the police station in the morning, I did not see the Rising Sun waving from the flagpole. No Japanese police or military were anywhere in sight. After the events of the previous night, that did not strike me as strange. But by late afternoon the Japanese were out in full force as if nothing had happened, enforcing their rules in and out of the ghetto.

I believe it was the next day that an American plane flew low overhead dropping leaflets signed by the Supreme Allied Command. These stated that Japan had surrendered, but that Japanese authorities would still be in charge until the appropriate military authorities arrived on the scene, probably within the next few days.

What followed was an unbelievable series of events. Riots broke out all over town. Some were spontaneous food riots by thousands of hungry Chinese, but others were obviously fomented by political activists. Heavy fighting broke out on the outskirts of Shanghai, mainly in Pootung, between Chinese Communist guerillas and the Japanese. The guerillas had controlled the countryside for a long time, while the Japanese held the cities. Consequently, the Communist underground, which had cooperated to now with the Nationalist Chinese, wanted to take over the area before the Nationalist troops could reach Shanghai, and the defeated Japanese had to hold them off in the interim.

What I saw a few days later really put the entire situation into perspective. There was an automobile caravan coming up Nanking Road. I had seen similar caravans with honor guards before when high Japanese official came to Shanghai. But this one was different. It consisted of a lead armored car followed by an open top convertible limousine in which eight Japanese soldiers sat stiffly holding fixed bayonets. This was followed by another open top limousine with two American and two Japanese officers. All this was followed by two more cars like the ones in front. Had I not known better, I could have believed the Japanese had captured two highranking Americans.

Nationalist troops began to make their appearance during the following week. They surely did not look like victors. Most were barefoot or wearing straw sandals, a terrible odor about them all. Many did not seem to know how to carry a rifle. These were flown in on U.S. cargo planes from locations thousands of miles away. All spoke a dialect which the local people could not understand, and they surely did not try to win the hearts and minds of the population.

American troops also arrived, first by air, later by troop transports. We were surprised how many of the U.S. personnel looked as if they had yellow jaundice until we learned that they had taken Atabrin, an anti-malarial medication which turned their skin yellow. Within a short time, there were three well armed armies assembled in Shanghai, one Japanese, one Nationalist Chinese, and one American.

This was obviously a very explosive situation but relatively little happened. As soon as troop strengths were adequate to provide security, Japanese troops were disarmed. Much of the heavy armament was brought to a sport stadium for safekeeping. One day it seemed like the war had started all over again. Bombs went off and shook the city, rifle and machine gun fire interspersed with rocket fire created an ear-splitting racket, and everyone started to run for shelter. As it turned out coolies working in the sports arena accidentally dropped a box of hand grenades which set off the whole explosions; but then again perhaps it was sabotage.

What surprised everybody was the discipline of the Japanese soldier. Here was a very well trained and equipped army with a core of battle-hardened fighters who had been through many fights in their long war against China, and in addition young draftees, all of whom had been brainwashed to die for the Emperor. Everyone was primed to defend the gains made over many years. Then suddenly, from one day to the next, they surrendered their weapons to a ragtag army of Chinese coolies interspersed with American soldiers.

Much later we learned what really had happened. Once the Japanese headquarter received the message that the Emperor had surrendered the top commander called in his officers and told them of his decision to obey the Emperor. He then proceeded to commit *hara-kiri* – ceremonial suicide. Several other officers joined him. The rest selected a new chief whose orders were that the Emperor had spoken, discipline would be maintained, and each officer would be responsible for the conduct of his troops. Once the Japanese were disarmed, they were put to work by the Americans to fill the holes in the sidewalks and other similar tasks.

Mostly American GIs supervised the work details. By chance I observed an interesting episode. Several GIs were supervising a work detail and one of them started to pick on one of the Japanese. The GI was about two hundred pounds, the soldier perhaps 130 pounds. The Japanese soldier motioned that he did not want to be slapped, which infuriated the G.I. Next thing the G.I. was lying on his back, flipped over by the little guy who picked up his shovel and continued to work. None helped the G.I. and he just walked off. I am sure that, had the shoe been on the other foot, there would have been a dead G.I.

Within about a month, repatriation of the Japanese army started. Troop carriers brought more American personnel, and some of the empty vessels took prisoners of war back to Japan. A long chapter in the history of China was ended, and a new one began to unfold.

Theodore H. White, the American journalist most acquainted with events at that time, wrote an account of what happened in his book "In Search of History" published in 1978. I found it fascinating to relive events that I personally experienced, described so accurately by White, and to learn about the political environment in which these events took place. Of course, at that time I knew practically nothing of the struggle between Mao Zedung and Chiang Kai-shek for control of China, even less about America's complex relationship with both of them during the war. Nor did I know about the Potsdam agreement under which a "free China" was promised Chiang after the war.

Prior to Pearl Harbor, around 1940, the American journalist Ernest O. Hauser wrote a book entitled "Shanghai, City for Sale". It is an excellent account of the city's history. Hauser wrote that Shanghai as he knew it, would cease to exist after the war which he saw coming. Either Japan would win its war against China or China would, somehow be victorious. In either case, Shanghai would never again be what it had been, a haven for foreigners on Chinese soil. China or Japan would drive the Westerners out and Hauser was absolutely right.

The Japanese detention camps, established to imprison enemy aliens during the war, were emptied. The ghetto was no more. People once more moved about freely, but it was not like it used to be. Before long, American soldiers dominated the scene, and Shanghai became a center for U.S. soldier's *R&R* (Rest and Rehabilitation). To a certain extent this meant going back to the days of lawlessness. Prostitution and gambling were flourishing again, supplemented by the quickly established black market for products brought in by American soldiers; from nylons to Parker pens, from "C" rations to candy bars.

But gradually the Nationalist Chinese began to control the infrastructure of the city. For a while, some pre-war foreign administrators returned to the International Settlement's Shanghai Municipal Council and the French Concession, but they were only caretakers until the official Kuomintang party was ready to dispense patronage.

As always in times of such political instability, entrepreneurs flourished. China was starving for merchandise, Shanghai was its central supply port, and Schetelig & Co. was sitting in the right place at the right time with the right connections. As the former managers of the Hong Kong & Shanghai Bank reopened their Shanghai branch, they greeted my boss with gratitude and affection. Their first move was to offer him on very favorable terms a suite of offices in the Wayfoong House, an office building in back of the bank building itself. The move was symbolic of their new relationship.

My little Red Cross operation was shut down and I became involved with the process of importing merchandise from all over the world. Gum Arabic from Sudan, caustic soda from the U.S., essential oils for making perfumes as well as pharmaceuticals from France, and from Switzerland watches and silk bolting cloth for sifting flour just to name a few of the products we imported within the next few months.

I was given the job of supervising the cargo's arrival and its clearance through Customs. I began to spend half of my time on the docks, cajoling and bribing wharf bosses to make sure stevedores did not "accidentally" drop cargo nets onto the concrete pier damaging our goods. Having secured the merchandise, I then had to negotiate with the Customs inspectors what duty would be levied against it.

All of us worked long hours trying to keep up with the avalanche of goods and activities. After a day at the docks, I would come back to the office to write my reports, letters to suppliers to protest short shipments, or letters to banks authorizing release of funds from letters of credit. It was exhilarating for a young fellow of twenty-three.

Still, there was time for some fun. I rejoined the YMCA and went swimming three to four times a week. Fritzi and I were still going together, but there was less time and our get-togethers were limited to weekends.

Oriental businessmen have the pleasant custom of throwing a party every time a contract is signed. These parties were lavish and at times I had the feeling their cost exceeded profit. Being young and single, without family obligations, I was often asked to participate in these parties to represent the management of our company. For a while I went to one or more of these parties every week. It was rough.

Most of my friends found employment with the American Armed Forces. Walter, Richard and Franz moved to Nanking for a while to work for the U.S. military. They roomed together and before long each had live in female help. Later on, Walter worked in the officer's club at a hotel formerly housing the Japanese High Command in Shanghai. All of them would come back with wild stories of their escapades. Others became drivers, chauffeuring U.S. officers all over town. Paul became a driver as well and later advanced to civilian chief of the military motor pool. With that job he had free access to vehicles. He would bring a jeep home on weekends for riding about town. Even Fritzi hung up her ironing board for a while to work for the Americans. She liked her independence but the money was too good to pass up. My cousin Horst also went to work for the military, but I do not remember what type of job he had.

China was depleted of everything after many years of wars and internal strife. The United States poured money into the corrupt Chiang Kai-shek regime, not only in the form of credits but also directly in the form of gold bullion. On my way to work in the morning I would occasionally see lighters unload cases of gold bullion and coolies carry their precious cargo across the Bund to the Bank of China. Special troops, guns at the ready, guarded the transfer. The lighter would shuttle back and forth between the jetty and an American ship anchored midstream.

Unfortunately, much of this gold found its way out the back door of the bank located on Szechuan Road, where the small shops of currency dealers disposed of the loot. All this was common knowledge and whatever little faith people had in Chinese currency gradually vanished. As a result, we saw rampant inflation, which made what we experienced during the war seem like child's play. Prices of consumer goods soared to astronomical heights. Larger transaction generally took place in U.S. dollars.

When a government sets a pattern of corruption, it soon permeates the entire fabric of society. Of course, bribery had a long history in China. It was an accepted practice not only of doing business, but also in one's private life. What emerged was a situation which became totally intolerable. To conduct any kind of business, one had to bribe even the lowest officials. I can cite but a few examples to demonstrate the pervasiveness of the practice. Meter readers of utility companies obtained their jobs by bribing supervisors. To recoup their "investment", these meter readers would then turn to clients for a bribe so that the meter would be read correctly. For those who refused, the reader would develop a sudden inability to read the meter, and he had to "estimate" the monthly usage. Similarly, obtaining a drivers license was impossible unless the clerk received his cut for providing an application form, the examiner his for passing your test, etc.

Doing business in Shanghai at that time became the art of the possible. This made my job more challenging. One comic episode typifies the situation. It involved a sample shipment of drugs from the Upjohn Pharmaceutical company, which Schetelig & Co. represented. A shipment of prescription medications came through the mail and was held up in customs at the General Post Office. To obtain the required import permit would have taken months of negotiations with the authorities and cost a bundle. Instead I "handled the matter" with the postal inspector. He allowed me to inspect the shipment in an empty office. I took out the drugs, replacing them with old books, then refused the shipment and sent it back to Upjohn, who must have been utterly confused when they received the books.

Somehow word got around of my ability to get things done and I was contacted by others for assistance. I was approached by a businessman from New York. Jack was a real operator who asked for help to clear a shipment through customs. It was a lift van that he said contained personal household effects. He was a smooth talker and although there was really no reason for us to get involved with personal goods, he convinced us to help. I obtained his shipping documents as well as his passport. To my surprise it was marked as "By Special Assignment for the U.S. Government." In answer to what that meant, he explained that he came to Shanghai from the Philippines where he met some military people. To allow him entry to some bases, he bribed a sergeant to stamp his passport and have it signed by a colonel. It sounded plausible.

The customs inspector and I found the van sitting on the docks and on a hunch he pried a board lose to peek inside. Inside the van he found a green Buick automobile, worth about US$15,000 on the local market, a fortune at the time. Furthermore, an import license was required for such automobiles. This was another situation that called for a lot of "negotiating" with the inspectors and a host of other petty bureaucrats to pave the way for delivery of this treasure. Lamont paid, got his Buick and probably still made a bundle selling the car on the black market. By the way, our bribes were never paid in cash but watches, which were, of course, as good as cash for the recipient. Being agents for Rolex watches, our currency was a gift of either a Tudor watch, which was cheaper or a Rolex for more valuable transactions.

Undoubtedly, such corruption paved the way to the eventual take-over by the Communists, who promised and brought clean government. For the moment though, we were reasonably secure. Having survived the war, we now benefited from the sudden rush of prosperity. I even saw a future for myself working for Schetelig & Co., although my parents did not quite see it that way. We still lived in Hongkew under miserable conditions, renting to people who, like most, were eager to get out of Shanghai as soon as possible. Once they left, our income would be drastically reduced because it would be difficult to re-rent these rooms owing to the increasing numbers of vacancies. The money we invested in a long term lease would have been lost.

Evolving events made the decision for us. Having gone through the German experience, our antennas were especially sensitive for picking up political winds. Gradually these gained momentum, sensing an ill wind blowing from the Communist North, which might sweep us away. During the latter part of 1946 we decided to leave.

The mood had changed in the U.S. about letting immigrants come into the country. The horrors of the Holocaust had begun to sink into the American psyche, probably creating guilt for not acting to save at least some of the unfortunates. Also, the postwar economy started to take off and jobs were more plentiful. The quota system, which kept us out before the war, was temporarily modified to open the gates to receive most of the Shanghai immigrants. Quotas, which had not been used during the war years, were now made available. As I recall, *UNRRA* (United Nations Relief and Rehabilitation Administration) certified that all of us in Shanghai were true refugees from the war. This expedited matters greatly. Not everyone went to America. A few, mostly mixed marriages between Jews and non-Jews, returned to Germany, as did some who were Communists, who went to East Germany, of course. Others went to Australia and Israel to join relatives.

Pulling Up Stakes Again

Now, the process of pulling up stakes started all over again. It was almost like running a movie reel backward. Again there were long lines in front of the American Consulate as well as the shipping companies. My parents asked Uncle Eric, who now lived in New York, to reactivate the affidavits (guarantees) which he had obtained for us before the war. His own situation had changed a lot. Before the war, Eric was a self- assured, cocky bachelor, who even took on the Nazi Chief of Police in Berlin at the time of his arrest. Emigration, the time he spent in Cuba, and his lack of success in New York changed him into a bitter person. He married a fellow immigrant whom he met in Cuba. My aunt Gertie was a sweet lady without much of a will of her own, totally devoted to Eric.

In a long letter, Eric explained that he was a poor now, working in a bakery as a shipping clerk, and that Gertie worked as a seamstress in a clothing factory. He offered to reactivate the guarantees and to bring some of Gertie's wealthy relatives into the picture to assure approval by U.S. authorities. He asked, however, that we provide some evidence that we would not become dependent on anyone once we were in the U.S. In February 1947, my parents transmitted US$1,200 to him and thereafter things moved quickly. Obviously, by that time, we had saved some money. The very fact that we had saved this amount since the end of the war indicates how well off we were at that time and why we had contemplated staying in Shanghai for a while.

Eric's affidavit indeed indicated that he was not well off financially and Gertie's relatives provided the back-up guaranty. It should be understood what such affidavit involved. First, it required that the guarantor bare his financial condition, which included the latest income tax statement, bank statements, etc. Secondly the guarantor has to attest to providing full financial assistance, if necessary. Of course, these were the days before health costs could bankrupt a family, nevertheless, a guarantor took on quite a responsibility. In spite of this impediment, many people were willing to provide the guarantees for total strangers. That is something which often is not recognized or remembered today, even by some of the refugees themselves, now that it is time for them to step forward to help others who are in similar situation.

Again, as in Germany, we needed an affidavit that we had no police record, as well as a doctor's certification that we were free of contagious diseases. This time, though, it did not take long to obtain our clearances.

There was a lot of freighter traffic across the Pacific Ocean to replenish goods missing from retail shelves since before the war.

However, there was as yet no passenger traffic. All passenger ships had been converted to troop carriers during the war. Now, these were pressed into service for civilians. In the beginning of 1947, we managed to obtain a booking for the troop carrier *SS General Meiggs*, to leave in early June of that year. This gave us a few months to wind up our affairs. We still had the long-term lease on our house in Hongkew, which really was not worth much now. Because so many immigrants were in the same situation, there were a lot of houses on the market. We finally managed to find someone to take the lease off our hands.

Having been involved in the import-export business, I tried to make contact with a number of exporters with the idea of representing them in the U.S. Paul had joined his father's firm, and he offered me the U.S. agency for his firm. I obtained several other agency rights that seemed to have a lot of potential. I also obtained a number of letters of introduction from Schetelig & Co., as well as other businessmen I knew, to help me make business contacts in the United States. Thus armed, I faced our move to America with some feeling of security in spite of Uncle Eric's dire warnings that the streets were not paved with gold in America.

Saying goodbye to friends was difficult. Some immigrants had left already, using the first opportunity to go either to the U.S. or elsewhere when things opened up. Fritzi and her mother went back to Austria to lay claim to her father's pension and some of the assets left behind. Walter stayed behind a few more months. My Chinese co-workers gave me a party, my last Chinese meal for quite some time.

Four

AMERICA, THE PROMISED LAND

Voyage to America

I do not know the exact date we left Shanghai, only that it must have been during the early part of June because we arrived in San Francisco on the Fourth of July, 1947. I also cannot remember how much luggage we had, but this exodus was nothing like the one from Germany, since we had relatively little luggage. The *SS General Meiggs* was a big ship, holding more than one thousand passengers, painted gray, and definitely not equipped for luxury cruises. The ship was docked at the same pier we arrived at almost eight years before.

Much had happened during that time. I arrived an inexperienced youngster and left a mature adult. I had seen and experienced a great deal; learned things not taught in school. I was now a young man of twenty-three, ready to tackle the world. In spite of all the hardships of the war, we were never bitter nor ever complained about the time we lost in Shanghai. It was a haven without which most of us would not have survived. Even the mistreatment by the Japanese never matched anything the Nazis perpetrated on Jews, or what the Japanese military did to political prisoners or to captured enemy soldiers.

As we came aboard the SS Gen. Meiggs, men were separated from women and assigned sleeping areas. Women occupied the fore and men the aft sections. Cargo holds had been converted into dormitories, with rows of three high metal bunks filling up the space of holds. The tops of holds, through which cargo was normally loaded, were left open to allow light and air to filter down.

By the time my father and I came on board there was only room left at the bottom level, but we were lucky as we were located near the cargo hold. Actually, the bottom level was the better ride because it was closer to the ship's center of gravity. The *heads* (toilets) were located directly over the ships propellers which made them extremely noisy with lots of vibration. There was absolutely no privacy on board.

Because of the crowded conditions, people spent most of their waking hours on deck. Food was plentiful, typical Navy chow. For instance, breakfasts alternated between reconstituted powdered eggs, chipped beef on toast, or heavy pancakes - shades of things to come during my college years. Food was served cafeteria-style on stainless steel trays with indentations for soup, entrée, and dessert. The mess hall was probably the noisiest place on the ship. All sound reverberated from the low metal ceilings. The constantly blaring radio accentuated the sound level to make it almost unbearable. We spent as little time there as possible.

Our first stop was Kobe, Japan where the ship dropped off some personnel and picked up a number of Japanese-American youngsters. These kids were caught at the outbreak of the war visiting relatives in Japan and were finally on their way home. Most were from Hawaii. Some spoke only broken English, having been very young when the war began; probably coming from immigrant families where mostly Japanese was spoken. I am sure after the traumatic experience in Japan these kids had an equally traumatic reentry into American life.

Before long, I became interested in a young lady who spent most of her time with her mother and a young fellow I assumed was her brother. She was tall, good looking and just what the doctor ordered for a shipboard romance. I befriended the brother and soon spent all day with the three of them. Joan had an unusual background. Her father, from a wealthy family in Germany, contracted tuberculosis and was sent to the best tuberculosis hospital in the world, which at the time was located in Denver, Colorado because of the fresh mountain air. It was a relatively new hospital called The National Jewish Hospital for the Treatment of Tuberculosis (now called National Jewish Health Hospital). As in California, Jews came to Colorado with the Gold Rush of the 1860's and did well enough to fund the hospital which took patients from all over the world.

He returned cured, full of tales about Denver and the West. Once home, he fell in love with a pretty young lady he met on a streetcar, proposed to her and pursued her until she said yes. He was Jewish, she was not. Against all odds, the marriage worked. Classified by the Nazis as a Jewish family and in danger, they escaped to Shanghai. Because of the poor health conditions there his tuberculosis returned and he died shortly thereafter, leaving his wife and two kids nearly destitute.

The non-Jewish wife had the option of returning to Germany with the kids but she threw her lot in with the other refugees, considering herself one of them. Toward the end of the war, the son also contracted tuberculosis, but managed to obtain clearance from the U.S. consulate by faking it. Understandably he was very nervous on board ship about possibly being rejected when our ship arrived in Hawaii.

Meanwhile, I was in no hurry to get to the U.S. because I had fallen in love with Joan and enjoyed every minute of the trip. We sat at the bow for hours, holding hands and watching the fish jump out of the water. Once we surprised a couple making love in one of the lifeboats. We knew them well, which made it very embarrassing. They were married and this was their only opportunity to have some privacy, until we showed up.

Arriving in Honolulu very early in the morning a message was read over the loudspeakers to the effect that all immigrants should remain on board to await a representative of the local Jewish community who would give them further instructions.

Once the boat docked, we could see busses and private cars lined up on the pier. Soon we were informed that the entire day had been planned for us with sightseeing tours, lunch at the Jewish Community Center, and assistance for anyone who needed it. Again, as during our exodus from Europe, local residents stood by to help their fellow Jews. I do not believe these people were ever adequately thanked for the support, moral and otherwise, which they extended our group as well as all who preceded or followed us. Some, like my parents, decided to explore on their own and took a bus to explore Honolulu. They were befriended by a young couple, both teachers, who showed them around town. The rest of us had a nice lunch and then did a little sightseeing. By five in the afternoon, everyone was back on board ship, ready for the final leg of the journey.

To our surprise we found some bunks occupied by roughneck Hawaiians. They were deckhands for an oil barge that was to be picked up stateside and returned to Hawaii. As long as they played their ukuleles they were relatively peaceful, but as the night progressed they started to drink and things became pretty rough. We tried to stay out of their way whenever possible, which made them mad because they felt discriminated against. They managed to spoil the rest of the journey by keeping everyone awake with their constant carousing. Unfortunately, they were all giants so that nobody was willing to tell them off and risk injury.

An officer of the U.S. Immigration Service had come aboard in Honolulu, and during the intervening time before we arrived in San Francisco he processed our papers. Having been battered as we were, it was only natural to be apprehensive about the unknown process. What if the immigration officer found something wrong with our papers? What if our health clearance was inadequate etc., etc.? To everyone's relief, there were no rejections, and late afternoon of Thursday July 3, 1947, the SS General Meiggs picked up a pilot at the Farallon Islands. The most exciting part of our trip was about to begin.

By the time we reached the Golden Gate, it was dusk and the bridge with all its lights looked truly golden. It was absolutely the most spectacular sight I had ever seen. The sun was setting in the west as we sailed under the Golden Gate Bridge, and all of us were stunned by the sights. The ship dropped anchor in the middle of the Bay and we tried to find sleep before entering the "Promised Land" the next morning.

Our arrival coincided with the Fourth of July, which fell on a Friday that year. That meant we could disembark, but had to wait until the following Monday to take delivery of larger pieces of luggage. Willy and his family had arrived in San Francisco about two month before us, but by the time we arrived they had moved to Tacoma, Washington. We were met at the ship by a representative of the San Francisco Jewish Family Service who had arranged for a room at the Hamlin hotel on Eddy Street, in the middle of San Francisco's Tenderloin district. The following Tuesday we had an appointment with the Jewish Family Service. We made it to the U.S.A. finally!

Strangers in Paradise

At Jewish Family Service we learned that we were on our own. Having paid our own way from China to San Francisco, we were not eligible for assistance. Furthermore, we were asked to reimburse them for the cost of the hotel. They did offer, however, to be of assistance in finding housing and employment.

Within a few days we moved to a room with kitchen privileges on Eddy Street near Fillmore. The lower Fillmore district was an area in transition at that time. It had been a heavily Jewish neighborhood for many years. But with the influx of many Southern Blacks to work in the wartime shipyards, the district had changed significantly. By 1947 it was an ethnically and racially mixed neighborhood.

Our room was located in a house owned by an elderly Jewish couple who had arrived as immigrants from Russia in the early thirties. Like ourselves in Shanghai, they rented out rooms to defray their own housing costs. One other immigrant family by the name of Meyer rented there. Years later their son, who was about my age, became a successful hotelier.

The following weekend this young fellow took me to the Jewish Community Center on California Street, where Jewish singles danced every Saturday night. I met a number of young people I knew from Shanghai. Standing in a corner talking to some of them I was approached by a young man. He asked whether I was from Berlin. When I confirmed that I was, he asked me to come along because an old friend wanted to see me. He then introduced me to a young lady, about eight months pregnant, who held her arms wide open and shouted: "Ernie, don't you remember me?" My first inclination was to say: "you have the wrong guy, lady." But she looked vaguely familiar. She turned out to be my former classmate from Lessler Schule in Berlin, Ellen Rothschildt.

After reminiscing a bit, the conversation turned to employment. I explained that I had just arrived and was looking for a job. I described my checkered past in Shanghai which prompted her husband to tell me about a possible opening for a fabric cutter at his sister's place of employment. A garment cutter's job was well paid, he explained, and I should go after it immediately. He would call his sister the next day and alerted her about my interest in the job. I protested that I had cut neckties in Shanghai, not garments, and I had been away from it for a long time. But being an aggressive salesman he persisted, and the next day I received a telephone call from his sister.

She explained there was, indeed, an opening for a cutter at her place of work. She had spoken to the shop foreman about me and arranged for an interview the next day. I told her of my considerable doubts, but she gave me a lot of encouragement. After all, what did I have to lose?

The next morning at eight, I introduced myself to Mr. Greenberg, the foreman. He was a typical New Yorker, an older man, sleeves always rolled up, wearing suspenders and a belt. After a few preliminaries he put me to work to see what I really knew. At the end of the day he came over to tell me in his heavy Brooklyn accent: "Oynee, you're no cutter, but I like you and we'll teach you. Go see Jenny downtown for a card and come back tomorrow."

Jenny Matyas became my guardian angel. She was the executive director of the local *ILGWU* (International Ladies Garment Workers Union). But she was much more than that. A women in her late forties, she had a doctorate in sociology, was involved in local politics, on a first name basis with civic leaders as well as the newsboy on the corner. She was also a fighter, having come out of the New York sweatshops as a union organizer. She was married but had no kids. Most importantly, she had the ability to make people feel comfortable and good about themselves.

Jenny saw to it that I obtained my Social Security card, gave me a work permit, and explained how the union operated. As time went on, she took a liking to me and involved me in union activities and politics. For me all this was quite an education. The campaign for the 1948 mayoral was in full swing. Jenny worked for the democratic candidate, and before long I was stuffing envelopes, running errands, learning politics from the ground up. It was heady stuff for someone who had only arrived in San Francisco a few months earlier, and I enjoyed it thoroughly.

On the other hand, my work was boring. The constant repetition of spreading layer on layer of fabric, chalking around paper patterns, cutting the fabric, only to repeat the whole process over and over again, left me very dissatisfied. I began looking around for greener pastures, and as luck would have it, I ran into a friend from Shanghai. When I complained about my situation he promised to look into possible opportunities for me in my old field.

By then I had already exhausted all the contacts I made in Shanghai and because of the political situation in China, my hopes of becoming a sales agent never materialized. A few days later I heard from my friend about an opening with a customs clearing house. Hoyt, Shepston & Sciaroni was an old firm, located on Sansome street near the old Customs House. It counted some of the oldest San Francisco trading companies among its customers. The work was a direct continuation of what I had done in Shanghai, only here the customs officials were not "on the take." I began working for a man named Rivera, a former Golden Glove amateur boxing champion. He took me under his wing and introduced me to the inspectors. I was a quick study because of my previous experience, and before long I operated pretty much on my own.

Shortly after I started to work on my first job, I decided that I needed to buy in an automobile. In reality the need was more imagined than real because the San Francisco Bay Area had an excellent public transportation system at that time. But the automobile represented independence, freedom, affluence, status and a new challenge, since I did not know how to drive. I was offered a car from a private party and bought it on the spur of the moment. So without a driver's license, not even a learner's permit, I made the plunge and invested about half of my assets in a used car. In retrospect, it was foolhardy, even crazy, to jump into car ownership. But it attested to the optimism I had in the future and the determination to enjoy my new freedom. I was fortunate. A friend offered to teach me how to drive, and he was an excellent teacher. He had the patience of Job and must have suffered agonies as I stalled the car in traffic, held up cars behind me, accelerated at the wrong times; all the mistakes all new drivers make. But shortly thereafter I had my license and the world was my oyster.

The car turned out to be a real gem. It was a blue '41 Hudson, the last model year before World War II, and it was well built. It was roomy and very comfortable. It lasted me for eight years, by which time I had taken the engine apart several times and knew every one of the car's vital innards.

Weekends were for exploring. Before long, most of my Shanghai friends had automobiles and a caravan left nearly every Sunday morning from a common gathering place for a day of new discoveries. Once, shortly after I received my license, we drove to Muir Woods in Marin County. I had my parents and a couple of friends in the car. On the way back, we ran into terrible fog, where one cannot even see the markings on the road. I was terrified but did not let on, and we had a party that evening to celebrate "our survival." The Shanghai crowd spent practically every Saturday evening together, meeting at one or another's apartment. Since all of us were constantly in new surroundings all week long, exposed to a host of new impressions and experiences, these gatherings were like a quiet harbor where one could compare notes, get new ideas on how to cope with life in America.

My parents and I were befriended by an older couple, who had been given our name by the Jewish Family Service. He was a real estate investor who had several properties in and around San Francisco. Occasionally they enjoyed picking us up on Saturdays and drove considerable distances to show us the area surrounding San Francisco. He was active in the Jewish community and through him we learned about Jewish life here. I believe both, husband and wife, were born in San Francisco and enjoyed talking about the wonders of the Bay area. Here was another instance of people befriending us and reaching out to help us.

My father's job search led to the Sealy Mattress Co. where he found employment as a shipping clerk. Obviously this was quite a blow for someone who had not worked for anyone else since his youth. Of course, not knowing much English did not help the situation. He lasted on the job about a month. For the next few months my father was at loose ends. Finally he came to the conclusion that the only thing for him to do was to get back into his own business, with a line of products with which he was familiar.

The situation was helped when my mother found employment. She was approached by a rabbi, probably through contacts with the Jewish Family Service, to take over the management of the *Mikve* (ritual bath). He told her they were looking for somebody reliable and honest and she was highly recommended. The job entailed making sure the place was clean and shipshape whenever someone wanted to take a bath, and that she would be available at odd hours.

The *Mikve* was located adjacent to an orthodox synagogue on 19th Street in the Mission District near Mission Delores. A small two-bedroom apartment came with the job, together with a small salary and tips. There was a large concrete patio behind the ground floor apartment and I remember spending a good deal of time there cleaning engine parts of my Hudson to keep it in good running order.

Removing the cost of housing lifted a big burden off my father's shoulders and gave him time to develop his own business. I contributed to the household, and things worked out reasonably well. Occasionally he would be asked to participate in the synagogue service to make up a *Minyan*. In Jewish tradition everyone can pray for himself, but it takes ten men, praying together, to constitute the community necessary for religious services. Orthodox Jews pray each morning and evening at the synagogue, and it happened occasionally they were short a man, in which case they would call on my father.

The climate in the Mission District is probably the best in the city since it is sheltered from much of the fog. At one time it was dominated by Scandinavians and Irish, with a pocket of Jews. Then, during the war, rural whites from the South moved in, which changed the complexion of the neighborhood. Later, some people from South and Central America arrived on the scene and started the trend toward Latinization. Now, with the influx of internet technologists, the area is being gentrified, in transition again from being the principal Latino neighborhood of San Francisco.

My father began to develop his business in earnest. He arrived at the first product in a curious way. My parents had re-established contact with Frau Rehmer and our maid Ella in Germany. Frau Rehmer had lost her husband during the last days of the war. Wanting to send packages to both of them, he went to five-and-dime stores and hardware stores to find some wrapping twine. All he could find were large balls of twine, much more than needed for his purpose. So he decided that he would start out with the introduction of small balls of packing twine. After all, this was something with which he was well familiar, even though he did not know the English language.

He obtained the addresses of twine manufacturers at the public Library. Never one to think small, he next went to a printer and ordered some letter heads for Glaser Cordage Co. Next he asked me to write letters to the twine manufacturers requesting catalogues and prices. Most of the responses were not too encouraging, except one in New England who suggested he contact their local representative. He then asked me to call to make an appointment for the following Saturday, when I would be free.

That weekend we met with the sales manager, a man in his late forties. I explained the situation, somewhat apologetically I am sure, since I was convinced the whole idea was hair brained. The gentleman quickly assessed the situation, recognized the businessman in dad immediately, and they connected even though communication between the two was difficult. He explained that in their experience there was no market for small balls of twine, but the factory would be willing to make a special run for truckload quantities.

This news did not faze my father, but he decided that some further market research was warranted before ordering such a large quantity. Consequently, he bought two fifty-pound reels of twine to take home and convert into smaller hanks.

For the next few evenings the three of us were busy winding ten and twenty-five feet lengths of twine around a pieces of wood to form hanks. My father typed little blue labels to attach to each hank. He then offered these to hardware and five- and-dime stores. They were an instant success! Obviously, a lot of people were in the same situation as my parents, wanting to send packages to Europe without having to buy a large ball of twine for just a few shipments.

That was all the encouragement Dad needed. Shortly thereafter we were back to order a truckload of twine. Of course we had to pay cash, but the manager really got a big kick out dad and bent the rules to accommodate him. In due course, the two of them became good business friends.

Before long, a truck arrived in front of the *Mikve* to deliver the twine. My father had converted a small area in the back of the apartment to store the merchandise. But it had to be wheeled from the street, through a very long corridor and the apartment to the back; a task the truck driver must have relished. On Saturdays, as soon as services were over, my job was to deliver the twine in my trusted Hudson. I was amazed how many orders Dad was able to obtain, and the variety of outlets he covered all over the Bay Area.

Once all potential customers had been contacted in San Francisco, he started to cover these in surrounding townships. To understand this challenging task, one has to remember that he covered the entire area by public transportation. He left early each morning to call on customers, ate a brown-bag lunch, returned home for dinner, only to then process the orders received during the day. For him, a day did not end until he had everything ready for shipment, including the typed invoices. My mother did the necessary bookkeeping.

The introduction of the small twine packages opened the door to many stores. That my father was able to sell without knowing the language, attests to his supreme salesmanship. People liked him, made allowances, and tried to help. It should be remembered this was before national chain stores dominated the business. Practically all such stores were privately owned at the time. Before long, he was looking around for additional products to sell. Back to the public library he went, this time to look for suppliers of dust mops, wet mops, etc. Again, he was determined to buy direct, if possible, not through a local wholesaler.

On his previous attempt to buy twine directly, the manufacturer inquired about the Glaser Cordage Co.'s Dunn & Bradstreet rating (a credit rating company). This gave Dad the idea to contact Dunn & Bradstreet's San Francisco office to obtain a listing. He dug out all his old business records from Germany, his old firm's letterhead, which stated his bank connection and that he was a member of the Berlin Chamber of Commerce, all to attest that he was a legitimate and trustworthy businessman.

He visited the Dunn & Bradstreet offices and asked whether there was someone who spoke German. Yes, one of the secretaries could speak German, a refugee from before the war. He told her the whole story, requesting, a D & B listing. She explained things did not work that way. One of their subscribers had to request information about a company, and only then would they investigate credit worthiness. This prompted Dad to ask whether they had any objections if he would use Dunn & Bradstreet as a reference on his contacts with suppliers. He was told to go right ahead.

On my next visit home, I had left for school at U.C. Davis by then, Dad asked me to compose a letter of inquiry to a number of manufacturers. Each letter cited Davis Cordage Co. and Dunn & Bradstreet as references. At least one large supplier, in Alabama, offered to supply without prepayment, i.e. on credit. Dad was off and running.

My own career took a decidedly different turn. I was happy with my job as a customs broker and saw a future for myself with the company. Uncle Sam, however, had different ideas. My parents and I had filed our first papers to obtain U.S. citizenship, and this made me instantly eligible for the military draft. In due course, I received a postcard to report for my army physical examination.

A batch of about thirty potential recruits were processed at one time, which meant we had to strip to our socks and stand in line for various examinations. The last of these involved bending over and spreading our buttocks; I was last in line for that particular inspection. The medical officer looked me in the eye and said: "How do you like my job? For this I went to Med school. Awfully inspiring, isn't it?" I really felt sorry for him. Shortly thereafter I received my draft classification. I was 1A, eligible for the draft.

I was twenty-four years old with a two-year hitch in the army staring me in the face. Having wasted the years in Shanghai, I was apprehensive about my career and looked for ways out of the military. Being a student was one way to at least defer the draft. It was an alternative that suddenly intrigued me. Having flunked out of high school in Germany, I acutely felt I lacked a proper education. Older and more mature, I was more motivated to study. Of course, without a high school diploma, I might not be accepted in college, but it was worth a try.

I visited the admitting office at U.C. Berkeley and told them my tale of woe. I lied that I was a high school graduate but had lost my records during the emigration. Furthermore, my school no longer existed, so there was no way to prove I graduated. After hearing my story, the lady was very understanding but school policy was not to accept anyone without a diploma or its equivalent. She suggested I apply to San Francisco City College (SFCC) as a special student. She thought I could take my freshman and sophomore courses there and, provided my grades were acceptable, transfer to the university for my junior year. Shortly thereafter, I started college life at SFCC: a new chapter in my life.

Of course, Dad wanted me to follow in his footsteps. As an independent businessman I might have been deferred too. He just could not understand why I would want to do anything else when there were such great opportunities in his line of business. But both of us were stubborn. He never stopped talking about the "great possibilities," and I never seriously considered the option.

San Francisco City College

In order to obtain draft deferment, I had to attend college on a full-time basis. This meant giving up my job and finding part-time employment. Again my friends came to my aid. One of my Shanghai friends had found employment in his old line of business, the clothing industry. He started as a shipping clerk in a small men's clothing factory that specialized in sports jackets. Before long, the owners recognized my friend's abilities and promoted him to plant superintendent. He gave me a job working afternoons and Saturdays as a shipping clerk. I managed to get by, working 25-30 hours per week together with some odd jobs. I loaded frozen food trucks at night for a small food distributor, a horrible job, worked in sales for a department store during Christmas, did some market research for Field Research Corp, and took inventory at night at I. Magnin.

One Easter vacation, cousin Willi asked me to join him at his work place. It was quite an experience. Upon his return from Tacoma, Willi first found employment in the shipping department of Levi Strauss & Co. He then switched to an operation that serviced bread baking pans for large bakeries. The service consisted of stripping pans of encrusted residues by immersion in a series of hot baths, drying them, and ultimately coating them with a bread-release agent. The company had been started on a shoestring by a couple of chemists, but after some initial struggles it managed to do quite well.

The process involved the use of large quantities of very hazardous chemicals such as caustics, chromates, ketones, in an environment which was inadequately vented. Today, it would be closed by the Operational Safety and Hazards Agency in an instant. But who ever heard of OSHA in those days? I remember standing over a large hot tank wearing a large rubber apron and rubber gloves, immersing huge baskets full of dirty pans. Several other Shanghai immigrants worked there, all of them helped by Willi.

Seeing Willi close-up at work was an interesting experience. Never, before or after, did I see anybody work as hard in good spirits. If he ever was discouraged, and surely he must have felt that way sometime, it never showed. His good humor was infectious and made that horrid place bearable.

College was fun, and looking back on those years it was quite enjoyable. I concentrated my studies in general science, not quite sure where it would take me. I even found time to become active in *Hillel*, the Jewish student organization. It was a small organization, perhaps twenty-five students. Our faculty advisor was professor Zacharin at whose home we held evening meetings.

Hillel Graduation Dinner at the Sir Francis Drake Hotel

I had my first exposure to campus politics. A small clique of kids, who had gone through high school together, held all the key jobs in the campus club which did not sit well with the rest of us. I became the ringleader of a reform group that finally wrested leadership away from the clique, but not without a lot of political infighting. To fend off constant disruptions, I had to learn all about Robert's Rules of Procedure in a hurry. Ultimately things calmed down and I made some new friends.

Among those active in Hillel were a brother and sister who, to escape the Nazi's clutches, together with their parents, fled to Italy from Yugoslavia. They were hidden by Italian non-Jews throughout the war. In 1944 the Americans brought them to the U.S., after their liberation in Italy. Margarete studied to become a teacher. Before long I started dating Margarete. In many ways she was the exact opposite of Hanne, who by now lived in Denver with her mother and brother. Although Hanne and I grew close after we met on board ship and even closer after our arrival here, things had fallen apart even before her move to Denver.

Margarete lived with her parents She was not one to rush into anything. Nevertheless, she was fun to be with, did not date anybody else to my knowledge. Her mother wanted to marry her daughter off and made it very clear to me that we should either make up our mind to get married or Margarete should date other likely prospects. The more the mother pushed, the more I backed off.

As an older student, I took my studies more seriously than others and was able to earn good grades. I enrolled in a remedial English course to come up to speed. All classes were University of California equivalents, which meant the course work paralleled that taught in the university system. Also, in order to be able to transfer grades from City College to U.C., class performance was graded on an absolute basis, not in relation to the performance of the rest of the class. When I finally reached the end of my sophomore year, I was readily accepted by U.C. Davis, and given full credit for my studies at City College. I had overcome my earlier scholastic handicap.

Of course, eventual military service was still a possibility, so when a fellow City College student approached me with the proposition of joining his Marine Intelligence Reserve outfit I was intrigued. His sales pitch was he was assigned to a language intelligence unit which allowed him to stretch his military service over a seven year period while going to college. His service consisted of summer training assignments. He was of Italian extraction and spoke French and Italian fluently. He thought my German together with a little French and Chinese would be adequate to get me into his unit. I struggled long and hard with the decision, but finally went with my father's suggestion: "*Geh' nicht zum Kaiser wenn Du nicht gerufen bist*" (Don't go to see the Emperor until he calls you). As it later turned out, this was excellent advice, because when the Korean War broke out my friend's unit was called up. He fought around the Pusan Reservoir and his outfit suffered substantial casualties.

I stayed in touch with Hanne in Denver, throughout this time. "Absence makes the heart grow fonder" and I came to the conclusion that she would be the right person for me to marry after all. We corresponded a lot and occasionally spoke over the telephone. She too had not met anybody and we were both convinced that we could be happy together. Consequently, I traveled to Denver during Christmas vacation, to see each other and to make arrangements for getting married before my transfer to U.C. Davis. I spent a glorious two weeks in her company and came back to San Francisco engaged and ready to marry the following April.

I knew my parents were less than enthused about the prospect of our marriage, but to their credit they put up a good front. I made arrangements for married student's housing at Davis after learning I was accepted. However, strange noises began to come out of Denver. It started very quietly but gradually worked up to a crescendo. The message became clear: Why we would have to live in Davis? "Can't you continue your studies in Denver?" From my perspective this meant being totally absorbed into her family's household, which was run by her brother.

Economically, it would have made good sense, but I felt my future would have been structured to suit them not me. I gave Hanne an ultimatum, either agree to move to California or else. She explained her loyalty to her family was more important to her than her own happiness, considering what they had gone through together in Shanghai. This was one of the few times in my life when I broke off a relationship without any future contact whatsoever. I was quite heartbroken for a while, and I immersed myself in my studies to forget this setback.

I now needed to revise my plans for summer vacation to save some money in preparation for entering Davis in the fall. Summer jobs were scarce, especially well paying ones, and it was relatively late in the game to apply. Through the school's employment office, I was put in touch with a lady at the State of California Employment Office for an interview. She was looking for somebody to work during the summer for her brother-in-law who owned a restaurant at Lake Tahoe. It was just what I was looking for, room and board, a little salary and tips. Work rotated between the kitchen, mainly dishwashing, and waiting on tables.

I did not participate in the graduation ceremony at San Francisco City College, rather I packed up immediately after my last examination in May of 1950 and moved up to Tahoe. My new boss was a former teacher, as was his wife. He had been advised by his doctor to switch to an outdoor profession for his health. He became a carpenter and over the period of several summers built himself a nice restaurant on the South Shore of Lake Tahoe. The rest of the year he worked in San Francisco on construction jobs. I shared a loft with some other fellows, all of whom had worked in the restaurant before. Looking back at that period of my life, it was probably one of the best. It was like a paid vacation. There definitely was hard work which started every morning at 6 a.m. and lasted sometimes until 12 midnight. But there was plenty of free time between meals, good food and good company.

Tahoe was heavenly those summers. The air was crisp and clean, and in spite of tourists driving up by car there was no trace of pollution. The water in the lake on the South Shore was a deep blue, clean and relatively warm. Swimming was delightful, especially toward the end of the season. Bijou, a resort near the Nevada State Line, was overrun by young people. There were dances every weekend and a lot of parties throughout the week.

I learned my lesson on gambling early on. Having saved my tips during the first week, I joined a group of fellow workers and their friends to try my luck at the gaming tables across the border in Nevada. I devised an elaborate system that was absolutely fool-proof in my estimation. A few hours later I was a lot wiser after having watched my hard earned dollars being raked in by the croupier, and I swore to myself never to gamble again.

I dated a lot, as much as time would allow. During the week I met mostly college kids, many like myself spending their summer working. On weekends the supply of potential dates would increase dramatically with secretaries coming up from Sacramento. Since I would attend U.C. Davis in the fall, which was located near Sacramento, I tried to develop Sacramento contacts for later on.

By the end of the summer I was tanned, happy to have a few dollars in my pockets, and full of expectations toward my next adventure, life at a real university. So, shortly after Labor Day I packed the few belongings into my trusted Hudson and drove to the University of California at Davis to register for the fall semester.

Despite the Denver setback, I was satisfied with life and my achievements. I had proven to myself that in spite of having flunked out of high school I would be able to study at a world-class university. Furthermore, I expected to be able do it financially, a big question in my mind a couple of years earlier when I started my studies in San Francisco. I had a lot of adventures and experiences during the first twenty-five years of my life. There were many close calls that helped me mature and sort out what was important in life. I felt on top of the world!

University of California at Davis

My grades were more than adequate, so I could have chosen either U.C Berkeley or U.C. Davis. So why pick Davis? I think I just wanted to get away from home. Davis was far enough from home to be on my own and still be able to quickly check on my folks, should the need arise.

I had embarked on a science curriculum at San Francisco City College. Science had intrigued me since my high school days, sparked by outstanding teachers like Herr Neufeld and Herr Preuss. U.C. Davis had science departments with a worldwide reputation and food and agriculture held a special interest for me for a long time. Probably owing of my years of deprivation in Shanghai, food was foremost on my mind. Moreover, I had a goal to work ultimately for the United Nations Food and Agriculture Organization (FAO).

I moved to Davis right after Memorial Day 1950. My roommate for the next two years, Dean, had already checked in and gave me a friendly welcome. The two of us could not have been more different, yet we struck up a friendship that has lasted to this day. Dean hailed from Hilmar, a farming community in California's San Joaquin Valley.

While my life experiences were as unstable as they could possibly be, his were the exact opposite. Of Swedish extraction, he was born and raised on a dairy farm in an area made up mostly of first and second generation Swedes, with a sprinkling of dairymen from the Portuguese Azores. As all youngsters in that community, Dean got up every morning before dawn to help his father milk his sixty or so cows, only to continue with other farm chores after he returned from school. His mother was the principal of the high school he attended

Our dormitory, West Hall, was a building dating back to the beginnings of the university campus. A "Berkeley Shingle" firetrap, it was scheduled for demolition. Our room was dark because it fronted a wide veranda. My new home away from home had a bed on each side of the room with a small desk in front of each bed and the barest minimum of storage space. Since there was no air-conditioning, the veranda became the sleeping porch during the hot months. There was a pool table in the hall downstairs together with a soda vending machine and an old jukebox. Very old beat-up sofas and easy chairs provided the only comfort. Yet the dorm was loved by all and, when it was finally torn down two years later, every one of its former occupants felt a real loss.

When enrolling in San Francisco City College two years earlier, my motivation had been solely to stay out of the draft. But along the way I developed a real interest in learning. Now, enrolled as a sophomore at Davis, I had to focus my studies deciding on what I was interested in doing with the rest of my life.

Again, circumstances made the decision for me. Even though tuition costs in those days were very low ($35.00 per semester), I needed to pay for food, housing, transportation and entertainment, which meant that I needed to work. I soon learned that good jobs were available for students enrolled in the dairy industry program. So I picked Dairy Manufacturing as my major with a minor in General Agriculture, and landed a weekend job in Sacramento with the Golden State Dairy Co. I had to join the Teamster union and was paid $2.25 per hour, which was high pay in those days. Work started at 6 a.m., so I was free after 3 p.m. and had afternoons and evenings for myself.

Although the choice of major was dictated by my need for well-paying employment, I was again fortunate. Unlike most curricula, this one overarched a number of sciences. It involved food engineering, bacteriology, nutrition, organic and physical chemistry as well as agronomy, animal husbandry and physiology.

Classes were small and there was a very close relationship between professors and students. I developed a friendship with Prof. Walter Dunkley who taught dairy engineering and manufacturing. Walt was not much older than I; he being a young professor and I an older student, and our friendship extended to his death.

I also managed to land a job working in the dining hall so all my meals were free, and I did housecleaning for one of the professors. Later, I obtained a job as a shipping clerk in a mail-order business owned by another professor. The way I was hired was interesting.

A fellow student in agronomy class approached me one day asking whether I would be interested in a part-time afternoon job. It entailed packing and shipping an unique instrument to dehorn cattle. It was a patented method, invented by a professor who set himself up in business as a side-line. The work entailed assembling and packaging orders, all done by students.

During the job interview, the professor asked me whether I was a Mormon. When I told him I was Jewish, he said, "good, because I told the foreman not to hire another Mormon". In subsequent conversation, I learned my contact, the foreman, was an Elder in the local Mormon church and gave job preference to fellow Mormon students. When I asked him why he picked me he said, "you are Jewish, so we are first cousins and the next best choice after the professor told me, not to hire any more Mormons".

Today's UC Davis university cannot be compared to that of 1950. It offers studies in all the major faculties and its student-body has risen from about four thousand to more that thirty-five thousand.

Since agriculture was not of primary interest to American Jews, it was not surprising that the number of Jewish students at Davis at that time was minuscule. Actually, there seemed to be more Israeli than American Jewish students in attendance. I joined the Hillel chapter, and we probably had no more than ten members, in the beginning.

I was also active in the Blue and Gold Dairy Club and was elected president, probably because I was one of the older students. As it happened, during my tenure Holland experienced a terrible flood with a great deal of damage to property and loss of dairy cattle. Hoping to combine the good with the useful, I promoted the idea of a fundraiser on campus to help the victims and obtain publicity for our club.

Somehow, I learned that an Air Force band stationed at a nearby base would play at such events and they readily agreed. Having met a Dutch immigrant girl at one of the Jewish Community Center dances and knowing that she belonged to a Dutch folk dance group in San Francisco, I approached her about participation of the group in our event and they agreed to come as well.

Needless to say, our dance was a big success, we raised quite a bit of money which we turned over to the Holland Flood Relief Fund, which Mrs. Chester Nimitz, the widow of Admiral Nimitz and Honorary Chairperson acknowledged in a very nice letter to the club.

I had a good time at Davis, and between various jobs and with free meals, I was able to save some money. I came home to the City between semesters and worked one summer at the Safeway Dairy operation at East 14th Street in Oakland making ice cream. The next summer I worked at Speckles Dairy in San Francisco. In both instances it helped being a member of the Teamster Union, not only in obtaining the jobs but also with the rate paid because of my work in Sacramento.

During Easter recess 1952, Professor Dunkley arranged a field trip during which the class of dairy students visited a variety of one-of-a-kind dairy processing plants. I will not enumerate all the plants we visited, but need to single one out because it played an important role later in my life.

Avoset Food Corporation was unique in a number of ways. It was the first manufacturer of commercial aseptically packaged milk. As such, it had a patent on ultra- high heat treatment with minimal flavor change, which resulted in shelf-stable milk for shipment into areas without refrigeration. During the Second World War, the military was a huge market for this product and Avoset became their sole supplier. With the end of the war, Avoset looked for new markets and applied this technology by aseptically packing aerosol whipping cream. Professor Dunkley wanted show us this unusual production line. Little did I realize I would be president of the company twenty years later!

Goal Change

As I entered my senior year, I had a conversation with my advisor about my career direction. Professor Cook was a bacteriologist in the School of Veterinary Medicine who had taken an interest in my background. He told me that he made inquires about job opportunities with the United Nations Food and Agriculture Organization and learned it did not hire people directly. Instead they recruited through other governmental organizations like the U.S. Department of Agriculture.

He asked me think about of a possible career in the USDA. "You are a big city boy," he said, "foreign-born and Jewish, and you want to tell American farmers how to grow crops or raise cattle? Don't you think that would be an uphill fight? Perhaps you should think about reorienting your studies". His advice made good sense and the logical conclusion was to move into food technology, a related field. The Food Tech Department had just moved from the Berkeley campus to Davis, and they accepted all my Dairy Department credits, so I was in luck again.

I was now in my senior year, interviewing for positions after graduation. It soon became evident that the dairy industry was extremely conservative with few good entry level opportunities. I discussed this with my boss, the plant superintendent at Golden State, knowing he had graduated from Davis. His answer was to the point: "If I had to do it over again, I would spend the time getting a Master of Business

Administration because the closer you sit to the cash register the more money you make." That sounded like good advice.

In subsequent conversations with Professor Cook he thought my boss was right. He urged me to apply to the top business schools, stating my grades were good enough and my background unique enough to be of interest to them. He suggested applying at Stanford and Harvard.

Before long I received a letter from Dean Jackson of the Stanford Graduate School of Business asking me to come for an interview. As Professor Cook assumed, the dean was interested in my background as well as my studies. The school never had a Food Technology student in its program. After some conversation, he asked how I planned to finance my way through Stanford. I replied that I had saved some money from various jobs and I hoped to find some work on campus.

The dean smiled and said that he had worked his way though Harvard. He advised not to work during the first quarter: "Establish yourself as a good student first. If you then have to work, professors often will give you the benefit of the doubt when grades slip a little. Furthermore, Stanford has a policy of not kicking out any student for monetary reasons. There are always funds available for such eventualities.". "Of course, he said, "this is on the assumption that we accept you".

A few weeks later I received a letter of acceptance from Stanford, but by then I had to make another decision. Davis offered me a scholarship in Dairy Science if I decided to stay for advanced studies, an option I had never really considered. After much soul-searching I decided that I did not think an academic career suited me.

Stanford University

I arrived at the Stanford Graduate School of Business in September 1953. The student body was of a totally different caliber than at

Davis. Classmates came from the top schools across the country and most were top students in their class. I believe we were about one hundred and forty students, of which about eighty were naval officers who had won scholarships in competition. The latter were a tightly knit group, most of them married. They were older, studied together, had access to old tests saved by former naval students, so they set a very high standard for the rest of us.

We were housed in Menlo Park, a short drive from campus. My roommate was from Seattle. He was an exceedingly bright engineer. Adrian never studied yet received top grades. When he was not reading mystery novels, he did puzzles or just talked to people. I soon learned to find a quiet corner in the library.

Before long I was part of a small group who pretty much bonded throughout the two years. After dinner we usually had heated discussion ranging from politics to religion.

The curriculum was totally different from that which I experienced in undergraduate school. Stanford "Biz" School used the "case method" originally developed at Harvard Business School. Homework consisted of an actual business situation encountered by managers when a decision had to be made on the basis of limited facts within a short period of time. For instance, we might receive a report containing all the information available to the actual decision-maker and told to recommend our course of action by next day or the following week. Late work was not accepted.

The whole idea was to learn to make logical decisions quickly under conditions encountered in the business world. There were no right or wrong answers. We were graded on the logic of our argument. The cases were usually reviewed in a following class when our recommendations were compared to those actually made by the manager and what the final outcome was.

By the end of the first quarter, I started looking for work. As at Davis, I landed a job in the cafeteria "hashing" for meals. This time I started washing dishes, but after a while the lady in charge took pity on me and put me behind the cash register.

Through the Biz School I was also able to find afternoon work at the Stanford Research Institute, a Stanford affiliate. The Institute published a Chemical/Economic Handbook that provided economic data to industry. My job was to accumulate data on the world's use of chemical fertilizers and study the implications.

Somehow I found time to have a girl friend, an undergraduate student much younger than myself. She was pretty, intelligent and fun to be with. She once told me that if she married me she would have to expect to be dressed in gingham dresses from Sears Roebuck. She lived in a Row House, a former sorority house. Sororities had been outlawed on campus a few years earlier after some girls committed suicide when rejected for membership.

Our romance fell apart after the summer recess, and she married another Biz School student. About ten years later, I ran into the two of them on a business trip to Japan. Her husband was located there working for an American oil company.

I profited greatly from attending graduate school. It is difficult to point to any specific instance; rather the sum total not only prepared me for positions in management, but also taught me approaches to problem-solving with universal applicability, giving me an increased level of self-confidence.

Unlike my experience at Davis, we never established close relationships with our professors. But I have to single out Professor Kreps, not because I got to know him well, I did not, but because of the influence he had on me and most other students. Professor Kreps was the head of our economics department. He prided himself for being the only Democrat in Biz School. He served on the Council of Economic Advisors during the Roosevelt Administration. He said, he saw his job at Stanford to: "Expose you to thinking about another side than the one you were brought up with by your parents who brainwashed you with Republican philosophy from early on". Professor Kreps must have done a fabulous job because my classmates cited him decades later as the one professor that most influenced them.

With the beginning of my second year at Stanford, I began job interviews. A number corporations interviewed on campus, among them General Mills. During my first interview they raised the Jewish question in passing and I thought nothing of it. During my second interview they went deeper into the subject, wanting to know which of the three branches of Judaism I belong to, etc.

Finally, I was asked whether I had any question, and I inquired about the significance of being Jewish. They responded that in my case it would not play any role, but raised the issue because the company had some unhappy experiences with orthodox Jews "who just did not fit ". As I recall, I did receive a job offer from them, but by that time I had already signed with Continental Can Company of Chicago.

At the end of May 1955, I packed my worldly possessions into my Packard (the Hudson had finally given out), said goodbye to my parents and friends and headed East. I was so eager to begin the next phase of my life, I did not even participate in the graduation ceremony.

With my proud Parents

A New Life in Chicago, a Wonderful Town

For the first time in my life I was totally on my own, without friends or relatives in the vicinity. True, Uncle Martin and family lived in Indianapolis, but I had not been in touch with them since I was a kid.

Checking in for work at Continental Can Co., I had the very pleasant surprise of being told that upon reviewing my qualifications they decided to increase my salary. Because of my science background, I was assigned to the Research and Development Division as a management trainee. At the moment the division was located on North Avenue in a section of an old manufacturing plant. But construction of a research campus was under way on the South Side, so I was advised not to look for long term housing.

I answered an ad for a bed and breakfast accommodation located on Lake Street run by an elderly Irish couple. It was quite an experience. They had bought on old mansion in a good neighborhood bordering Oak Park and rented out rooms to young fellows like myself. As I recall, I was the only non-Irish person in the house, so I was introduced to a very Irish ambiance. The owner was an operator of one of bridges over the Chicago River. He hated the British and could not stop talking about the atrocities perpetrated by them on the Irish. I suspect that he was also involved with the IRA (Irish Republican Army; labeled by the British as a terrorist organization)

His wife was deeply religious, attending church every morning before making breakfast for her tenants. She would constantly badger me to eat more, and had I followed her advice I would have probably gained fifty pounds.

This being summertime, before television and air conditioning became ubiquitous, we would sit in the evening on the screened-in veranda and I received a thorough indoctrination on Irish culture and history. Occasionally, we would experience spectacular Mid-Western thunderstorms.

At work, I was very fortunate with the manager to which I was assigned. Bernie and I soon struck up a friendship that lasted until he passed away decades later. Bernie had a Master's degree in bio-chemistry, which was really his second career choice. He was the product of the Catholic Parochial School system and had a thorough grounding in Greek, Latin and some Hebrew. He went on to study for the priesthood, but half way through changed his mind. Bernie played an important role later in my career.

A few months later, my division moved to the South Side. I rented a small apartment in South Shore, about ten minutes from my place of work and said goodbye to my Irish friends.

In comparison to my previous location, the new research center was heaven. For one, it was air-conditioned, which was a blessing during the unbearably hot l summer months. It also had the latest scientific equipment, much of which was entirely new to me. Work consisted of investigating container problems reported by customers as well as evaluating new types of materials for containers. It also involved a lot of fieldwork, working with customers on problems or new ideas, and supporting our sales people on calls.

Stockyards in Chicago, Omaha, Kansas City and St. Paul were still in operation with adjacent slaughter houses and canneries, so I became well acquainted with such operations. A number of these places dated back to the early part of the 20th century and must have served as sources for Upton Sinclair's book on the meat industry entitled "The Jungle".

Occasionally, I was sent to Southern California to work with the tuna canneries located on Terminal Island or to the San Francisco Bay area to work with fruit and vegetable canners.

All in all, the training I received at Continental Can Co. over more than two years was invaluable, but I let it be known that I was ready for a step up.

It came in a direction I did not expect. Manufacturing speeds had not increased over decades, limited by the need to solder the side seam of tin containers. Production speeds averaged 800 cans per minute, but the engineering department had developed a welding method to replace soldering, and this line produced cans at the rate of 1500 to 2000 per minute. This improvement made it possible to develop a continuous can-making line in which a coil of steel could be enameled, slit, formed, welded and cut without interruption. I was picked to head up this project. It was a fantastic opportunity!

Settling Down

Stanford had been true to its promise, and I was able to augment my meager incomes with loans at very low interest rates. Now I was determined to rid myself of debt in the shortest time possible. My expenses were low. Bed and breakfast with the Irish couple was inexpensive, and dinners at the company cafeteria cost little so, before too long I managed to be debt free.

For entertainment, I attended Saturday night dances at a temple on Sheridan Avenue where I met several very nice ladies. Before long, I was dating Joan regularly. She was an intriguing individual. Her father was Egyptian (his name was Sharif), her mother from somewhere in the Southern U.S. Neither was Jewish, but Joan had it in her head that she wanted a Jewish husband. Her father had abandoned her mother, who raised Joan. Judging from photographs, she resembled her father. She had a striking appearance, which was accentuated by her clothing; not flashy but very much in style. She was the private secretary of a company president and had a relatively good income. Being very goal-oriented, she must have thought I had potential; if not why bother with a poor college graduate fresh out of school.

On occasion, I dated another young lady I met at the temple dances. Her father was a psychiatrist, and she was still going to college in Milwaukee. But she faded out of the picture after a while. The reason might have been my interest in another person I met.

As mentioned earlier, my job was transferred to Chicago South Side. There, my boss' laboratory was just one of many, each involved with different types of corporate research. One day, one of the engineers came to my office to introduce himself. He had heard of my background, and being a refugee himself, he wanted to meet me. Otto was about my age and had spent the war years safely in Lichtenstein, a tiny principality. Obviously, he came from a very comfortable background because he was educated in private schools there. Otto played the violin in a Chamber Orchestra and, living in the Hyde Park area, he and his wife were part of the University of Chicago scene. A lot was going on at that time and both were quite active in local and national politics.

After learning that I was by myself in Chicago, Otto invited me to his home for High Holiday dinner. As it happened, one of the guests was alone at the time because his wife visited her family in Minneapolis. When he learned that I was unattached he offered me the phone number of a lady, living in his apartment complex, who he thought I might enjoy meeting.

I soon followed up his suggestion and my life changed from then on. I was still dating Joan, but here was someone who shared my values, had a charming personality, was intelligent and had experienced life. The fact that she was good looking did not hurt. Eleanor came from very poor background. Living in a small town, her widowed mother raised four very young children on her own with some help from the local Jewish charity. To contribute, Elly started work at a very young age.

At age 20, she enlisted in the Marine Corps to get away from home. Upon discharge, she went to the University of Michigan under the G.I. Bill. She married at school and moved with her husband to New Zealand. While there, she finished college and graduated in absentia from the University of Michigan. After a brief stay in Australia, the two went to Europe, then youth hostelled in England before returning to the United States. Along the way, she decided her marriage was a mistake and she divorced soon after her return.

Chicago had a great attraction for Elly because, being stationed at the Great Lakes Naval Station while in the Marine Corps, she experience the warm hospitality that Chicagoans extended to all members of the Armed Forces during the war.

By the time I met her she was in a secure position as secretary to the president of the National Congress of Parents and Teachers living in a beautiful apartment overlooking Lake Michigan. Here was someone that I could relate to easily, who had experienced hard knocks in her life, and had raised herself up by her own bootstraps.

Just coming out of an unhappy marriage, Elly was unsure of herself. Consequently, I continued to date Joan occasionally, although I spent more and more time with Elly. And here is where I ran into difficulties.

Elly had gone out of town on a working convention, but before she left I promised to pick her up at the train station upon her return. We had not made a date beyond that, but to Elly's mind that was a foregone conclusion. I should have known better, but I made a date that same evening. When I picked her up and told her I had a commitment the rest of the evenings she felt jilted. Here was again proof that men could not be trusted. She would not talk to me for several months, but I could not get her out of my mind. A few months later I moved to a studio apartment and called Elly to invite her to see the place. She must have been sorry about the break in our relationship too because she readily accepted and from that point on we started to date regularly.

We joked about how Elly's dinners played a decision making role. There was no company cafeteria at the new location but I found cheap, nutritious meals at the nearby YMCA. However, I soon found that Elly loved to cook, and after a few dinners at her place I made it a point to call her for a date right before dinnertime. The conversation always ended with an invitation to join her for dinner that evening.

When I proposed marriage a few months later Elly was still very hesitant, understandable under the circumstances. She just did not want to make another mistake. Finally, my argument prevailed: with goodwill on both sides we should be able to overcome all future hurdles; mutual trust, love and respect were really at the base of our relationship. We rented a very nice apartment on Marine Drive near Foster Avenue and moved our furniture there over a weekend.

We had disagreements and, yes, fights over the years but our love, trust, and respect for each other never wavered over the more than nearly sixty years of our marriage. To my great sorrow, I lost Elly not long ago and I am still trying to cope with her passing. More on this later.

Neither of us had relatives nearby. Elly's mother had remarried and lived in New York, her three brothers also lived in the East, while my parents lived in San Francisco. None of them could afford a trip to attend our wedding, nor did we have the funds to have such an event, so we decided on a very simple ceremony. I learned through the immigrant grapevine that Rabbi Swarsensky from Berlin was now the rabbi of a reform congregation in Madison, Wisconsin, and I contacted him. He was glad to hear from me and offered to officiate at our wedding, but we would have to come to Madison.

It was a memorable wedding. I believe the Weil's were on vacation overseas so we looked for witnesses. I had made friends with one of the secretaries at work whose artist husband worked as a designer in Continental's art department, and they agreed to accompany us to Madison as witnesses. Neither were Jewish.

By that time, I was the proud owner of my first brand new car: a Karmann Ghia, which was a fancy Volkswagen in reality. It was a great car, black top, red body and it was rare enough that fellow owners of Ghias would wave at each other as they passed.

We took off Saturday morning in our cars. They drove a Corvette and brought along their big shaggy dog. As we arrived in

Madison and started looking for a motel for the night, we found there was a dog show in town and motels that would accommodate pets were unavailable. Finally, we found one at the outskirts.

We arrived at the synagogue late in the afternoon with Rabbi Swarsensky waiting. Everyone wanted to change into more suitable clothing for the ceremony. As Elly tells the story, as the bride she had to help the helpless bridesmaid into her dress instead of the other way around. The ceremony itself did not take very long, and when it was over we went to a very nice restaurant for dinner. The next day, everyone went home and that was it.

A delayed honeymoon began a couple of months later when we drove to San Francisco so Elly could finally meet my folks. I remember Elly being very excited about visiting San Francisco, a city she fell in love with when working at a PTA convention.

By now, my parents received small monthly checks from Germany as compensation for the damage done by the Nazi regime, and this income allowed my mother to give up the job in the *Mikve*.

My parents welcomed Elly into their apartment on 48th Avenue. My father and Elly hit it off from the start. The same could not be said about of mother, who was a more difficult person in any case. That mothers and daughters-in-law do not mesh is not an unusual situation, but my mother suffered from a number of problems that influenced her behavior as she aged.

When my parents heard of our plans to visit the Grand Canyon, they wanted to come along. It was not exactly the usual request on a couple's honeymoon but we agreed. They would have to take the Greyhound bus and meet us there since our car would suffice for sightseeing, but could not accommodate four people over long distance.

We had decided to return to Chicago via the Southern route to visit Elly's brother, Al and his family in Oklahoma City. Although I had met Al in Chicago on previous occasions, I had not met the rest of his family. All I remember about that visit in Oklahoma City was how excited Elly's three nephews were with my new "bubble car", as they named it.

On the way home, we decided to start our own family since both of us were already in our thirties. Nine months later we welcomed our first baby, Bob – officially Robert Benjamin Glaser.

My work had changed from customer service to project management. Aside from increasing my responsibilities and salary, it had some other major advantages. Whereas customer service was a necessary operation, the company was in the packaging business and making cans was a major profit center with more opportunities for advancement. As my friend from college days said: "the closer you sit to the cash register, the more money you make".

Parenthood

Back in Chicago, we settled in, waiting for the new arrival. Elly continued to work almost to the end of her pregnancy.

I also took a weekend job to have a little more income. There was a part-time job opening at Weiss Memorial Hospital, a few blocks away from where we lived, and I applied. The job was of an admitting officer, which meant receiving patients, assigning them rooms, and completing all necessary paper work. Being a private hospital specializing in certain types of surgery, meant a heavy influx of patients over the weekend in preparation for surgery during the week. It was interesting work, dealing with people under a lot of stress.

During the week I was settling into my new assignment. It involved supervising five researchers engaged in the development of can coatings that would dry exceedingly fast. As mentioned earlier, high speed can production was seen as the future of the industry, and fast-drying coatings were an integral part of the "coil-to-can" program which was to take us into the new era in making cans. It was exciting work with high visibility.

I soon found myself confronted by a sticky personnel problem. One of my subordinates, a fellow in his early twenties, was not pulling his weight. He came to work late and could not be found much of the time. I tried to motivate him, but to no avail. I learned that he performed in similar ways for other supervisors.

He told co-workers nobody would dare fire him because he was related to somebody high up in the organization.

I took the issue up with my boss, taking the position that such behavior was very bad for morale and could lead to other problems. He agreed and said that he would check this out and let me know. At our next meeting, he told me yes, the fellow was well connected, but not to worry about it; his relative would take no action on his behalf.

I confronted the fellow and fired him, judged my action justified and that it would be the last I would see of him. I was wrong. Next morning he was there, on time, asking to talk to me. He said he thought about it, that I was right in my action, that he saw his error and wanted to correct it if I would let him return to work. I did and he turned into an excellent employee. It was a good lesson for both of us.

Elly and I were now looking forward to becoming parents; she more than I because the baby was kicking a great deal. We had taken a Red Cross course on birthing and parenting, but her pediatrician had warned her not to bother calling him with false alarms. Consequently, she was afraid of contacting either him or me at work when contractions started. When she soiled her housecoat, she laundered and ironed it, all the while being terribly uncomfortable.

The doctor had arranged for her to go to Michael Reese Hospital where he was on staff. It was the best and most modern facility in town but it was located on the south side of town. When

I finally came home from work she was pretty far along. I quickly loaded her into the car and rushed her to the hospital, all the while she worried that it might be a false alarm. Once at the hospital, the nurse took one look at her then rushed her to the birthing room without any preparation. Shortly thereafter, on Thursday, May 29, 1958, our son Bob was born. Mother and son were doing great, and I was a very happy and relieved father.

Contrary to today's practice, new mothers stayed in the hospital nearly a week and Michael Reese's Lying-In department was the place to be. It was spacious and cheerful with newborns kept in the mother's room much of the time; hence the term Lying-In. Also, the food was far superior to ordinary hospital food. Elly felt like she was staying at a fancy resort hotel. She needed that rest for what awaited her at home, as it developed.

News from San Francisco was discouraging. My mother had fallen and apparently broken her hip. Having worked in the Weiss hospital for a while, I realized that this could be the beginning of the end for an elderly person. By that time, I had befriended several doctors at the hospital and I discussed it with one of them. My mother's doctor in San Francisco had recommended an operation to pin the hip, which is standard procedure, and the Chicago doctor suggested he look at the x-rays as a second opinion.

The doctor studied the x-rays and concluded that the hip was not broken, that it had a tiny fracture which would heal itself in time. Of course, I was greatly relieved but convincing my parents of this was another matter. What if her doctor was right and mine wrong? I knew my doctor and his reputation, and I was convinced that he was right. In discussing the matter with Elly we decided I should bring my mother to Chicago.

But that was easier said than done. I flew to San Francisco and, after convincing my parents of this course of action, I met with my mother's doctor who was vehemently opposed to moving her.

Whether it was out of conviction, pride, or greed, he refused to discharge her from the hospital, but after a lot of cajoling he relented, but not before he made me sign a disclaimer.

Now came the task of transporting my mother on a stretcher. Today, medical transports are handled on small jets and are very expensive. But in those days it was possible to put stretchers on commercial flights, some of which still offered sleeping berths. Jet planes had not yet replaced propeller-driven ones. Because planes flew at lower altitudes the trip took a long time and was very noisy and bumpy. On arrival, I was able to check her into Weiss Memorial.

Elly's week long stay at Michael Reese came to an end just about that time and, contrary to my frantic drive to the hospital, I suddenly became a very careful driver with Elly and the baby in the car. We decided to cede our bedroom to my parents and sleep on a couch in the living room close to the baby's crib. My mother was discharged from Weiss within a few days and so began a very stressful period for Elly.

While I was away at work, Elly, insecure with taking care of a new born baby, had also the daily care of her in-laws; not a good way to start motherhood.

Unfortunately, the baby had trouble digesting milk and became very colicky. Elly managed to work through it all, not wanting to burden me. I did not notice her tension until my parents went back to San Francisco. It all came to a head one evening when the two of us went out for a fancy dinner to celebrate our first anniversary. All of a sudden she broke down crying inconsolably. "I wanted the baby so much and now I don't enjoy him at all," she said. All of her suppressed anxieties and frustrations spilled out and I felt helpless. In retrospect, I could have been more helpful had I been more observant.

I should not forget to mention our Thanksgiving trip to New York that year. I won a frozen Thanksgiving turkey at work and on the spur of the moment we decided to visit Elly's mother who lived in the Bronx and had not seen the baby. We packed the turkey into the luggage compartment thinking that it would be defrosted by the time we got there. But we ran into very cold weather and we arrived in New York on Thanksgiving with a block of ice.

Elly's mother lived in one bedroom apartment with her second husband; an unhappy marriage she entered into when still in Michigan because she was very lonely when her kids had moved away. Her husband was a very rough, uncaring individual who ran a home delivery milk route when these were still in operation. It was depressing to see Elly's mother under such circumstances. The next time I saw her was on a much happier occasion in Chicago, at the birth of our second boy, Bill.

Back home again, my daily commute from the North Side to the South Side took a lot of time and my parents' crowded visit convinced us to look for larger quarters on the South Side. We found a second floor, two bedroom apartment in South Shore on Coles Avenue. It had a sunroom and an all-purpose room in the back. It was just what we needed, but best of all, the landlord and his wife lived downstairs, were Catholic and loved kids. Noise never bothered them. When I asked for permission to install a jungle gym in the backroom they readily agreed. By the spring of 1959 we were happily ensconced in our new, spacious quarters.

What we needed was furniture. This kindled my latent interest in cabinetmaking. I passed a Technical High School on my way to work every day so I enrolled in an Adult Education evening course. The school was very well equipped, and I was fortunate in being assigned to an outstanding teacher. He recommended I undertake a practical project that incorporated many furniture-making functions. Elly had bought an old Singer sewing machine that was in good shape except for the cabinet that housed it. So the project I chose was easy: a Scandinavian-design sewing machine cabinet.

I attended classes twice weekly and was able to complete the work within one semester. The cabinet lasted about forty years and we were both sorry to part with it at the time of our latest move. My second project involved making bunk beds, the design which I copied on a visit to a furniture store. Walnut lumber was still plentiful and cheap, so I decided to make the beds of solid walnut.

At work, my group had made a lot of progress and it was decided to build a pilot facility in one of the commercial plants. Space was available at our San Leandro, California plant, and since the project was expected to extend over many months, I was asked to move there temporarily. The company offered to pick up extra living expenses.

By fall, the three of us were on our way to California. We first checked into a motel in San Leandro while I looked for permanent quarters. A friend I knew from Stanford lived in Danville, and through him we were able to rent his neighbor's furnished house. She had just lost her husband and was delighted to be able to get away from that home for a while.

Elly was pregnant again and, not knowing how long the California venture would last, she had a gynecologist and a pediatrician in each location. That worked out well but we had other problems. We had only one car which I drove to and from work. This left Elly without transportation, dependent on my friend's wife. The location of the house was almost rural, without any sidewalks, so she could not take the baby out in a stroller for any distance. And then the rains came, and Elly was really shut in. It seemed like the rains would never stop.

I was called back to Chicago for a progress report and took Elly and Bobby with me. It was good to be home, if just for a few days, but we were unprepared for the soot and grime that had settled on our furniture during our absence. It was winter by then and coal-fired heaters were still very common. I remember Elly doing house cleaning during our visit, but it seemed a fruitless task. Even during the rainy season California looked better.

Elly was now in the eighth month of her second pregnancy. When I mentioned this to my boss he suggested that it might be better if she came home and I visit her every second weekend. After all, the project was almost completed. By early February, Elly was home in Chicago.

We were now coming close to the date projected by the doctor, so we arranged for Elly's mother to be with her during my absence, and I came home the weekend following my birthday. To celebrate, Elly prepared roast duck and chocolate cake and we had a real feast that Saturday evening. A few hours after going to bed Elly woke me up to tell me that she did not feel good. We both thought that perhaps she should not have eaten the duck. But, the pains did not subside, and we drove to the hospital to have her checked out. Again, we arrived at the hospital just in the nick of time and our second son, Bill, made his debut without giving the nurses time to prep Elly. Fathers were not permitted during birthing, contrary to today's practice. Very shortly after settling in for a long wait I was told the good news.

Changing Jobs

On the West Coast, I attended a Food Convention in San Francisco and ran into my old boss, Bernie. I knew he had left Continental Can Co. but I had not seen him since being transferred to the pilot project in California. Bernie now had a position as the Director of Research for the Grocery Products Division of Armour & Co., a very responsible job.

He explained that he felt stymied at Continental and jumped at the challenge to develop new products for Armour. The meat packing company was under new management and heading in new directions. Bernie asked me to join him at Armour. It was tempting to go back into the food business and to work for a great guy like Bernie. But I also liked my current boss and I did not want to leave the project without completing it. Bernie understood, and even though I turned down his offer he left it open.

By April 1960, my pilot plant was operating successfully and I was waiting for another assignment. What Continental's management had in mind for me was another engineering project for which I did felt unqualified. I came to the realization that advancement within the company required an engineering background because their profit base was all machinery-related.

Consequently, I asked Bernie whether his job offer was still open. A month later I was on Armour's payroll. I loved the job, the only drawback being its location in Bellwood, quite far north and west from where we lived in Chicago. It was a recently built research facility which provided state-of-the-arts equipment for processing and testing. Our projects ranged from aseptic packaging of meat products to a new freeze-drying operation; from development of new types of hot dogs to new dog foods.

After about nine months on the job, I read in the company paper of a new position in marketing. I told Bernie I was interested in that job, only to learn that he already submitted my name. A month later I started in the marketing department, which in time would lead to my becoming the assistant director of New Product Marketing and Acquisition.

Armour was one of the three giant meat packers in the U.S., but it was also involved in many other businesses. Its Grocery Products division handled foods and non-foods, from canned meats to Dial deodorant soap. Dial is still a major brand but it was really the only product of its kind on the market at the time and very profitable.

We bought a privately held company, Appian Way Pizza, that sold a packaged pizza mix which included tomato topping and grated cheese. We also bought Parson's Ammonia Co., a logical extension of our non-food business.

Describing the many other projects in which I became involved would go beyond the scope of this autobiography; suffice it to say during my four years at Armour I was exposed to many of the revolutionary developments in the food industry, primarily aseptic packaging and freeze-drying. As it turned out, aseptic packaging would be my focus for much of my career.

Throughout this time, I kept my eyes open for possible job opportunities in California. We continued to live on Coles Avenue, never bought a house, always ready to move if an opportunity opened up. Each time my travels took me to the West Coast, I returned raving to Elly about the weather and life there, and how foolish we were freezing during Chicago winters and sweltering in summer.

Then, one day, I answered an ad in the *Wall Street Journal* for an R & D director position in Northern California. I was asked to interview in Oakland for a position in Gustine, a little town in the San Joaquin Valley, and Elly and I flew there over a weekend. In many ways it was the kind of company I was looking for. It was small enough so I could have a real impact, yet part of a conglomerate which provided security and good benefits. It was a leader in aseptic packaging of dairy products; apparently there was plenty of funding for expansion.

The president of the company seemed a bit peculiar, but I would report to the executive vice president, who seemed easy to get along with. Gustine was a town of about four thousand not far from Modesto, which had a population of about one hundred thousand. The Bay Area was about sixty miles away.

However, as we started to discuss details of the position, I saw their ideas and mine were widely divergent, the location undesirable, and by the end of the interviews I was convinced I would not be happy there. Elly and I returned to Chicago very disappointed, but she backed me all the way in my decision. Shortly afterwards something else developed.

IMC Interlude and Home-Ownership

I received a call from the management consulting firm Booz, Allen & Hamilton inquiring about my interest in a top level position in Skokie, Illinois. Whether this was a coincidence, or word got around I was job-hunting I will never know, but the opening was very intriguing. A division of International Minerals & Chemicals Corp. was being restructured by the consultant, and they wanted to fill the positions of director of marketing and director of new products. The division made a single product, the food flavor enhancer monosodium glutamate (MSG), marketed under the brand name "Accent." They had national distribution and wanted to extend the brand into a line of flavor-enhancing products.

Elly and I talked it over and we decided I should not pass up this opportunity. We also decided to settle down and finally buy a house. We drove around the North Shore and decided on Highland Park as the most suitable location. It was an easy commute to Skokie, with good schools and a generally pleasant environment. In 1962, we bought a three-bedroom house in a relatively new development on Summit Avenue, north of Day Road. With it began a new lifestyle for us of suburban homeownership. We had settled down, or so it seemed.

Since I needed our car to commute and public transportation was insufficient, we decided Elly should learn to drive and we should buy a second car. Elly was in her late thirties then and had never driven. Also, having been in a car accident as a child she was fearful. When my driving lessons almost led to divorce, she continued lessons in a professional driving school. We bought a second hand Renault that turned out to come with many problems.

After a while, Elly felt secure enough to brave even icy roads, but she never liked driving, and she was always apprehensive at the wheel. Most of her driving involved shopping in the neighborhood or taking the boys to activities, but on occasion she dropped me off or picked me up at the airport. This was difficult even for a good driver in Chicago under the icy winter conditions.

At work, my department had about five people developing products and designing new types of packaging. Monosodium glutamate (MSG) is an interesting product. Oriental cooks had made use of it as a flavor-enhancer for centuries. It is part of the natural fermentation process in making soy sauce. In its pure form it looks like tiny glass splinters and has no odor or flavor. Convincing American housewives to use this product to give meat more flavor had been an incredible success story.

IMC was basically a fertilizer producer that mined potash and phosphates all over the world. A number of years earlier, the chairman of the company discovered MSG in Japan during one of his trips, then convinced his board to diversity into manufacturing food additives generally, and specifically MSG. He was in love with the product and no expense was spared in its marketing. Top advertising and public relations firms were utilized to introduce the product and once established to support sales.

In this environment, I had the good fortune of meeting and working with people who were leaders in marketing and advertising. After thorough investigation, we decided that better new marketing opportunities existed in Latin American markets such as Mexico and Puerto Rico than in the U.S., because MSG was especially effective in bean dishes. As a result, I spent time in both areas in preparation for market introduction, which actually happened after I left the company.

As the Director of New Products, I was also given the opportunity to participate in negations with Takeda Chemical Co. This company developed two ingredients which extended the flavor-enhancing properties of MSG and exhibited some unique attributes of their own. These compounds could open the market for the use of MSG far beyond that in existence at the time.

After some initial discussions with Takeda in California we were invited to visit the company at their headquarters in Japan. I accompanied my boss, Mr. Hamilton, and two lawyers to Osaka. As was usual in the Orient, business negotiations extended into social affairs. We were entertained royally in an outstanding restaurant with a banquet served by geishas who then performed dances and sang. Negotiations extended over several days but came to naught in the end. Apparently, Takeda decided to make the investment of breaking into the U.S. market on their own. Knowing the outcome of their effort, I am sure we could have done a much better job for them.

Takeda Party

My leaving IMC was brought on in part by internal politics. Booz Allen brought in a new head of marketing at the same time I joined IMC. Steve was a fast- talking Southerner whose smooth exterior concealed his aggressive nature. From the day he and I met, he judged me his chief rival for the top position in the company. He did his best to undermine my work, much of which overlapped his. Obviously, there were no harmonious work relations and the two of us had several run-ins. The irony is I recognized his management capabilities early on and would probably not have minded working for him, but under the circumstances that was out of the question. Our boss was nearing retirement and I could see the handwriting on the wall.

Again, fortune came my way when I received a call from the Executive Vice President at Avoset Food Corporation. Visiting

Indianapolis, he asked me to join him. He was one of the men who had interviewed me in California. I learned from him. that the company had filled the position with someone who did not work out; probably for the reasons I had pointed out to them earlier. Top management had reviewed the situation and came around to my view how the position should be structured. About one month later we were on our way to Oakland. Elly was delighted, as were my parents, who finally had their grandchildren close by.

Avoset Food Corporation

Eleven years had passed since I had left the Bay Area and a lot happened in that time. I had a wife and two boys I loved, not to forget our dog. I was now embarked on a new job that would ultimately take me to the top of the company, which, of course, I could not know at the time, and I was close to my parents who were getting on in age.

There were two aspects to the job: one involving administration; the other development. Our research facility, which fell under my jurisdiction, was located in Gustine. Consequently, I visited there three days a week on average and spent the balance of my time in Oakland. Since Interstate 5 was not built yet, my trips there could take as much as two and a half hours each way in bad weather. Nights were lonely, spent at a motel in Modesto or Los Banos. Modesto was further away but offered Spanish language night school classes I attended.

Absence from home was not my only problem. I had to face a number of difficulties with existing personnel. But my biggest headache was the company president, Mahlon. Although I nominally reported to the executive vice president, I soon learned everyone, from the janitor on up, reported directly to the president.

He was a conflicted man. He was an exceedingly intelligent chemical engineer by profession whose two main problems were people and money. Born in Philadelphia, he was closely related to the founders of one of the world's largest pharmaceutical manufacturing companies. Being a liberal, with a Quaker background, he was in conflict with his family's values. When a job opened up with a subsidiary in California in the late 1920's, he saw his opportunity to get away from home.

The subsidiary, the California Milk Company, had undergone a number of changes over the years. Originally it manufactured ingredients for pharmaceutical products made from byproducts of California's emerging dairy industry. But by the time he joined the operation, these ingredients were no longer needed. With an enormous supply of cottage cheese whey, the California Milk Co. switched to the production of lactose and casein for industrial applications. Before long, they were the world's largest supplier of these ingredients. It was a very profitable operation and headquarters in Philadelphia did not bother him.

But things never stay the same. Dutch manufacturers found ways to produce casein and lactose much more cheaply, taking business away from California. Not wanting to leave the West Coast, he needed to find another business. Mahlon heard of a newly patented system to produce shelf-stable milk with good flavor. His plant was located in the heart of California's milk production; perhaps he could use this new method to take the milk industry in an entirely new direction: non-refrigerated milk distribution. He bought the patent rights without ever tasting the final product!

Mahlon was convinced he could make a go of it, and for the next couple of years he experimented with aseptic packing in glass. Another invention bailed him out. A small engineering company in San Jose developed a canning machine to fill and seal tin cans aseptically. Here was the answer to Mahlon's problem. One of the very first Dole Canning Systems was installed at the plant in Gustine and he was on his way. But was he? Who needed the product? Housewives liked fresh milk, not canned stuff that did not even taste like fresh milk.

But luck was with him. With the outbreak of war in 1941 and unreliable milk supply overseas, the military looked for just such a product, one that did not require refrigeration and was palatable. Before long, the Gustine plant, now called Avoset, was humming and for the next several years Mahlon's business was flourishing again. But, with the end of the war came an end for the need of Avoset's product. Again, it looked like he had come to a dead end, and again he recognized an opportunity which bailed him out.

A new product had come on the market. Called "Reddi Whip", whipping cream sprayed from a seltzer water (soda water) dispenser instantly producing whipped cream. An entrepreneur in St. Louis took the concept and franchised dairies throughout the U.S. Because of its convenience for restaurants and bakeries, the product caught on quickly. It was easy to use, tasted good, but it had one major drawback: it soured quickly so dairies experienced high returns.

Enter Mahlon, his aseptic canning system, and with a young laboratory assistant. Bob had two years of college when he went to work for Mahlon, but he was a very quick study. Working with a manufacturer of aerosol cans, he demonstrated that cream could be sterilized by the Avoset system and packed aseptically for long shelf life.

To Mahlon's credit, he recognized Bob's capabilities and he let him run the project. The new product was named "Qwip" and Bob travelled the country trying to sell it. In a few markets it sold well, but distribution problems hindered wide market penetration. Soon Bob recognized that Avoset did not have the capabilities to market Qwip successfully. That was when he came up with the idea of offering dairies the opportunity to market aerosol whipping cream, produced by Avoset, under their own brand. This would solve the dairies' spoilage problem and give Avoset large production volumes with national distribution. An ingenious idea indeed!

Avoset did well and so did Bob. He was now in charge of national sales, and before long he was appointed executive vice president. He also knew how to handle Mahlon. The latter, though married, had no kids and Bob became his surrogate son, groomed to ultimately take over the company.

With success came competition. "Reddi Whip" was badly hurt by Avoset's private label packing, but they had a strong brand name and they knew marketing. They also figured out how to extend the shelf life of their product. There was talk that they were working on a cream substitute that could be sold at a lower price. Bob needed to beat them to the punch with his own imitation whipping cream.

Avoset's research staff had dairy training, but knew little about the chemistry of vegetable fats. More importantly, they resisted the whole idea of developing a cheaper non-dairy whipping cream. I was brought into the company to move product development in this new direction. It was soon obvious that I was heading toward a confrontation. Development work had heretofore been conducted by the laboratory director, a chemist who had been with Avoset for many years.

Early on, I sensed his resentment of my coming into the company. Discussing the matter with Bob, who advised not to let it bother me and do what I had to do. After nearly four years' experimental work, he had nothing to show for it. Finally, when I asked to see his laboratory notebook, he lost his temper, started to throw things around and quit. His sidekick and friend stayed another year but by then things had changed significantly within the company.

Mahlon had a fatal heart attack when vacationing in Maui, and headquarters put Bob in charge. But before this happened, I had a run-in with Mahlon as well.

Without first checking with Mahlon about the expenditure, I bought a piece of equipment for about two thousand dollars to advance a project quickly. He called me on the carpet and before he was through I was fired as I had not checked with him first.

I had finally obtained an interesting job in California and even though I worked for a difficult person I did not want to make a change. I also had my family to think about.

After thinking about it for a few hours, I marched into his office and told him that his action was penny wise and pound foolish. Knowing how tight fisted he was, I explained it had cost him a lot of money to bring me and my family to California. Furthermore, our project was on the right track, and his pride of not being asked to approve the equipment purchase must have gotten the better of him. He mumbled something and I left his office. A little while later Bob came to tell me to forget the whole thing.

Later the production vice-president, told me that Mahlon explained the incident to him saying: "The son-of-a-bitch wouldn't let me fire him". True.

With Mahlon's death and Bob's taking over the company, I was given greater responsibilities including supervision of the quality control department. I was elevated to vice president within the year. As such, I gained some exposure to top management in Philadelphia, and I sensed that Avoset had a pretty low standing there and Bob was not very well liked.

The reasons for this were obvious. Mahlon was thoroughly disliked and resented at headquarters. Bob was seen as his alter ego, so their dislike for Mahlon was transferred to Bob. I was seen as a newcomer, an outsider, unaffected by any of this.

Apparently, Bob was well aware of their attitude, having made some comments to that effect. It must have bothered him a lot because he started to drink heavily. His wife tried to talk Bob into retiring, but he would not hear of it. He was still relatively young and I believe his pride got in the way.

I began to enjoy my work; in large part because the company was making considerable progress introducing new products which were developed under my supervision. I hired a young man with experience in fat chemistry, and he developed an entire line of imitation cream products. This allowed us to bid successfully against a number of competitors that had sprung up. But I was after an entirely new market.

Heretofore, Avoset's packaging capabilities were primarily limited to aerosol containers, and we still packed dairy products for the military. As a matter of fact, during the Vietnam War we shipped carloads of canned liquid mixes of soft serve ice cream to the army. For the moment, our profit still came from our aerosol products, but the market was saturated.

I wanted to take the company in a new direction and Bob backed my efforts all the way. With the introduction of aseptically packed dairy products in Europe, I was convinced here was an opportunity for Avoset. The problem was that in the U.S., the dairy industry was regulated at federal, state and local levels. This meant any new dairy product required innumerable approvals. Aseptically canned dairy products on the other hand were generally exempt from such regulations because they were considered part of the canned foods industry, supervised by the Food & Drug Administration not the U.S. Department of Agriculture, which covered milk products.

For the next year my job entailed proving that aseptically packed cream in flexible paper or plastic containers was as safe to consume as that packed in rigid containers. To describe how we ascertained this information is extremely interesting but goes beyond the scope of my autobiography. Suffice it to say we succeeded. As expected, I ran into a lot of opposition from state dairy interests who wanted to keep California milk products out of their state. It took a lot of politicking as well as help from SmithKline's legal department to finally gain approval, at least in major segments of the country. In the process, I got to know many decision-makers in the dairy industry, which stood me in good stead in later years. Avoset became a major supplier to our dairy customers of all types of cream products in conventional dairy cartons.

Frozen food distributors were located all over the U.S., but there were only a few distributors for liquid dairy products other than dairies themselves. Having supplied these dairies with aerosol whipping cream, Avoset had essentially a nationwide distribution system for refrigerated products.

When flying around the country, I noticed the airlines served frozen coffee creamers that often were not thawed when served. There was only one manufacturer of these little one-half ounce portions of cream substitute, and it seemed like an opportunity for Avoset.

In discussing this idea with Bob, he readily saw the opportunity too and agreed with me to investigate this further. I came across French equipment used to produce portion-sized jams and jellies.

Within a month, our plant engineer and I were on an expedition visiting a number of plants in Europe that used this new type of equipment. In the process, we noticed some other equipment, so we visited not only France but England, Denmark, Switzerland and Germany as well.

As an aside, it was my first return to Germany and it was traumatic! While I readily spoke German in Denmark and Switzerland, I just could not get myself to do so in Germany, and I stayed there for the shortest time possible.

The engineer and I saw the possibilities of modifying the French equipment and our report to Bob was very positive. However, this involved a very large investment, and he wanted to obtain approval from Philadelphia before embarking on the new venture. So Bob and I flew to headquarters, made our presentation to SmithKline's president, and received his blessing.

Receiving ready acceptance from our dairy distributors, Bob obtained a contract from United Airlines and we were off to the races. Within a year, we bought a couple of additional machines, Bob wrote contracts with several other large airlines, and we were producing about one million creamers a day. And that was not all. Now that the airlines were happy with our product, they asked us to supply them portion controlled salad dressing as well. They were willing to supply us specific formulas they had developed. It all sounded easy but it turned out not to be so.

Our packaging materials were not suitable for salad dressings, they disintegrated during storage. This meant that we had to start from scratch. Our job for the next few months was to work with several material suppliers, and we finally succeeded in putting together laminates that functioned well. Now our business was booming. Avoset was the only manufacturer having contracts with all major airlines and a network of suppliers that could deliver nationwide.

However, we soon learned our supply lines were getting too long and costly. Shipping bulky products all the way to the East Coast turned out to be prohibitively expensive, so we decided to open two additional plants, one in Ohio and one in Newburg NY We converted two defunct milk processing plants to aseptic operation, and my additional job was to deal with all the regulatory agencies that had to approve our new operations.

I had been dealing with most of them when we shipped products into the areas under their jurisdiction, so I thought I would have no problems obtaining plant approval. But I was wrong. When bringing product from California into another state, we had the protection of Interstate Commerce laws, but now we wanted to manufacture in their backyard and we were looked at in a totally different light. This was especially true in New York, where I soon found politics playing an important role.

The milk business in New York City, though regulated by the city's health department, was in reality controlled by what was called "the Dairy Mafia," a few milk processors who essentially divided the business between themselves. My task for the next few months was to convince that group to let us come in and serve their market. I cannot go into the details of our negotiations; suffice it to say that we ultimately reached agreement.

But in the process of negotiations, I had my first exposure of New Yorkers' "attitude" and it was quite an experience. I soon learned one's assertiveness plays a vital role in successful negotiations. New Yorkers try to intimidate you if you let them, but they back down when people assert themselves. I had many a shouting match, something I never had before, and mostly had my way in the end. But I suspect they often just enjoyed giving me a bad time.

Promotion

As mentioned, shortly after Mahlon's demise, my responsibilities expanded to include all technical aspects of the business, including quality control. The latter was a relatively small department but, because of its interaction with production, a constant source of conflict. Production wanted to move as much product as possible into the market and quality control, true to its mission, wanted to stop production lines whenever quality was jeopardized.

Heretofore, the quality control department reported to the production vice- president, and he resented my taking this responsibility away from him. It took a lot of time, diplomacy, and effort to deal with this issue, and it was not resolved until much later.

In the meantime, I had a few interesting experiences. Word got around the dairy industry that Avoset had developed an innovative processing technology. With the end of the Second World War, European milk processing and distribution systems were revamped, and we were frequently contacted by overseas processors. Two of these contacts are worth mentioning here.

The first one involves a couple of Englishman, Hans, the moneyman and Ernest, a Member of Parliament and the former Postmaster General of England. They wanted to license our aerosol cream technology. After a visit to our Gustine operation, they invited me to England for further discussions.

The trip took me to England's largest dairies (these two men had the connections) with the idea of having one of the dairies manufacture aerosol whipping cream under an Avoset license for the two. They wanted the distribution rights for all of Europe.

The MP insisted that I stay at his London residence. Since the stay extended over the Boxing Day weekend, a national holiday, he arranged for me to accompany him to an official Boxing event taking place in the ballroom of the Intercontinental Hotel in London. It was a very formal event, and he provided a tuxedo for me to wear.

There were no more than a couple of hundred people in attendance and I was seated next to Lord Derby, who was the Queen's representative and the one offering the required toast to the Queen. A great honor, indeed. The boxing match seemed a mere formality; it was very short and uneventful.

But the end of the story is more interesting. About a month after my visit, the technical vice president of England's largest dairy company came to California to finalize our arrangements. From comments he made after a few drinks, I got the impression that his opinion of the MP was less than favorable, so I was not surprised when headquarters called Bob shortly thereafter to warn him about our upcoming English venture. They had made inquiries through their London office, which came up negative.

Our second possible European involvement started in Philadelphia. The international ventures department of the Chase Bank contacted headquarters in Philadelphia about Avoset possibly licensing its technology to East Germany. Chase, under contract to the East German Government, made all the arrangements, and since they picked up expenses I asked Elly to come along, at our expense of course. We were put up in the fanciest hotel, by communist standards, in East Berlin. But what we remembered most was an incident that happened at breakfast. As usual, we ordered coffee, as part of the meal. When Elly asked for a re-fill, the waiter did so grudgingly. But when Elly asked for a third cup, he refused. When told we would gladly pay for it he said, "Two cups is enough, nobody needs more than that". Nothing could explain more the difference between East and West then this waiter's response.

The commissar for the dairy industry of East Germany took me to a number of dairy plants which he thought might be suitable to use our technology. He was in his late thirties and very personable. We had a chauffeured car. Understanding their conversation, I was amused by their use of the familiar "Du" and "comrade", while each being mindful of their status.

I was very impressed by the commissar, and came away with the opinion that, had he been born in the U.S., he would have been equally successful there. Nothing ever came of the trip as it was obvious the quality of their raw materials was substandard.

Time for a Change

By 1972 I was in a secure position at Avoset. I enjoyed my work, so why did I want a change? There were probably many answers to this question. I sensed things were not going all that well between my boss and corporate management in Philadelphia. I also observed him drinking more during the day than before. Furthermore, whenever he returned from a conference in Philadelphia he seemed especially tense. Consequently, I feared for the future of the company, which meant my job as well.

I started looking for alternatives. I was well versed in all aspects of aseptic packaging, so I thought of starting my own business. I wrote a business plan and started shopping around. The city of Milpitas was trying to bring in new industry. Parts of it were run down and parts were swampy, but it had a great location. They had received funding from the Federal Government to build an industrial park, and they offered low cost manufacturing facilities. They were even willing to help financing new ventures.

Within a few weeks, I had everything lined up, and I had a long talk with Bob. To my surprise, he told me his job was too strenuous, he had difficulties in Philadelphia, and his wife wanted him to retire. In the next sentence he offered me his job. His close relationship with his predecessor was at the root of his problem, and he thought I would get along with headquarters just fine.

Of course, I was flattered and intrigued with the offer. I had to make up my mind whether I wanted to take the risk of going out on my own or step into Bob's shoes, provided top management approved my promotion.

In retrospect, I think what prompted me to stay with Avoset was the security of being part of a huge conglomerate. But I also had many ideas for operational improvements and new product opportunities. Now, instead of just thinking about them, I could actually bring these about.

After a month, the head of corporate personnel came to Oakland. He spent considerable time interviewing each of us in top management. From my discussions with him, I was unable to ascertain what my future status would be with the company.

A short while later, I was invited to come in Philadelphia to discuss my future with top management. It soon became evident that they knew very little about Avoset's business other than we used to be quite profitable. Our declining profitability over the last couple of years was a major concern, and they wanted to see that trend reversed.

I was to be named president of Avoset Food Corp. and report to a corporate vice-president who supervised five other subsidiaries. I was expected to come to Philadelphia every quarter with an operational report. Their sole interest was profitability as I soon learned. They had no interest in future plans or opportunities whatsoever. I met with the corporate president, and SmithKline's chairman, both were very cordial and wished me well.

I also met with the head of personnel, the person who had earlier interviewed us in California, and was told of some personnel changes he would like to see. Principally among these, he wanted to bring in someone to replace our vice-president of finance. He felt the man currently in the position was not qualified. Although I personally liked the man, had actually been helped by him on a number of occasions, I had to agree that the position outgrew the man. They insisted on bringing someone out of the Philadelphia office to Oakland: Frank, a man I had dealt with on a number of occasions, had an excellent background and had made his career at headquarters since graduating from Wharton Graduate School of Business. As it turned out, Frank and I worked well together over a number of years.

The year was 1974 and I was on my way. I was in charge of a large operation headquartered in Oakland with plants in Gustine, California, Washington Court House, Ohio, and Newburg, New York.

Aging Parents

After the initial euphoria of having located the family once again in California, reality set in. I traveled a lot when we lived in Chicago and later in Highland Park, but my new job involved much more travel. In the beginning I was away from home three to four nights a week. This meant that the task of moving into our new home, getting settled and raising the two boys fell principally to Elly. It was very tough on her and it was a strain on our marriage; but we managed to live through it. This was especially true during the months we lived at the Hillside Motel in Lafayette while searching for a home.

The house we bought in Moraga was slightly larger than our home in Illinois, and it was located close to schools. Elly loved the place and felt very comfortable there.

Although we sent our kids to the Temple Sunday school in Highland Park, we ourselves did not belong to any temple or synagogue. Suddenly, Israel's Six Day War broke out in June 1967, and we felt at such a time of crisis all Jews had to stand together. What better place to be than a synagogue? We went to Temple Isaiah in Lafayette, liked what we saw, especially the Rabbi, and joined shortly thereafter.

Elly's mother was living with her second husband in New York and had had a stroke. While we were in the state a flux, Elly's brother Al, who lived in Indianapolis, was well connected with the Jewish community through his job with Israel Bonds. He arranged for their mother to be admitted to a Jewish rehabilitation facility in Indianapolis which specialized in the treatment of stroke victims. It was a godsend, bringing her back from near death to many more years of life, though with severely impaired speech and mobility.

When Al was transferred to Seattle in 1979, Elly and I moved her mother to the Home for Jewish Parents in Oakland, which offered better care than she had received in Indianapolis.

My father was still active in his business but it became evident my mother was having severe memory problems. At first we thought it might be best for them to be closer to us, and we made a down payment for a house in Moraga, which was being built. But by the time we had to finalize the deal, we realized this would not be a solution.

Although we saw my parents almost every other weekend, neither Elly nor I realized how much of a strain taking care of my mother was having on my Dad. By then he had given up his business and, as we learned later, he was totally devoted to taking care of her since she was incapable of taking care of herself. It was an enormous reponsibility and strain and it obviously affected his health.

My parent's marriage was very complex. As I mentioned, they were deeply in love with each other but had difficulty showing it. My father's jealousy led to frequent conflicts, but somehow these were always resolved. My mother, high-strung and quite self-centered as she aged, was not an easy person to live with. But they adjusted and as she grew older they seemed ever closer to each other.

I see this in retrospect now. At the time, I was involved with my own family and career, and my parents' lives, although I worried about them, were not foremost in my mind. So it came as a terrible shock when my father suddenly had a massive heart attack. He was taken to St. Mary's Hospital in San Francisco and I rushed over to see him. He was in terrible shape and I consulted with his doctor, who I knew he trusted and was quite close to. The doctor indicated there really was very little he could do other than keeping him sedated and free of pain.

I had a terrible dilemma. I was to make a presentation to the board of directors the next day in Philadelphia. My father knew about it. I said I could cancel, but weak as he was he indicated he wanted me to go. Whether it was the Germanic sense of duty he tried to instill in me, or whether it was that he did not want me to be present when he passed away, I will never know. It might have been a little of both, at any rate, the doctor assured me that I could make the trip and he would last at least that day. He did not make it.

I left on a midnight flight to Philadelphia, arrived early in the morning only to be met by Frank at the airport, who transmitted Elly's phone call to him that my father had passed.

To my mind there were two possibilities, either he had an agreement with the doctor to help him into the next world or, strong-willed as he was, he just turned to the wall and willed his own death. Of course, I will never know, but I still wonder to this day.

The Board could not have been more understanding. Frank had informed them earlier of the situation, and each came over to express condolences. I quickly gave my presentation and took the first available flight back to San Francisco.

I was very close to my father and his death, though not unexpected, came as a terrible shock to me. I miss him to this day. He was a complex man, a reflection of the times he lived through. He made friends easily, yet not close ones. With a twinkle in his eye, he could be very charming, but also cruel and destructive at times. For example, on several occasions when in Shanghai he was frustrated with my childish behavior, he stated that I was stupid and would never amount to anything. An expression of love was not in his vocabulary, yet he loved his family deeply and his actions spoke louder than words. Devoted to my mother he would often insult her, thereby venting his own frustrations on her.

German to the core, he had an unshakable sense of duty and of the importance of hard work in building character. With many prejudices including the belief in German superiority, a product of his early upbringing, he nevertheless had obvious feelings of inferiority, undoubtedly owing to his lack of a formal education. He was a self- made man in the truest sense.

We soon realized that my mother had greatly deteriorated and her dementia had taken over. Although we never knew how much she understood, it appeared that she was unaware of her husband's death. Having had a good experience with the care Elly's mother received, we decided move her into the Home for Jewish Parents, which turned out to be a mistake.

Several months after the move, Elly received a call my mother could not be found on the premises. She had wandered off to who knows where. I immediately rushed there, only to be told that the police had been notified.

I cruised the neighborhood on foot and by car, thinking in her confused state my mother could not have walked very far, but I was wrong. Finally, after hours of cruising in ever widening circles, I saw my mother standing on a corner disheveled, crying, and totally confused.

Obviously, the Home was not suitable for her needs. Luckily, we found a woman in Concord who ran a very small caregiver service in her home. There my mother received round-the-clock supervision, good food and personal care. The woman was a Christian Fundamentalist with many anti-Jewish biases, as we later learned, but she was very good to my mother. When the woman moved to Fresno a couple of years later, we transferred my mother to the Orinda Convalescent Center, which was not far from us. By that time she was totally bedridden. She died in her sleep.

My mother had devoted her entire life to my father and to me. She had had a very difficult life. She married relatively late, during extremely unstable times and at the height of German inflation when money was absolutely worthless. Deeply in love with her husband, she had to endure his frequent fits of jealousy after his many absences. A well-educated woman with many interests, she became a home maker and a devoted daughter to her domineering widowed mother. As a mother, she insisted on not repeating her mother's mistakes, but did.

Shortly after my mother's move to Orinda, we decided to locate Elly's mother there as well. Both received excellent care until the end. Elly's mother also died there in her sleep.

Elly was better to my mother than I. She visited her frequently to check up on her. Since my mother had lost her memory, there was no possible verbal communication with her, which bothered me a lot. Nevertheless, Elly would spend time sitting with her. This is all the more remarkable, since Elly never received any warmth or affection from my mother in earlier years.

I loved my mother and knew the many hardships she had endured throughout her life. Dominated by her mother, then by ther husband, she struggled through depravation in early life, the horrible Hitler and Shanghai years, and finally an adjustment to a new country. All this for someone with early ambitions that went unfulfilled, tremendous internal tensions and conflicts. She showered affection on me, and I am afraid I did not reciprocate adequately. I guess children never do. With all her ailments, and she had many, she did not suffer in the end and passed away peacefully. The loss of their grandparents must have been the first real shock in the young lives of our two boys.

We moved to a larger house in 1971. It was located practically around the corner for our first home in Moraga, and turned out to be one of our major mistakes. The house was built on two levels on a steep hillside. As usual, I was out of town when a major rain storm flooded the lower level owing to poor drainage, and

Elly was stuck coping with the problem. Nevertheless, we lived there for six years.

Our boys were not boys any longer, they were young men. When our elder son, Bob, graduated from high school, he decided to take time off and live in Israel on a Kibbutz for a while. He was eighteen years old. Upon completion of his stint there, he decided to make a few stops on the way home and he visited Rome, Florence, Zurich and Paris. To our great delight and surprise he returned the day of our wedding anniversary. Elly looked out the kitchen window and could not believe she saw Bob walking up the driveway unannounced.

Our second son, Bill, followed in Bob's footsteps and also spent time in Israel but did not stay quite as long. Before long, Elly and I were by ourselves, "empty nesters", another phase in our lives.

Life Goes On

It sounds harsh, but life does go on. The loss of one's parents is traumatic and one never quite gets over it; at least I did not. To this day I occasionally dream of one or both of my parents, and I find myself reminiscing about them frequently as I get older. And yet one cannot, and should not, dwell too long on their loss.

Fortunately, our parents lived to experience our boys' *Bar Mitzvahs*. Even though they were not really very religious, this rite of passage was very meaningful to them. Our two boys were close to my parents, had spent a week with their *Omi* and *Opa* while Elly and I moved from Chicago to the Bay Area, and, of course, received the royal treatment at that time. Both boys meant a great deal to our parents and these feelings were reciprocated.

Bob and Bill were growing up fast, spending less time at home. We still did many of things together, such as travel, then Elly became interested in activities outside the home. At first she started to work as a freelance writer for the *Moraga Sun* and the *Jewish Post and Opinion*, which was published in Indianapolis. Then she became a docent of California history at the Oakland Museum, and she wrote a column called "Honorable Menschen" for the East Bay Jewish Federation's weekly paper. Ultimately, she was hired by the University of California's Regional Oral History Department in the Bancroft Library at Berkeley as an interviewer/editor, a job she enjoyed tremendously.

We always travelled a lot. One of our most memorable experiences was a visit to Israel with the boys in 1971, right after Bob's Bar Mitzvah. I felt it was important for them to see at an early age what they learned in Sunday school had some basis in fact. We rented a car and criss-crossed Israel, visiting some of the places mentioned in the bible. It was a great experience and occasionally we talk about it to this day.

As mentioned, business travel had taken me back to Germany for the first time since leaving as a refugee, and the difficulty I had speaking German there. Yet a year or two later, on the occasion of the ANUGA food exhibition in Cologne *(Allgemeine Nahrungs- und Genussmittel-Ausstellung)*

I took Elly and the boys with me to Germany to show them from where I came. By coincidence, we were in Berlin during the time of the High Holidays and we attended services at the Fasanen Strasse synagogue, the one that my grandmother and I watched burn November 9, 1938 and which had been partially rebuilt by then.

We stayed at the Kempinski Hotel across the street and had dinner there on *Erev* (the evening before) Yom Kippur. Eat your heart out, Hitler!

The next day's service at the synagogue was one that neither Elly nor I will ever forget. When the cantor recited the names of the death camps in the midst of congregants, all of whom were Holocaust survivors, there was not a dry eye. It was a heart-breaking experience.

Why would people continue to live in Germany after all? It was an obvious question both of us asked people we met. The answers differed, but mostly it involved economics. The overwhelming majority were East European Jews who, in spite of everything, felt more secure, more welcome then where they came from, and were offered financial incentives to settle in Germany. Whether their children, who grew up in Germany, would stay was problematic. Most felt their kids would probably migrate to Israel. A few answered that Jews came to Germany with the Romans, that they belonged there and that the new Germany needed the Jews. A Germany without Jews meant victory for the Nazis.

Business Experiences

As the incoming president of Avoset, I had to be mindful of people's feelings and attitudes. Here I was appointed to a position several old-timers thought was rightfully theirs. Both the vice president of production and the vice president of sales had been with the company some thirty years, had helped build the company, and each felt he was much better suited to fill that post than this young upstart (Jewish at that!) who had taken it away from them.

Furthermore, each man all along had developed their own following, people who had hitched their own careers to these managers. On the other hand, I had few if any enemies among the rank and file employees, having made an effort to establish personal relationships all along.

When Frank, the comptroller, and I poured over the books it became evident the company was not in very good financial straits. As I analyzed the situation, it was clear what had taken place. In many corporations, top management wants to build sales at any cost because their remuneration is usually tied to how much product is sold. My predecessor was no exception.

Avoset Food Corporation specialized in manufacturing for others. Dairies and supermarket chains sold products under their own brands, but often had other manufacturers produce these products for them because they could do it more efficiently. Avoset was the biggest of these "private label" manufacturers in the dairy business in the U.S.

Originally, Avoset had specialized in cream products because their unique technology extended the shelf-life of such very perishable products. Cream constitutes only a small fraction of a dairy's total production and short runs are costly to produce. Because Avoset produced nothing else, it was very efficient.

But times had changed, and as people became mindful of cholesterol, cream sales had plummeted. Bob sought to increase sales by offering dairies low-cost production of other dairy products, such as half-and-half, which constituted a very large volume. This would allowed dairies to cut their costs. How was Avoset able to come in below the dairies' own production costs?

Bob reasoned such large volumes would offer him very efficient twenty-four hour production runs. Since he already had the necessary production equipment and a fixed overhead, his actual costs would be limited to raw materials, packaging and labor. Safeway Supermarkets immediately signed on and soon production was humming around the clock. Of course, with little downtime for maintenance, equipment broke down faster and new investment was required for cold storage, etc.

Before long profits, heretofore pretty high, began to sag and red ink appeared on the balance sheet. But Bob was no dummy. He and the comptroller did some creative accounting losses which were not evident in the short run. Now it was obvious to me why Bob drank more than was good for him and wanted to retire; he saw the company in a dead end. My first move was to step away from unprofitable business and go back to eight hour shifts; not a popular move with workers who loved the extra hours. It also required a number of management shifts and forced retirements, which were equally unpopular. I began to feel a lot of pressure.

Fortunately, I received support from headquarters in Philadelphia who, once Bob left the company, realized what had happened, supported and understood my actions. I was given a free hand to make the changes I felt were necessary.

With cream sales down, I was desperately looking for ways to generate profitable new business. In my role as new products' director, we had developed cream substitutes for which we had received a patent. The cholesterol scare had not only cut into cream sales, but other high-cholesterol products such as the sale of eggs, so the thought of an egg substitute, akin to our cream substitutes, was logical.

Chemically, egg yolk is similar to cream: an emulsion of water, fat, protein, and minor nutrients. Take our cream substitute, add egg color and flavor plus some vitamins and *voilá*, you have a phony egg yolk. Now add egg white to it and you have an egg substitute. Sounds easy, but it isn't, because egg white coagulates at relatively low temperatures and chemical treatments are illegal. I cannot go into details here, but to the process we developed was sufficiently unique to be granted a U.S. Patent.

United States Patent [19]

Glaser et al.

[11] **3,928,632**

[45] **Dec. 23, 1975**

[54] **EGG SUBSTITUTE PRODUCT**

[75] Inventors: Ernest Glaser, Moraga; Philip F. Ingerson, Merced, both of Calif.

[73] Assignee: Avoset Food Corporation, Oakland, Calif.

[22] Filed: July 31, 1974

[21] Appl. No.: 493,450

[52] U.S. Cl. 426/72; 426/73; 426/614
[51] Int. Cl.² A23L 1/30
[58] Field of Search 426/196, 72, 73, 211, 212

[56] **References Cited**
UNITED STATES PATENTS

3,475,180   10/1969   Jones 426/185

3,563,765   2/1971   Melnick 426/211
3,594,183   7/1971   Melnick et al. .... 426/211 X
3,806,608   4/1974   Perret 426/211

Primary Examiner—Raymond N. Jones
Attorney, Agent, or Firm—Joseph A. Marlino; Richard D. Foggio; William H. Edgerton

[57] **ABSTRACT**

A liquid egg substitute product which is virtually cholesterol free and comprises in combination egg white, polyunsaturated liquid vegetable fats, and a fatty acid lactylate alkali metal salt.

5 Claims, No Drawings

A New Venture

Avoset's relationship to headquarters had always been strange. As mentioned the Corporation was one of the largest pharmaceutical conglomorates in the world. Consequently, the company's orientation was to health and the medical world. More than fifty percent of its business was prescription drugs, the balance split between over-the-counter drugs, veterinary drugs, clinical/analytical laboratories, ultrasonic devices and Avoset's food business. Consequently, they felt distant, tended to ignore us, and I wanted to change that. As a token of their interest, or so I felt, they put me on the corporate management committee on which I served as the one president of a single subsidiary, all others being group vice-presidents and corporate officers. It was a great honor and exposed me to much of what went on inside the corporation. I also learned a great deal about the pharmaceutical business and over time established excellent relationships. I am still friends with at least two members.

Larry was one of the committee's group vice-presidents heading up a chain of clinical laboratories. He befriended me and with his help Philadelphia became a more familiar place for me. Larry even went so far as to take our son Bob to several of the historic battlefields around Philadelphia when Bob accompanied me on trip to headquarters. We still count Larry and his wife Wendy among our friends.

My first aim was to attain the level of group vice-president; and to this end I looked toward suitable acquisitions. One company we came close to buying was Estee Candy Co., which marketed sugar-free candy; a possible bridge to SmithKline's health- oriented business. It was a family-owned company, but the family was not quite ready to sell at that time.

Acquisitions can be time consuming and I was in a hurry. So I went back to my roots: new products. The egg substitute, which was fully developed by that time, seemed like a product that could move Avoset in a new direction and could possibly bring us closer to headquarters.

Contrary to cream substitutes, which easily replaced regular cream, a liquid egg substitute was a new concept; there was no liquid real egg on the market. Consumers needed to be educated. It was not a product for private labeling and to educate consumers required a lot of expensive advertising money which I did not have. But SmithKline had more than money, they had a missionary sales force that could drop coupons, talk to doctors about the merits of the product, and through them create consumer demand.

Here was something management in Philadelphia understood. Once I sold them on the basic concept, they were willing to provide funds for advertising. They even offered to put their in-house publicity department at our disposal. Now the fun could begin!

When Avoset first tried to market Quip, an aerosol whipping cream, they used a small, local advertising agency which had done some very innovative work. I had known Warren, the president, for some time, and I approached him with my idea for marketing our next product. At the same time, Philadelphia transferred one of their up-and-coming marketing people to help develop plans. He and his associates came up with the name "Second Nature" for the product.

Second Nature, Imitation Eggs

Warren suggested we use Arthur Godfrey as our spokesman, and thereby hangs a long tale. Arthur Godfrey was a well known TV and radio celebrity. With an Irish twinkle in his eye, a unique personality and sense of humor, a distinctive voice and a ukulele, he had captured the hearts of millions of women in America, his primary audience. They trusted him, especially older women who were the ones we needed to convince of the merits of our product. He had been the first to come up with the idea of a talent show and several other innovative television programs. His voice was instantly recognized by millions. He advertised "Lucky Strike" cigarettes for many years and, a heavy smoker himself, contracted lung cancer. After the removal of one lung and many cancer treatments, the disease was in remission and he had become a health nut.

Arthur also made a lot of enemies along the way and had the reputation of being a very difficult person with which to deal. He was also known as an anti-Semite. Obviously, if we wanted to use him I had my work cut out for me. By the time we got to Godfrey his career was on the wane and, like all celebrities used to being in the limelight, it frustrated him.

Warren contacted Arthur's agent in the spring 1973 and was told Arthur dealt only with principals not advertising agencies. He arranged for me to meet Arthur at the Pan Am Club in New York City. Why there? Arthur was a well known pilot, had his own plane and, as a member of the club always conducted meetings there.

My job was to sell myself, my company, the product, and finally secure him at a cost we could afford with limited funds. At the height of his career Arthur could command millions for a product endorsement on his show; but times had changed.

I thought I had came up with an idea the night before the meeting that might appeal and I sprung it on him. He was used to the usual arrangement by which the celebrity is paid a large fee up front for production of commercials with a graduated percentage of sales to follow once the product is marketed. The more was sold, the smaller the percentage. I told him that although we were part a large conglomerate, we were essentially an entrepreneurial operation with very limited funds. Therefore, I offered him a different kind of arrangement. We would pay all costs for making the commercials, travel, and promotional meetings, etc. He would invest only his time.

Furthermore, his initial percentage on sales would be nominal but – and here was the kicker – the more we sold, the higher the percentage. It all depended on him. The obvious reasoning was that the more we sold the more profit we could share with him. It was a new approach and it appealed to his entrepreneurial spirit.

We had a signed contract the next day, and I must say Arthur put his heart and soul into the project. We even developed a certain friendship, in spite of his anti- Semitism. I learned later, he hated a lot of people, not only Jews, generally anyone he considered either below or above himself, except those very much above himself like corporate presidents, whom he respected tremendously.

For the next few months, Arthur and I spent a lot of time together. First there were the radio commercials and he was a perfectionist. He demanded a specific studio, identified the technicians he wanted and insisted on his own direction. He drove Warren crazy with his demands, but then he was equally hard on himself. He would do innumerable takes of the same commercial until satisfied. I believe we spent three days from early morning to late at night just making commercials.

Next there were meetings with our brokers. We had done some market research which convinced us consumers were eager to buy the product, so we faced the decision whether to test market the product or roll it out quickly, i.e., offer it nationally as quickly as feasible, from region to region. By now, word was out in the trade of what we were up to, and a frozen product was being introduced under the brand name "Egg Beaters" by Nabisco Company. That forced our hand. No time for test marketing; go national as quickly as possible.

On the Road with Arthur

As luck would have it, there was a food broker convention in San Francisco that year, and we invited our broker sales force to a sumptuous breakfast and meeting with Arthur. Of course, we served "Second Nature" egg substitute.

With late night partying at conventions, breakfasts are always poorly attended, but not this time. Arthur brought them out and they even brought their wives for an eight o'clock breakfast! And they were not disappointed. He gave them a half-hour show with jokes, his ukulele and Irish charm. He really fired them up. It was a joy to watch a true professional showman.

The next step was to back up our efforts with publicity. I knew Barbara from my days at "Accent" in Chicago and we had become friends. I brought her in to help with our product launch, and she too did a tremendous job. Barbara and her sister had bought one of the largest public relations firms in the food business. They had a full staff working on recipes, which then went to food editors across the U.S. She also had a string of health professionals who gave testimonials and others made presentations at professional meetings.

The next important step was to make sure product found its way onto supermarket's shelves, for unless consumers could buy the product in stores all other efforts were in vain. To this end we invited chainstore buyers and their wives for "Dinner with Arthur Godfrey," at which each dish contained some "Second Nature." Arthur did his usual shtick and of course everyone wanted his autograph.

Then we started airing Arthur's radio commercials; radio because it was cheaper than television and turned out to be incredibly effective. Because of a fluke the commercials started airing just about the time of the oil embargo in the wake of the 1973 Arab-Israeli war. Long lines of automobiles were sitting at gas stations waiting for their turn at the pump with their radios blaring, Arthur's commercials could be heard every few minutes. We could not have designed the exposure any better.

And business was good, at least for a while. Then Nabisco really started pumping money into advertising, and we found ourselves in a spending contest we could not afford. "Second Nature" had a strong market position in the Western U. S. and for the next few years split the business with Nabisco. They dominated the East, we the West.

By that time, headquarters was preoccupied with a revolutionary ulcer medication that had been developed in their facilities in England. Every spare nickel and dime went into speeding the introduction of their new product. It was a smashing success once it was on the market, but similar to "Second Nature" a later market entry stole the march on them.

Decision Time

Those were good years for Avoset: our product lines were profitable, our plants were running full shifts, our workers were happy, and Philadelphia reasonably happy with our financial contributions.

They were preoccupied with their new product and had no to complaints about with the way Avoset was run. Over the years, I had developed a personal friendship with my boss, Henry, and his wife Holly. Henry was on his way to becoming the corporate president. I believe he was executive vice-president at the time, so he had more on his plate than to worry about Avoset. I travelled to Philadelphia frequently, often staying with Henry and Holly or at the downtown corporate apartment on Rittenhouse Square, at times accompanied by Elly.

It was a high-pressure job; running a company is no picnic, even when one likes his job. There were constant meetings to prepare for, speeches to give, and decisions to be made based on few real facts. Just the stuff we learned about in Biz School.

At one of my discussions with Henry, I let it slip to sell Avoset to a larger food company which could better utilize its unique technology, perhaps to Kraft Foods, one of our customers. It was selfish, but not totally so. As I mentioned earlier, Avoset was a "fish out of water" within the corporation. But within another food company it would be able to grow organically, while I might have better growth opportunities. Henry would not hear of it.

Some time later, one of my Stanford graduate school mates had a heart attack and died. He was actually younger than I, as were other classmates who also ran into heart problems. This gave me pause, and I decided that I would rather live than be the richest man in the cemetery. On my next visit to headquarters, I told them I was thinking of taking early retirement at age fifty-five, giving them time to find a replacement I could train appropriately.

There was no immediate response, but during a subsequent visit to Philadelphia I was called into the office of the chairman of the board. He told me they had discussed my possible retirement and my suggestion of selling Avoset. He then asked me to stay and help sell the company. He explained it would undoubtedly be easier to sell it with its president in place. Since I was not in great rush to retire, I agreed. Now came a whole new phase in my life.

First, the legal department got involved with a contract covering my new duties and responsibilities. Then word spread among business brokers that Avoset was up for sale, and much of my time was taken up handling telephone inquiries. Then we were contacted by some principals directly inquiring about further details, all of which took even more time.

I was contacted by a venture capitalist in New York interested in financing a buyout, offering me partownership. As word got around, the city of Gustine offered to participate in financing a venture to assure operations stayed there. Of course, this was very flattering and I seriously considered the proposal. In the final analysis I decided against pursuing these offers. I reasoned that if the pressure was this great when employed, how much more pressure I would have to deal with under a buy-out situation.

There were a few serious contenders within about six months, two of which became finalists: the American company Anderson-Clayton and an English conglomerate. Anderson-Clayton's inquiry was interesting. They were the largest vertically integrated manufacturer of vegetable oil in the U.S., principally of cottonseed oil. They used much of the oil themselves in production of margarine and salad dressings. Their well-known retail brands were "Chiffon" and "Seven Seas."

Left over from the original oil extraction was cottonseed meal, a high- protein cattle feed. Anderson-Clayton's research scientists developed a bland tasting protein from the meal that was suitable for use in food products, including coffee creamers, hence their interest in Avoset.

The English conglomerate saw a totally different value in acquiring our company. Their source of income was the English brewing industry, which they supplied with yeasts and specialty ingredients. It was a profitable business but they wanted to diversify and they wanted to get into the U.S. market. Avoset was to be the first of a number of acquisitions of unique American companies, and they were as much interested in me as they were in Avoset. They stipulated they would only buy the company if I stayed on a minimum of five years and they offered me very attractive terms.

It finally came to a bidding war between the two companies. Personally, I was ambivalent about the English offer. On the one hand, it was very attractive, but on the other the principals had no experience with American business practices and there might be a clash of cultures.

I was not sorry when Anderson-Clayton won the bidding. I was asked to stay on at least a year, to which I readily agreed. SmithKline treated me generously and allowed me to retire from their company instead of retiring from Avoset. This turned out to be a very smart move on my part, but I could not have known that at the time. Here is what happened. Within a year, Anderson-Clayton's president was fired and the company, including Avoset, was sold to Quaker Oats. The latter did not know what to do with Avoset and sold it to Kraft Foods, which then merged with General Foods, which was taken over by Phillip Morris Tobacco Co. Of course, they did not know what to do with Avoset either and after a few years sold the company to an entrepreneur who started Morningstar Foods and put together a number of dairy companies. Such are the ways of American business.

On My Own Now

The year was 1978. We felt financially secure and I wanted to take some time off before embarking on something else. I hoped to travel and see the world; places we had not seen before. But then Elly came up with an interesting suggestion. "You are not the type that can go from museum to museum," she said: "You need a purpose in your travels." And I realized she was right. So we put our heads together and decided we should start a company that offered new packaging and processing technology overseas. Licensing of American know-how, technology transfer, was practiced by many large corporation but smaller companies, many with unique technology, missed out on profitable ventures overseas. We incorporated as Inter-Tek Licensing Corporation; just the two of us, with Elly as secretary/treasurer and me as president.

It so happened there was a technology transfer conference coming up in Sydney, Australia, and we signed up for it. Elly had lived in New Zealand years before and was interested in revisiting down-under, while the whole continent was new to me. For the next few months I was busy lining up suitable companies to represent and likely partners overseas.

We first went to New Zealand's North Island, a fabulous place, visiting dairies and other likely prospects; even a carpet manufacturer which was looking to dispose of mountains of carpet waste. In between times we were sightseeing. Then we went on to Australia where we repeated the process, finally taking in the conference in Sydney before returning home. It all seemed like great beginning for our new venture, but for a number of reasons further activities were postponed to a later date.

Before leaving California, we had made an offer on a house in Lafayette, a custom-built home we fell in love with, and had put our house in Moraga on the market. While overseas, we learned our house was sold and the Lafayette offer had gone through.

Coming home, then, meant a lot of new activity. Decisions had to be made as to alterations to the home in Lafayette, getting contractors, putting the Moraga home in shape for selling, and packing.

It was a stressful time. We had to move into our new house before the work had hardly begun, and I soon saw that while the workmen were excellent the contractor was not doing his job. I talked to his workmen who saw what was going on and they agreed to work for me directly without the contractor. It was a new experience for me and I learned a lot in the process, much of which stood me a good stead in later years.

Elly's mother was quite depressed and she wanted Elly nearby. She also expressed the wish to see all her kids and grandchildren again so we arranged for a family reunion in our new home once completed. Grandma was obviously delighted to see everyone again. We made sure to include her in as many family outings as possible, even though her mobility was greatly impaired.

Grandma passed away in her sleep later that year and is buried near my parents, as she wanted to be. Actually, she was quite close to my dad. They respected and liked each other, and I believe she found in him a kindred spirit.

She had had a very rough life. Widowed with four young children and no assets, she scraped by, first on welfare, which she felt demeaning, then by renting out rooms. Yet she managed to hold the family together, more or less. Elly always felt that her mother preferred her boys, but I believe that was more cultural than personal. Of course this matters little to someone trying to cope with the loss of her father only to feel rejected by her mother. Elly never got over the lack of support from her mother.

Five

A Japanese Adventure

A friend told us of a trip to Japan which intrigued Elly and me. He and his wife were included in a group of Japanese-Americans on their journey throughout Japan; akin to a non-Jew visiting Israel with a Jewish organization. We had approached the tour agent but he was not very encouraging because the tour was fully booked. Then we received a call on Labor Day, 1981 from Kosakura Travel. They had a cancellation and if we could be ready within a week they could accommodate us. Short notice? Yes, but we were ready and our flexibility paid off. The trip was all we hoped for and more. The itinerary was excellent, taking us to places most people had never heard of, much less visited. Above all, it was our fellow travelers who made the journey such a delight.

Sometime during our trip, I must have talked about my business experiences. When we returned to Tokyo at the end of the trip, I was introduced to a businessman who seemed familiar with my background. We spent an evening together, mostly talking business. After returning home, I received a call from a Japanese stockbroker in San Francisco. He asked me to see him, saying that an important client of his was potentially interested in hiring me as a consultant.

The gentleman was a friend of Mr. Ito, Chairman of ITOHAM, the second largest meat packer in Japan. It turned out he was on his way to San Francisco and, in a subsequent visit with the two of them, they spelled out where I would fit in.

It was explained the food business in Japan was changing rapidly, yet it was behind the changes taking place in the U.S. He needed someone to keep him personally posted on the latest developments in processing, packaging, marketing, and distribution. The same held true for changes at the supermarket and store levels. He explained, while they had a manufacturing facility in San Francisco, his Japanese staff was not tuned into such aspects of the food business. Would I be interested? Of course I was! And so, for next six years I was a consultant to Mr. Ito and visited Japan at least once a year.

Another Venture

Sometime in 1989, toward the a home construction project, I received a call from a fellow who used to work for me as a young salesman at Avoset. He had gone on to bigger and better things, and by that time he was on a new job with the California Milk Marketing Board. Prior to that, he did some consulting work, and one of his customers in the egg business was now was thinking of going into the egg substitute business.

The company, being California's largest egg producer and processor, supplied Avoset with egg whites. Therefore, I was familiar with the company and they knew me, even though the people I dealt with at the time had long left the company.

I was asked whether I would be interested in consulting, putting them into the product line I developed for Avoset. Of course

274

I was! And so for the next ten years I drove to Ripon, about 120 miles round trip from Lafayette each day. The distance did not bother me since I enjoyed driving. They gave me a nice car and I drove on their time, listening to the radio.

The Ripon plant was a really dilapidated operation. Management had invested very little in plant and equipment upkeep and realized that. I recommended they invest in brand new, state-of-the-art equipment, having the idea in the back of my mind that the same equipment could be used in production of a variety of products other than egg substitute. They readily understood my reasoning and approved the expenditures.

We were rolling. For the next two years I was busy with equipment suppliers and development of specifications while new buildings were under construction. Part of my job also involved training quality control and production personnel in the specifics of aseptic packaging.

Meanwhile, my friend decided that opportunities with his former client exceeded those of his current job and he joined the company as vice-president of marketing. He was instrumental in the subsequent success of our project, and it was interesting for me to see how much of what he had learned at Avoset he brought to this new entry into the egg substitute market.

With its own strong brand as well as under many private labels the operation was quite profitable until the competition decided not to give up the market without a fight. A price war ensued in which competitors, purchasing cheaper raw material outside California, had a decided advantage.

Fortunately, our processing and packaging equipment allowed us to supplement production with non-egg products, like coffee creamers and pastry toppings. So we were able to fully and profitably utilize our capabilities. That is until package innovations replaced the paper containers with plastic. Chain stores requested we followed suit. However, the board refused the necessary funds, had a falling out with the president, which prompted my friend to leave the company as well, and the company went through a retrenching phase under new management. I stayed another year or so, hired and trained my replacement as called for in my contract and left the company.

Six

COMMUNITY INVOLVEMENTS

Settling Immigrants

*F*or someone used to being on the job early every day, my new found freedom took some getting used to. To stay in shape and have a fixed schedule, I started jogging first thing every morning at a nearby high school track. I soon found this quite boring and switched to running around the Lafayette reservoir, which was much more enjoyable even though more strenuous. It was fun watching the seasonal changes, the wildlife coming out early mornings and seeing other walkers and joggers.

As mentioned earlier, Elly was working at U.C. Berkeley's Regional Oral History Office as an interviewer/editor. I often accompanied her to the university to make use of the vast technical and business libraries. This, and the many business contacts I had in the industry, enabled me to stay up-to-date with changes in the food industry for my reports to Japan. In many ways it was the best of all possible worlds.

But I also felt a strong urge to give back to the community. Elly and I joined the Temple Isaiah "Social Action Committee" and along with others member became involved in immigrant affairs. Being an immigrant, it appealed to me. It was during the time the Vietnamese boat people came to the U.S. and needed to be settled. Our temple signed on with the Jewish Federation's Committee for New Americans, which worked with HIAS (the Hebrew Immigrant Aid Society), and before long we were informed we could expect a Vietnamese family to arrive. Our group sprang into action, securing housing, furniture and all things necessary for setting up housekeeping.

When the Lam family arrived they were only three, a mother and two young boys as the father was forced to stay behind because of a lung ailment. It was an amazing experience for all concerned! They did not speak any English and communication was difficult at first, but they learned quickly. The boys were placed in local schools as well as being tutored by a member of our committee. As a matter of fact, when Elly took Mrs. Lam shopping on her second day here it took her no time at all to figure out that house brands were cheaper than name brands. Mrs. Lam was very bright, as were her boys, contrary to the father, who followed a few months later. He turned out to be good natured, but incompetent.

After a few years, the Lams moved to St. Louis where her sister had settled. They opened a restaurant and were quite successful. Years later they returned to visit, and the members who had helped them were invited to a sumptuous dinner at a local Vietnamese restaurant.

Next, our Social Action Committee was assigned a young Jewish couple from Leningrad (St. Petersburg). The Tsenters and their young son Dima arrived in Oakland after having travelled nearly two days from a holding camp in Italy, looking as fresh as can be. Svetlana Tsenter came off the plane looking like a film diva. Our committee had been able to obtain and furnish a nice apartment, but the thing that impressed them most was the telephone. They told us, in pretty good English, in Russia one had to wait years for such a luxury. I am still friends with the Tsenters.

Jewish Federation

The Jewish Federation of the Greater East Bay, to differentiate from the San Francisco Federation, covers three counties: Alameda, Contra Costa and Solano counties. While its main function today is fundraising, it was a major service provider to the Jewish Community at that time. As such, it owned and operated community centers, the Home for Jewish Parents, the Jewish Family Service, and a Jewish Board of Education. It also operated a public relations department and partnered with the Jewish Museum and the Board of Rabbis. At that time it received its funding in part from the Community Chest, the Federal Government, and, of course, from the Jewish Community.

A few years ago, it was believed the community could be better served by each service organization incorporating separately, becoming responsible for its own operation. But that was after my time. I was in opposition to this, still am, but lost out.

The New Americans Committee of the Jewish Federation was originally part of Family Service, but because of the avalanche of refugees it reported directly to the Board of Directors. As a refugee, I found this committee a natural avenue for community activity. This was the beginning of eighteen years of involvement with the Jewish Federation, some of that time as president.

But for now I was just a member of a group of involved people who wanted to help others. I was the only one in the group who had actual experience of not only being a refugee myself but also having participated in settling several families. In a crowd of blind people a one-eyed man is king, and so it was that I was asked to head that committee. This also involved membership on the Federation board.

The New Americans Committee was set up to settle the large number of Russian immigrants. Our task was not only to arrange for them to be welcomed and cared for by Jewish congregations in the East Bay, but also to negotiate with State and Federal agencies for the assistance they offered refugees under the law. It also involved securing health care, language and employment assistance, like writing résumés. We even created a warehouse and distribution center for people to drop off used furniture, etc., for the new arrivals. All in all, it turned into a big operation with several Russian employees to bridge the language gap.

At that time I began to realize the precariousness of Israel's position internally as well as vis-à-vis its neighbors. It barely survived the Six-Day and Yom Kippur Wars, and now it was being threatened constantly from across the border with Lebanon. Internally, there were constant terrorist attacks which, while not threatening its existence, were debilitating and degrading to morale. Our Federation, as did most other Federations throughout the U.S., increasingly sent funds and people to Israel in support. Our community had participated in "Operation Flying Carpet" to move Jews from Yemen and later from Morocco to Israel. Now, with the exodus of Jews from Russia, a high percentage of them going to Israel, our East Bay community again came through. It committed itself to guaranteeing several millions dollars for short-term loans. A very risky undertaking we all thought at the time, but a necessary one. As it turned out practically all loans were promptly repaid. The community rallied behind its Federation when some time later Ethiopian Jewry was airlifted to Israel in "Operation Moses."

By that time I had moved through the ranks of Federation leadership and was one of its vice-presidents. I was in charge of organizing several fund-raising events, including a very large one in Lakeside Park in downtown Oakland. It was very uplifting to see how many people participated without any coercion to make the event a smashing success.

So I was not surprised when the Federation president and its executive vice-president, asked me to accept the presidency.

It was a lot of work, but I enjoyed it. Over the years, with the Federation's pre-occupation with Israel and local service delivery, it had neglected to reach out to the religious community. So there was a lot of grumbling in synagogues and temples about the Federation. I saw it as my first task to rectify this situation and reach out to the religious communities. I spoke before many boards and attended more religious services than in all the years of my existence. There existed a lot friction between the religious and secular leaderships, both vying for the same charitable dollars. Gradually, the two began working together and the situation has much improved.

At the completion of my term as Federation president, I stayed involved, first serving on the board of the Community Foundation and then on several committees. But after a while I felt that I should take a hiatus. After all, I had been involved with Federation activities for nearly twenty years. Perhaps it was time to call it quits.

Temple Isaiah and AIPAC

I enjoyed tremendously the work with refugees, but as the tide subsided and their influx finally ceased, our group was disbanded. But work was continued by the Jewish Family Service. I continued serving on the Federation board as an ad hoc member.

By then I got to know many within the leadership of our temple and was asked to join the finance committee, a thankless task. Our work involved reviewing temple members' dues commitments, determine whether people pledged their "fair share" and then to negotiate an adjustment; not a way to make friends.

Subsequently, I was asked to chair the education committee, a job that had nothing to do with education but all to do with money; it mainly involved negotiating teacher salaries.

From my days in the German Zionist Youth organization, I was always deeply concerned about Israel's welfare. So it was not surprising that when asked to participate in the creation of the San Francisco chapter of a relatively new national Zionist organization, I readily agreed. AIPAC (American Israel Political Action Committee) was a lobbying organization whose aim is to educate, pressure, and cajole Washington legislators on behalf of American Zionists. As such, it employs professional lobbyists, arranges for educational trips to Israel for legislators and their staff, and provides feedback to the Jewish community on pending legislation of concern to Israel. Over the years, AIPAC has become a pre-eminent organization within the U.S. political power structure.

For my part, after serving on the regional board for a number of years, I moved up to the national advisory committee, which met in Washington. By that time, the political direction of the Israeli government had shifted to the far right, and I soon felt that a similar shift had taken place within AIPAC, especially within the committee in Washington. I also felt that the "advice" given by the national committee to the board of directors was generally ignored, so I resigned without regret.

California/Israel Technology Exchange

Shortly after joining the regional AIPAC board its executive director asked me to head up the creation of a new organization. Naomi Lauter, always well- connected, was a friend of Leo McCarthy from their high school days in San Francisco. Leo was by then lieutenant governor of the State of California with considerable political clout. Naomi convinced her friend to create a new organization to bring the State of California closer to Israel. After all, the two areas had similar climate, agriculture, and people with a pioneering spirit. Both also had an evolving Hi-Tech industry.

Naomi and I met with Lt. Governor McCarthy in Sacramento. He jumped at the idea for a number of reasons; not the least of which probably was his interest in the California governorship, toward which end Jewish support could be important. It was agreed we would put together a group of California businessmen with interests in Israel, and Leo McCarthy would lead the group on an exploratory mission.

The trip turned out to be a real education in how politics works. As the number two California politician, McCarthy, a long-time legislator and, I believe, the head of the California Democratic Party at the time, not to mention a potential future governor, no door in Israel was closed to him. He was lionized by the Israeli press and, having brought his own photographer, he made sure not to miss any photo opportunity. We met with Shimon Peres, Yitzchak Rabin and many top government officials. We were always accompanied by the AIPAC representative in Israel, who seemed to know just about everyone on a personal basis.

What really impressed me was the extent to which McCarthy absorbed the salient facts of the many meetings, asked intelligent questions, and seemed genuinely interested in learning as much as possible during the trip. I was also impressed by the man's stamina, since our days started early and ended late in the evening. Toward the end of the trip, it emerged that Israel's advanced knowledge of fish farming, especially of *Tilapia*, and its know-how in drip irrigation would be of considerable interest to California, and that these should be pursued.

Upon our return, I learned, not withstanding McCarthy's pleadings, the California Bureau of Fish & Game refused to issue permits for the importation of live Tilapia for farming, because these were considered predatory fish which could endanger domestic species. Strangely enough, enormous quantities of frozen tilapia are now available in supermarkets, produced in the orient. As for drip irrigation, an Israeli company located in Fresno started to market it here in California for agricultural applications and is widely used in orchards and vineyards.

American Jewish Committee

Probably because of my involvement with both the Federation and AIPAC, I was asked to join the local board of the American Jewish Committee. It was originally started in the early Twentieth Century by German Jewish business leaders as a civic-cum-public relations organization. Its aim was, and still is, to establish permanent contacts and relationships with non-Jewish organizations to combat discrimination in the work place and in the media. Its approach differed from the American Jewish Congress, which was created by businessmen of Eastern European origin with similar aims. AJC did not work in public very much, preferring to deal on a one-on-one basis with business and political leaders.

Board meetings had as much of a social as a civic component to them, with many of its younger members intent on networking. Although I served on that board for many years, I cannot say that I was ever very active in the organization.

Elly and I did, however, participate in an AJC mission to Germany. The mission was by the invitation of the German Government, so it was not surprising that our contacts were at the highest level, including President Weizäcker.

Of particular interest was our second visit to East Berlin,. It was still a dreary place, but this time we were there not on business, but as American Jews trying to learn more about that government's attitude toward Israel, the Holocaust, and its Jewish citizens. Our first contact was the Minister of Culture and Religious Affairs, Klaus Gysi (the father of Gregor Gysi, a leader of the Left Party in Germany today). As we learned later, his mother was Jewish but he did not let on. Dr. Kirschner, head of the Jewish community, was in attendance and, as during my observation a few years earlier, they addressed each other with the familiar "Du" and "Comrade." From him we learned that East Germany's affiliated Jewish community was quite small, although they admitted there were probably many more unaffiliated Jews. They were free to practice their faith, but there were few operating synagogues. As to the attitude toward reconstituting Jewish properties expropriated by the Nazis, the official position was that "Communists also suffered under the Nazis, Jews included". In other words, forget it!

The Reutlinger

But like an old fire horse, I start running whenever the bell rings. Years ago, I was asked to join the board of directors of the Home for Jewish Parents at their new location in Danville, now named "The Reutlinger". Since I might possibly end my days there I accepted. It was a new and interesting experience. However, the time came when I did not want to leave Elly alone evenings, which mandated my resignation from the board.

Seven

Construction

A ll my life I dreamt of building my own home. It never came to pass, but our home in Lafayette offered many opportunities to do home expansion and additions. Although I was quite involved in community affairs, most meetings took place in the evening, which left plenty of time for construction during the day.

The first project involved enclosing a space under a large overhanging roof in the rear of the house. An energy audit by the power company showed that considerable heat savings could accrue by allowing the winter sun to heat the enclosed area without adding to the heat load during the summer owing to the type of roof construction. Elly thought it was a crazy idea, calling it "our bowling alley" because the space was long and narrow. But she loved it once I had completed the work, especially since it gave her new space for an office.

The next project was much more complicated. A small room, more like an afterthought at the time of the original construction, was intended to be used for a changing for swim wear. Later a pool house was built, which obviated the use of this room. When we first bought the house, I had converted the space into a tiny Japanese room which was very attractive, but relatively useless.

Elly was in love with the house and swore she would never leave it so, with both of us getting on in years, I decided to gut the room and build a larger one with its own entrance, suitable for live-in help. Quite a project, and I am proud to say I did much of the work myself.

Our son Bob helped with digging the new foundation and placing the concrete forms that I constructed. Bill helped with the gravel work while I arranged for pouring the concrete. I also relied on an expert carpenter to place the roof trusses, a roofer for closing the roof, a plumber and an electrician. But I pretty much did all the rest of the work myself. It took a long time but when it was finished it was a very comfortable room where we spent most of our time, using it as our family room.

Travels

Elly and I always enjoyed travelling. Earlier I mentioned several business related trips and our Japan adventure, but I need to relate some other more unusual trips.

Elly and I had visited Israel over the years on a number of occasions, the first one with our boys; a really memorable visit that I mentioned earlier. Beyond that, I visited Israel several times on behalf of the Federation to participate in meetings and special missions.

Elly read about an archeological exploration in Israel to be conducted by Sacramento State University. We signed up for it as well as a preceding study trip through Greece.

Our accommodation at an agricultural school at Pardes Hannah in Israel was adequate but sparse, as was the food. But we came for the experience and on that score we were not disappointed. The dig took place at Tel Dor, a site on the Mediterranean

Sea shore dating back to Canaanite times. The *Tel* (mount) had been opened a few years earlier with several universities participating in the excavations.

Work started a five a.m. and ended by noon when the heat became unbearable. Classes started after resting in the afternoon and involved "pottery readings" i.e., an analysis of the importance (or the lack thereof) of what was dug up in the morning. Generally, pottery shards of little value were discarded and we were free to take some home with us. To go into a description of the many aspects of the excavation would go beyond the scope of this autobiography. Suffice it to say that both Elly and I came away from this experience exhausted but educated.

Another equally memorable trip took us through much of South America. With the exception of Venezuela, Paraguay, and Bolivia, I believe we visited every other country in South America. We travelled into the Amazon Basin, up the High Andes, down to the tip of South America, and out to the Galapagos Islands. It was too long and exhausting, but in retrospect I am glad we made the effort.

Another unusual trip involved a visit with my cousin Uschi and her family in Johannesburg, South Africa on the occasion of her eightieth birthday, which we followed up by going on several safaris. Uschi and I had been close as kids, lost touch over the years until she visited us in Moraga in the early 1970's. But as we aged we grew closer. Today she fills my need for the sister I always wanted.

Not knowing what to expect in South Africa, but having heard others rave about its scenery, we were not disappointed. We were pleasantly surprised by the friendliness of the people, both black and white, once we left the metropolitan areas. What has taken place there politically is truly amazing; a total transformation with practically no bloodshed.

Neither Elly nor I were great wild animal lovers prior to the trip, but we came away totally enchanted by what we saw and with a much better understanding of what is meant by "natural balance" and ecology.

More recently, not as able to climb, hike or carry as we used to, we've learned to enjoy ocean cruises more and more. One such cruise was both very touristy and emotional. It started in Bangkok and ended in Beijing, but it also included Shanghai, my first visit there since I left more than sixty years ago. Seeing Shanghai again after more than sixty years was obviously a deeply-felt experience. It allowed me to revisit the ghetto and it gave Elly a better understanding of what our life entailed at that time.

While Greater Shanghai today has very little in common with what it looked like back then, parts of Hongkew have not changed very much as yet. I say "as yet" because parts of it have been rebuilt already while other parts are being torn down for later rebuilding. Luckily, the immediate area where I lived has been untouched, and I found the last house in the ghetto we lived in practically unchanged. On the other hand, I was not really able to identify our house in the French Concession because so much had changed there. The two days we spent in Shanghai were totally insufficient and made me want to return again; probably an idle dream.

Eight

Another Move

With the end of my consulting work, I was at loose ends again. During the intervening ten years, a lot of deferred maintenance had piled up in our house and garden, and I was soon busy getting things in shape. But whether old age was catching up with me or just boredom with the repetitiveness of the work, I just did not enjoy it as much anymore. Elly sensed that something was amiss, and after discussing the matter, she suggested we move to the retirement community of Rossmoor. This was a major sacrifice on her part because she was very comfortable where we lived, hoped to stay there indefinitely, and Rossmoor was never on her agenda.

We have lived in Rossmoor for eleven years and have acclimatized well to the new environment. Rossmoor is a retirement community par excellence which provides a great variety of activities to suit anyone's needs. Since I enjoy woodworking, I spend a good deal of my time in the woodshop, which is equipped with the latest in commercial equipment. And I am back to how I began, making furniture.

Nine

I remember being taught at Stanford that an ideal life consisted of three phases: business, public service, and teaching. I guess by that definition I did not quite make it, though not for the lack of trying. I contacted several institutions after retiring, only to be told that without a teaching credential there was little opportunity. I suspect requirements changed during the intervening fifty years since my graduation.

Looking back over the entire span of my life, I can say that the only constant was change. Yet it could not have turned out better if I had planned it.

All told, I have been extremely fortunate; perhaps, lucky would be a better word. I had a pretty stable childhood during terribly unstable times, with parents that gave their all to me. We escaped Hitler's clutches, survived the war, and came to the "Promised Land of the West." I was given many opportunities and was able to utilize most of them.

More than fifty years ago I married the woman I loved and still love – perhaps more so today because I got to know her better in the interim. And we have two boys who now have their own families, all of whom I love dearly.

My only regret is that I did not, perhaps was not able, to spend more time with our boys during their early childhood, mainly leaving their upbringing and education to Elly. I tried to make up for it by including them in some of my business travels, but I know it was a poor substitute for parental involvement.

What advice can I give my children and grandchildren? There is a German saying that: "There is nothing sure or safe in this world, and you might lose anything you own by force or circumstance except that which you have in your head." In other words, learning is the only safe investment! What you have between your ears makes you free. I did not learn that lesson until I came to the United States, but it turned out to be true. There was an engraving over the main entrance to City College in San Francisco: "Give me a Base and I'll Move the World;" obviously I never forgot that motto.

Since we are going through difficult economic times, I want to conclude with a comment by Ben Stein I read in the New York Times:

"We are more than our investments. We are more than our year-to-year or our day-to-day changes in our net worth. We are what we do for charity. We are how we treat our family and friends. - We are what we do for our community and our nation. If you had $100 million or $100,000 a year ago and now have a lot less, you are still the same person. You are not a balance sheet, at least not one denominated in money." Words to live by!

Ten

*M*y life's narrative was written over many years, with many pauses and interruptions. However, it is as much Elly's story as my autobiography and I want to finish it in memory of Elly, who passed away peacefully on June 18th, 2016.

Elly and I were married for nearly sixty years and, thinking back, it is surprising to me our marriage was so successful. We were the "opposites that attract each other." She was a night owl and I was, and still am, a morning person. She loved to curl up with a good book and read for hours, while I could not sit still for very long. Both of us came from vastly different backgrounds: Elly lost her father at an early age and felt neglected by her mother; I grew up spoiled by both my parents. On the other hand, we both experienced great poverty and deprivation, yet managed to work our way out of it and, although Elly would never admit to it, she was as ambitious as I was.

Over the years, we developed a great and deep love for each other, enjoyed being together, loved watching our sons and grandchildren grow up, and then seeing the world. So it was heart wrenching seeing my very bright and intelligent wife lose her memory and her self over a seven year period.

Aware of the final outcome of this terrible disease, I had hoped to be able to cope with Elly's passing, but I find it difficult. Keeping active and having family, friends and community helps, but once the lights are out, memories crowd out sleep.

Early on, as Elly knew of her diagnosis and its inevitable outcome, she said: "Don't mope around when I'm gone!" I'm trying, honey!

In Loving Memory
Eleanor Glaser
October 15, 1923 - June 18, 2016

Eleven

POSTSCRIPT

This autobiography was written with my children and grandchildren in mind; to provide a basis for reflection and on which they might build their own lives. Thus it contains a lot of details which may be of little interest to other readers except perhaps to fill in some of the background. By the same token, I tried to include material which is not autobiographical because I believe it provides a broader understanding of the times and events through which I lived.

Looking back, these were extremely momentous times and I always try to relate today's events to what happened then. These were not isolated events, they were part of a continuum, and what affects us today can often be traced directly to what happened decades ago. In that spirit, I want to urge all readers to be mindful of past events, because history can and does repeat itself.

Twelve

ACKNOWLEDGMENTS

I want to express my profound thanks to Dr. Herbert M. Eder without whose help, suggestions, and encouragement this autobiography would not have been possible. His generous commitment of his expertise, time to review and edit my original draft made this printed version a reality.

I also want to thank Dr. Sylvia Asmus, Director of the "*Deutsches Exylarchiv 1933 – 1945*" at the *Deutsche National Bibliothek* in Frankfurt a/Main who took time to review this text and made suggestions.

Finally, I want to thank the many friends and acquaintances without whose encouragement this work might not have come to fruition; Sally Adams, Debbie Katzburg, and Sally Schubb among others.

Thirteen

SOURCE

Several Pictures have been copied from Prof. David Kranzler's book "Japanese, Nazis & Jews", published by Yeshiva Press in 1979, and former residents in the Shanghai Ghetto.

Made in the USA
San Bernardino, CA
07 September 2017